TURBULENCE IN THE PACIFIC

TURBULENCE
IN THE PACIFIC

Japanese-U.S. Relations
During World War I

Noriko Kawamura

INTERNATIONAL HISTORY

Cathal J. Nolan, William R. Keylor, and Erik Goldstein,
Series Editors

Westport, Connecticut
London

Library of Congress Cataloging-in-Publication Data

Kawamura, Noriko, 1955–
     Turbulence in the Pacific : Japanese-U.S. Relations during World War I /
by Noriko Kawamura.
          p.   cm.—(International history, ISSN 1527–2230)
     Includes bibliographical references and index.
     ISBN 0–275–96853–7 (alk. paper)
     1. World War, 1914–1918—Diplomatic history.   2. United States—Foreign
relations—Japan.   3. Japan—Foreign relations—United States.   I. Title.   II. Series.
D610.K24   2000
940.3′2—dc21   99–055034

British Library Cataloguing in Publication Data is available.

Library of Congress Catalog Card Number: 99–055034
ISBN: 0–275–96853–7
ISSN: 1527–2230

First published in 2000

Praeger Publishers, 88 Post Road West, Westport, CT 06881
An imprint of Greenwood Publishing Group, Inc.
www.praeger.com

Printed in the United States of America

∞™

The paper used in this book complies with the
Permanent Paper Standard issued by the National
Information Standards Organization (Z39.48–1984).

10 9 8 7 6 5 4 3 2 1

Copyright Acknowledgment

The author and publisher gratefully acknowledge permission for the use of the following
material:

Edward M. House Papers, Manuscript and Archives, Yale University Library.

For my parents
Shozo and Kazuko Kawamura

Contents

Series Foreword

This series promotes historical scholarship that is genuinely international in subject matter and approach, as well as multi-archival in methodology. The series fosters publication of monographs and edited volumes which focus on a wide range of topics in the history of international relations. These include studies of the political, military, and diplomatic relations among sovereign states, international economic history, the history of international law, and the role played by "non-state actors" in world affairs. The main focus of the series is the impact of internal political, social, and cultural developments on the formulation of foreign policies and interstate relations. But it also focuses on the effects of international events on the internal affairs of national societies.

In addition to international historians, within the disciplines of International Relations and Political Science there is a corps of scholars who are deeply committed to a historical approach to their fields. These scholars locate their research in a classical tradition of intellectual inquiry that examines the historical antecedents of international conflict and cooperation in order to better explain contemporary affairs. The research and teaching of these scholars suggest that the meaning of political, cultural, social, and economic events is most readily and richly revealed by historically informed study. These scholars pay particular attention to the historical genesis of the principles and practices that shape relations between and among peoples and states. What these scholars have in common is a commitment to moving beyond the confines of a particular society to explore the important connections between that society and the outside world.

Cathal J. Nolan, William R. Keylor, and Erik Goldstein

Preface

At the close of the twentieth century, having witnessed two catastrophic world wars and the half-century-long Cold War, we see how diverse the world is and how complex relations are among nations. Those in search of a new world order as a universal solution to international conflicts have been trying to resurrect the rhetoric of Wilsonian liberal internationalism. Yet, everlasting violence and frictions among nations remind us that the centrifugal forces that divided nations during the First World War still seem to be at work. President Woodrow Wilson might have been ahead of his time, but it is also possible that his vision of a new world order was based on a tenuous premise with limitations and fundamental flaws that prevented it from developing into a truly workable international system.

This study examines the reasons for increasing tensions between Japan and the United States during World War I as part of an effort to identify some of those centrifugal forces that frustrated the emergence of international federalism. We have a good understanding that the shortcomings of Japan's continental policy eventually led the country astray in the 1930s and resulted in the Fifteen Years War in Asia and the Pacific. But do we really know the consequences of the failings or limitations of Wilsonian internationalism? Although the main concern of this book is the effectiveness of President Wilson's policy in the Pacific, the book does not really concentrate on the analysis of Wilsonian foreign policy making itself. Instead, the troubling transformation in Japanese foreign policy that challenged the Wilsonian foreign policy ideals is discussed in detail. The examination of the motives and circumstances behind Japan's actions and how Washington perceived and responded to Tokyo's moves illuminates the weaknesses of President Wilson and his administration's handling of the East Asian problems, which are difficult to bring to light simply by looking at the American side only.

This book is the conclusion of a long journey I began as a graduate student in Seattle. I offer my greatest gratitude to my mentors, Professor Wilton B. Fowler and Professor Robert J. C. Butow. I am deeply indebted to Professor Lloyd E. Ambrosius, whose works redirected the course of my journey. He also read the manuscript and gave me valuable advice and encouragement. My sincere thanks are due to Dr. Ken Kurihara at the Diplomatic Record Office of the Japanese Foreign Ministry; Professor Jonathan G. Utley for his constructive criticisms; Professor Cathal Nolan, Dr. Heather R. Staines of Praeger, Alice Davenport for her editorial assistance, and Sarah Moore for making the maps; my husband, Roger Y. M. Chan; and my parents who made it possible for me to study in the United States.

Introduction

In the great drama of the First World War, what happened in East Asia was a sideshow, but these events permanently altered relations between Japan and the United States. The accord between the two countries deteriorated dramatically in the course of the war, even though they were fighting on the same side against a common enemy. Their wartime association was purely a marriage of convenience. In May 1918, the final year of hostilities, Vladimir I. Lenin, who had just withdrawn the newly established Soviet Union from the war, provided a Marxist economic explanation for an inevitable "clash" between these two capitalist countries for "the domination of the Pacific Ocean and the surrounding territories." He stated that "we must not forget that no matter how solid the imperialist groupings may appear to be, they can be broken up in a few days if the interests of sacred private property, the sacred rights of concessions, etc., demand it." Lenin went on to warn, "It may well be that the tiniest spark will suffice to blow the existing alignment of powers."[1] Even if one discounts Lenin's revolutionary propaganda for "the constancy of the tendency to war between rival capitalist countries,"[2] one cannot disregard the inescapable conflict of national interests between the United States and Japan in the Pacific that Lenin illuminated. Some prominent American diplomatic historians later echoed Lenin's economic interpretation and characterized U.S.-Japanese rivalry as conflict between two different forms of capitalist imperialism.[3]

The more orthodox and widely accepted explanation of Japanese-American estrangement, however, has been one of confrontation between Japan as an opportunistic imperialist aggressor in China versus the United

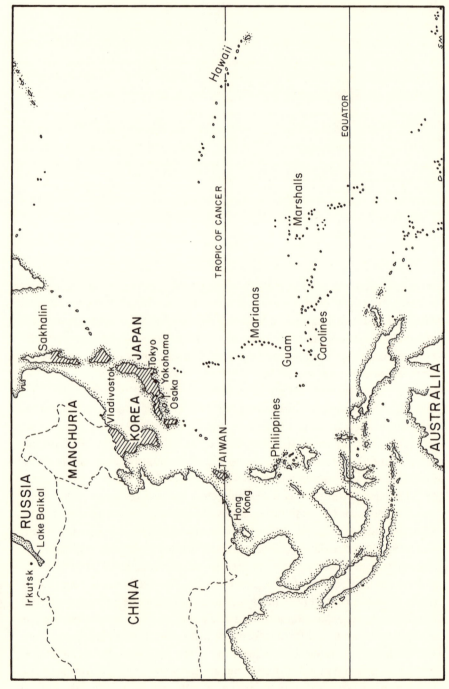

Western Pacific, 1914

States as a moralistic champion of the Open Door and the independence of China. President Thomas Woodrow Wilson of the United States was the most articulate proponent of this view. Ray Stannard Baker, Wilson's official biographer who served as head of the Press Bureau of the American Committee to Negotiate the Peace during the Paris peace conference in 1919, set down for history the Wilsonian crusade for the New Diplomacy against the Old Diplomacy practiced by imperialists of the Old World. Its implication in East Asia is the creation of the dichotomy between Japan's "Old Diplomacy" and America's Wilsonian "New Diplomacy."[4] This interpretation, however, oversimplifies the complex interactions between the two countries and perpetuates the stereotypes retrospectively created by the Americans in the 1930s and the 1940s. This study attempts to reexamine the reasons for the deterioration in Japanese-American relations during the First World War by inquiring into historical sources of both sides. It will pursue the twofold question of how and why Japanese-American tensions increased and eventually developed into antagonism by the end of the war.

As William G. Beasley, the author of *Japanese Imperialism*, has appropriately suggested, it is unrealistic to search "mono-causal explanations of complex historical phenomena."[5] This work will try to incorporate several factors into one chronological account. At one level, this study explains the reason for the increasing tension between Japan and the United States through the conventional method of factual analysis of their policy disagreements and their conflicts of national interests—geopolitical and economic. These occurred mainly over two regions in East Asia, namely, China and Siberia and, to a lesser extent, over the so-called German Southern Pacific Islands. The main events to be examined here are Japan's Twenty-one Demands on China in 1915, America and China's entry into the war, the Lansing-Ishii agreement concluded in 1917, the Siberian Intervention launched in 1918, and the Paris Peace Conference in 1919.

At another level, this work suggests that contingent historical developments and human factors further strained the already complicated Japanese-American relationship. Some developments were beyond the control of the policy makers in both Tokyo and Washington, such as the timing of the First World War and the international circumstances that existed at the time. Even at home, both Japanese and American leaders were often prisoners of domestic politics, economic conditions, and public sentiments. While in the United States President Woodrow Wilson provided sound leadership in his government during the war years, Japan underwent quiet but fundamental changes in its political power structure. Between August 1914 and November 1918, Japan experienced three cabinet changes and had seven different foreign ministers. Compared with the centrality of

President Wilson in America's foreign policy, Japanese foreign policy faltered repeatedly as new political factions came to power. Part of the problem in Japanese-American relations can also be attributed to shortcomings of human interaction, such as prejudice, misunderstanding, and mistrust on both sides of the Pacific. Rivalry and conflict over interests in China and in other areas often influenced the way policy makers in Tokyo and Washington perceived each other. When they attempted to settle differences, their negotiations were often exacerbated by excessive suspicion, continual misunderstandings, and lack of communication on both sides. When the two sides resorted to ambiguous compromises, these often became further causes of misunderstanding and mistrust.

Finally, and most important of all, this study is an attempt to reexamine the application of the dichotomy between the Old Diplomacy and the New Diplomacy to Japanese-American relations. If the incompatibility between the principles of the Old and New Diplomacy explains the Japanese-American confrontation in East Asia during the First World War, what then, specifically, were the basic differences in the ideological foundations of Japanese and American foreign policy principles and diplomatic practices?

Japan was perhaps the best student of the Old Diplomacy in the non-Western world. As a latecomer to the industrial age, which wanted to attain equality with the West and join the ranks of the great powers, Japan emulated its rivals by adopting their expansionist and imperialist practices overseas. Because of geographic proximity, Japan was eager to benefit from the treaty port system the Western powers had already established in the territory of its weak neighbor, China. Japanese leaders quickly learned to use alliances and secret treaties—and if necessary, armed forces—to protect and further their own country's national interests. However, they paid due respect to the existing rules and the international precedents of the imperialist game as established by the Western powers. Drastic action was not undertaken without first reaching some prior understanding with other major powers, especially with Japan's military ally, Great Britain. Therefore, Japanese government leaders considered themselves to be fair players in the arena of international competition.

President Wilson and his government, on the other hand, condemned the Old Diplomacy and predatory imperialism as the true cause of the Great War. The president concluded that imperialistic practices were a hindrance to the realization of higher purposes, such as democracy and world peace based on liberal internationalism. He was determined to put an end to the age of imperialism and bring about a new world order to guarantee universal peace through the creation of an international organization. Wilson's principles of the New Diplomacy were best outlined in his Fourteen Points. In

East Asia, the president applied his New Diplomacy to America's traditional Open Door policy. He revamped the meaning of the basic principles of equal commercial opportunity in China and reemphasized the preservation of that nation's independence. He categorically condemned the practice of making both public and secret arrangements among the great powers for the purpose of exploiting China. He considered the scrambling for concessions and the establishment of spheres of influence by the European powers and Japan to be infringements on China's sovereignty and violation of the Open Door principles. In his view, the Open Door policy was an implementing policy to bring about democracy and self-determination in China and, ultimately, peace in East Asia.

These two incompatible approaches to diplomacy, Old and New, may partly account for the ways Japan and the United States formulated and pursued diametrically opposing foreign policies in East Asia, but do not fully explain why the two countries could not resolve controversies. Their differences seem to be more than simple disagreements over diplomatic methods and behavior and go beyond any particular disputes over economic, territorial, or political concessions. Hidden behind the conflict between the Old Diplomacy and the New Diplomacy was the dichotomy between America's universalism and the unilateralism inherent in Wilsonian idealistic internationalism and Japan's incipient particularistic regionalism and the pluralism based on its own assessment of power relations in East Asia and its strong sense of nationalism and racial identity.[6]

As the United States was engulfed in the Great War in Europe, President Wilson justified American participation in the war as a crusade for democracy. To restore and maintain peace in the postwar world, he came to embrace idealistic liberal internationalism centered around the principles of open diplomacy, freedom, self-determination, and international justice. He believed that these were universal principles and ought to be the basis on which every nation conducted foreign relations. Wilson's universalistic idealism stemmed from his unwavering faith in Christianity and in the superiority of moral values, political sophistication, cultural tradition, and racial characteristics of Western civilization. Because the Old World was corrupt, he believed that Americans had the unique mission to lead a Christian crusade for the goals of freedom, democracy, and international peace and justice.[7]

Once Wilson assumed the universality of his ideals of liberal internationalism, nations that failed to adhere to the ideals were considered morally and legally wrong regardless of their reasons. He unilaterally applied his ideals to the East Asian situation without truly understanding the realities in that region. His knowledge of Japan and the rest of East Asia was limited, and was colored by reports from missionary friends and diplomats who shared his zeal for America's mission in East Asia.

The attention of the leaders of Japan at the time of the First World War, on the other hand, was narrowly focused on their country's security and on protection and enhancement of national interests and prestige. Having established Japan's foothold on the northeastern edge of the Asian continent through the annexation of Korea and the acquisition of a so-called sphere of influence in South Manchuria, Japan entered a transitional period in its foreign policy. Its leaders were searching for a new direction for their policy: something more self-assertive and appropriate for a newly emerging great power in East Asia. The outbreak of war in Europe provided them with a one-in-a-million chance to launch a vigorous policy of continental expansion.

In the course of searching for a new comprehensive policy toward the Asian continent, senior leaders in Japan gradually developed a regionalist approach to justify Japan's hegemony in East Asia. By focusing on both the geopolitical separation of Asia from the West and the differences in racial and cultural heritage between Asian and Western states, they were moving toward a particularistic and pluralistic stance. Their position was pluralistic in the sense that they questioned universal applicability of the Western standards to the Asian situation and began to believe that a nation's conduct was based on more than one set of values and principles. Japan's pluralistic approach apparently evolved partly because of the dilemma the Japanese were facing with regard to racial discrimination against Asian immigrants abroad, particularly on the West Coast of the United States. Japanese senior statesmen perceived the First World War as the result of increasing intensity in racial rivalry. To survive a future war between the white and yellow races, they began to argue that Japan must assume a regionalist stance of "Asia for Asians." Many political and intellectual leaders in Japan, from the outset of its modernization efforts, claimed that a "special relationship" existed between Japan and China. They pointed to obvious geographic, politico-economic, and strategic reasons, but some leaders (Genro Aritomo Yamagata, for example) derived the concept of a Sino-Japanese special relationship from the idea of a "common culture and common race" (*dobun doshu*) that the peoples of the two countries shared. Others, such as Genro Masayoshi Matsukata, argued in favor of a special position for Japan in China by using the idea of Japanese "tutelage" over China or the idea of the "yellow man's burden," which was espoused by Premier Shigenobu Okuma. Japan's wartime leaders saw in these arguments an ideological foundation for a Japanese version of regionalism in East Asia or an Asian Monroe Doctrine, and began to formulate policy slogans such as Sino-Japanese "cooperation" (*teikei*) and "coexistence and co-prosperity" (*kyoson kyoei*).

It is important to note, however, that because Japanese leaders came to assume the pluralistic attitude in response to Western discrimination against the Japanese abroad, they themselves did not espouse cultural pluralism within their empire or in their policy toward China.[8] The Sino-Japanese cooperation Japanese leaders envisaged was based on unequal partnership. As Japanese scholar Taichiro Mitani argues, World War I finalized the transformation that was taking place in the Japanese leadership's vision of regionalism. Many Japanese leaders had abandoned the old idea of regional cooperation between the Qing dynasty and Japan as equal partners after the Sino-Japanese War (1894–1895) and moved toward the concept of "vertically integrated regionalism." The intensification of racial rivalry that Japanese leaders thought the Great War symbolized made it easier for them to accept "the Asia Monroe Doctrine" with Japan as the superior leader and China as a subordinate.[9]

This study traces how the two different ideological attitudes held by the Wilson administration and the Japanese government affected interactions between the two countries during World War I. Contemporary Japanese-American relations did not create a spectacle of ideological conflict because both governments were still searching for a formula that would fit the new international order. The United States operated under the strong leadership of President Wilson with his unwavering faith in America's mission, and Japan's leadership vacillated between a self-assertive independent course in East Asia and the conventional policy of accommodating the wishes of Western powers. By the time the United States intervened in the war in Europe, Japanese leaders became so concerned about the relative increase in American influence over China in the absence of the vigilant eyes of the European powers that they began to question the need for cooperation with the United States. When Wilson announced the Fourteen Points and urged that his liberal internationalism be accepted as a universal goal, Japanese leaders, preoccupied with their regionalist goals, failed to understand the significance of the president's concept in a broader international context. They interpreted the Fourteen Points as rhetoric to conceal the Anglo-Saxon conspiracy against the non-Western world, especially against the newly emerging Pacific power, Japan. By the end of the war, Japanese and American leaders stood very far apart in terms of their visions of the postwar world.

These three aspects—policy disagreements and the conflict of national interest, historical contingency and perceptual problems, and the ideological dichotomy between Wilsonian universalism and Japanese regionalism—are incorporated into a chronological account of how and why Japanese-American relations deteriorated over the course of World War I. Chapter 1 examines Japan's aggressive diplomacy of the Twenty-one Demands on China. This event reveals Japanese leaders' willingness to venture on an assertive policy to establish Japan's supremacy in the Asian continent while Western powers were distracted by the war. Chapter 2 demonstrates that the crisis of the Twenty-one Demands became a turning point in Japanese-American relations when President Wilson emerged as a defender of China by elevating the principles of the Open Door and the independence of China into a moralistic and universal value to forestall Japan's regionalist ambitions. Chapter 3 examines Japanese-American rivalry over the question of who should guide China into the war against Germany. This episode shows that President Wilson's well-intended attempt to make the war a universal crusade against autocratic and militaristic Germany fueled Japan's determination to assume the leadership role in East Asia and assert its supremacy in China. In chapter 4, the examination of the making of the Lansing-Ishii Agreement reveals how the dichotomy between Wilsonian idealistic universalism and Japan's particularistic regionalism made it difficult for the two countries to solve their differences over China policy. The Siberian intervention is the subject of chapter 5. It demonstrates that the joint Japanese-American military expedition to Siberia further aroused their mutual suspicion and intensified their antagonism. Whereas Japanese leaders were concerned about their regional geopolitical interests, President Wilson was primarily interested in upholding the principles of open door and self-determination. Chapter 6 contrasts Wilson's peace program, driven by his universalist aspiration to create a new world order, with Japan's narrowly focused claims for the advancement of its own regional interests. Wilson's unilateral attempt to impose what he believed to be universal values failed to accommodate the realities dominated by the emerging regional power.

NOTES

1. Vladimir I. Lenin, *V. I. Lenin: Collected Works*, trans. Clemens Dutt, ed. Robert Daglish (Moscow: Foreign Language Publishing House, 1960–1970), 27: 367–368. Report on Foreign Policy Delivered at a Joint Meeting of the All-Russia Central Committee and the Moscow Soviet, May 14, 1918.

2. Giovanni Arrighi, *The Geometry of Imperialism: The Limits of Hobson's Paradigm*, trans. Patrick Camiller (London: Verso, 1983), 14.

3. William A. Williams, *The Tragedy of American Diplomacy*, 2d rev. and enlarged ed. (New York: Dell Publishing Co., Inc., 1972); Walter LaFeber, *The Clash: A History of U.S.-Japan Relations* (New York: W. W. Norton & Company, 1997).

4. Ray Stannard Baker, *Woodrow Wilson and World Settlement*, 3 vols. (Garden City, N.Y.: Doubleday, Page & Company, Inc., 1923).

5. William. G. Beasley, *Japanese Imperialism* 1894–1945 (New York: Oxford University Press, 1987), 12.

6. This dichotomy was formulated from the conceptual framework provided by the works of Lloyd E. Ambrosius: Lloyd E. Ambrosius, *Woodrow Wilson and the American Diplomatic Tradition: The Treaty Fight in Perspective* (New York: Cambridge University Press, 1987); and Lloyd E Ambrosius, *Wilsonian Statecraft: Theory and Practice of Liberal Internationalism during World War I* (Wilmington, Del.: Scholarly Resources Inc., 1991).

7. This interpretation of President Wilson's idealistic internationalism was based on the following sources: Lloyd E. Ambrosius, *Woodrow Wilson and the American Diplomatic Tradition* and *Wilsonian Statecraft*. Other sources include David Steigerwald, *Wilsonian Idealism in America* (Ithaca: Cornell University Press, 1994); Michael H. Hunt, *Ideology and U.S. Foreign Policy* (New Haven: Yale University Press, 1987); George F. Kennan, *American Diplomacy*, expanded ed. (Chicago: University of Chicago Press, 1984); Arthur S. Link, *Woodrow Wilson: Revolution, War, and Peace* (Arlington Heights, Ill.: AHM Publishing Corporation, 1979); Thomas J. Knock, *To End All Wars: Woodrow Wilson and the Quest for a New World Order* (New York: Oxford University Press, 1992).

8. The Japanese pluralistic attitude during World War I can be compared with the example of ethnic groups in the United States who were part of cultural pluralism but failed to espouse that concept toward other ethnic groups. See Milton M Gordon, "Assimilation in America: Theory and Reality," *Daedalus* 90 (spring 1961): 263–285.

9. Taichiro Mitani, *Kindai nihon no senso to seiji* (War and politics of modern Japan) (Tokyo: Iwanami shoten, 1997), 88–95.

China, Manchuria, and Siberia, 1914

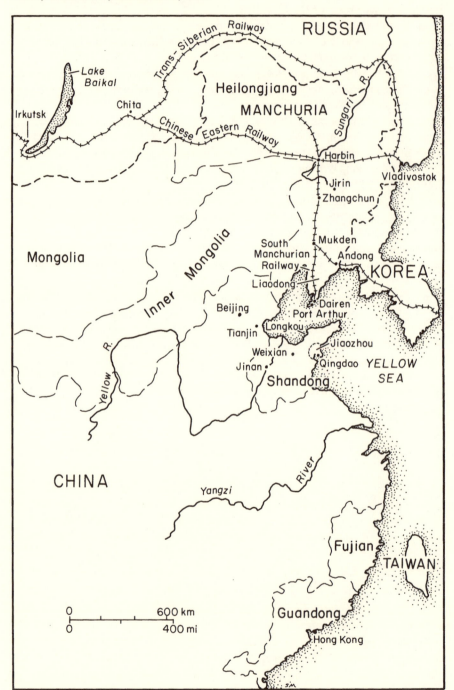

CHAPTER 1

Japan's Entry into the War and the Twenty-one Demands

The First World War that broke out in Europe in August 1914 provided Japan with an opportunity to venture on a self-assertive policy to establish itself as the dominant power in East Asia. Japan immediately joined the war on the side of the Allies with a view to expanding its foothold in China by eliminating Germany's sphere of influence in Shandong. It also took advantage of the Western powers' preoccupation with the war and attempted to settle its outstanding problems with China without European interference. The Japanese government formulated the Twenty-one Demands on China to fulfill these multiple objectives.

After the annexation of Korea in 1910, the primary goal of Japanese foreign policy was to establish Japan's dominant position in East Asia through an expansion of political and economic influence over Manchuria and China. On the eve of World War I, Japan had largely succeeded in securing South Manchuria as its sphere of influence, but Japan's economic and political foothold in the region was still unstable. The Japanese government had been trying unsuccessfully to negotiate with Chinese authorities to extend the expiration date both of the Guandong lease and the rights to the South Manchurian Railway from 1923 to 1997. Japan's position was even more precarious in China proper than in Manchuria. Japanese leaders, both civilian and military, not only were uneasy about Japan's economic competitiveness in China but also about the stability of the new government headed by President Yuan Shikai. With only a very limited amount of capital, Japan was at a disadvantage when competing for investments in China. Prior to 1914, the Japanese did not own any rights to major Chinese railways or mines south of the Great Wall. Japanese leaders were afraid that should the new Chinese government collapse, Western investors might intervene to protect their investments and divide the Chinese territory among themselves, thereby blocking Japan's access to Chinese markets and natural resources and excluding Japan from Chinese politics. Japanese Foreign Minister Nobuaki Makino, who resigned his office in April 1914, was concerned about the situation and left a memorandum for his successor, Takaaki Kato. Convinced that the East Asian situation had reached a critical stage, Makino urged the Japanese government to take decisive measures to acquire railway and mining rights and other interests in China.[1]

Given such concerns, the outbreak of the First World War in Europe was a godsend to Japan. Foreign Minister Kato, a former ambassador to Great Britain and the future president of the Kenseikai (one of Japan's two largest political parties), emerged as the architect of Japanese foreign policy, whereas Premier Shigenobu Okuma merely served as the symbolic unifying figure of the cabinet. When on August 7, 1914, the British government requested that the Japanese fleet "hunt out and destroy the armed German merchant cruisers" in Chinese water in accordance with the Anglo-Japanese agreement on alliance,[2] the Okuma cabinet decided within thirty-six hours to take this "one-in-a-million chance" to establish Japan's supremacy in China.[3] Foreign Minister Kato admitted that the situation had not yet reached the point where the terms of the alliance obliged Japan to declare war on Germany, but he argued that participation in the war was the best policy for Japan for two reasons: first, it would fulfill Japan's moral obligation under the alliance with Great Britain; and second, it would strengthen the Japanese position in East Asia by eliminating the entire German foothold in the region.[4]

Because Germany occupied an important economic and military position in northern China, Japan would greatly benefit from eradication of German influence in the region. The major German stake in China was a ninety-nine year leasehold in the territory of Jiaozhou on the Shandong peninsula amounting to about two hundred square miles. The lease included the city of Qingdao—the best harbor in China north of the Yangzi River. The Germans fortified the port of Qingdao and made it their naval base, as well as one of the largest trading ports in China. This leased area, which was surrounded by a neutral zone of thirty-three miles, became a virtual protectorate of Germany. Between Qingdao and Jinan, the Germans also built the Shandong Railway which connected with the main line to Beijing at Jinan.

However, though Kato was certainly convinced of the need for a vigorous China policy, he was also feeling pressure from both the genro and the military. The genro were Japan's most influential senior statesmen who had held, at various times, the highest positions in the government since the Meiji Restoration in 1868. Although most of the genro had retired from public service, their advice had significant bearings over any decision of national importance. Most notably, Prince Aritomo Yamagata, known as the founder of the Japanese imperial army and the cabinet maker, manipulated the government behind the scenes. Kato, who was trying to bring control of foreign affairs to the hands of the foreign minister, was fighting an uphill battle because the genro maintained loyalty both from the military and the government bureaucracy.

Soon after the war broke out in Europe, Genro Yamagata presented to the Okuma cabinet a written opinion stressing the necessity of a more vigorous regionalist foreign policy in East Asia. He urged the government to seize this "one-in-a-million chance" to solve all the unsettled problems with China, especially the issues concerning Japanese rights and interests in Manchuria; at the same time, he made a lengthy argument to promote closer cooperation with China, pointing out that the present war was part of the international trend toward "an increasing intensity in racial rivalry." Referring to the anti-Japanese movement in California and the discrimination against Indians in British Africa, Yamagata predicted that after the war the Western great powers would again focus their attention on East Asia to profit from the region. "When that day comes, the rivalry between the white and the non-white races will become violent," continued Yamagata, "and who can say that the white races will not unite with one another to oppose the colored peoples?" Now that Japan and China were the only two countries in Asia that somehow maintained their independence, Yamagata argued that "if the colored races of the East hope to compete with the so-called culturally advanced white races and maintain friendly relations with them while retaining their own cultural identity and independence, China and Japan, which are culturally and racially alike, must become friendly and promote each other's interests." He suggested some sort of Sino-Japanese entente or accord pledging "union and cooperation" in which China would promise to consult with Japan whenever it needed to deal with other foreign countries concerning political, military, and economic matters. He thought that Japanese financial assistance to the Yuan government would facilitate such an arrangement. Yamagata argued that the crux of the matter was the necessity for Japan to win China's confidence and trust through persistent persuasion and guidance.[5]

Another important player in shaping foreign policy during this period was the general staff office, which was actively involved in the civilian government's decision-making process from the very beginning of the war. When Russia mobilized its forces on July 30, 1914, the vice-chief of the general staff, Motojiro Akashi, who practically ran the office, wrote to the most influential army general, Masatake Terauchi, then the governor general of Korea and a future premier. In his letter, Akashi expressed his concern over the increased presence of German military advisers in north China and stated that he was watching the developments in Europe very closely because they would likely provide Japan with an opportunity to establish its authority in northeastern China. Akashi also urged War Minister Ichinosuke Oka to push the government to make a decision to enter the war against Germany so that Japan could take the German-leased territory in Shandong. Thinking that the Allied powers would most likely defeat Germany, Akashi feared that the Russians might take Jiaozhou and connect the port of Qingdao with the Russian-owned Chinese Eastern Railway. While Akashi was urging his colleagues to take action, younger and lower ranking officers in the general staff office, such as Giichi Tanaka, favored a more vigorous policy toward China and were flooding their superiors with war proposals. The ministers of war and the navy, in turn, pressed the foreign office to make a speedy decision for war. Genro Yamagata at one point worried that Foreign Minister Kato might resign because of the pressure that the military was exerting on him.[6]

Tokyo's diplomatic exchanges with London during this period show that the Japanese government was determined to pursue its own war objective—that is, occupation of the German territories in Shandong and the Pacific. However, concerned about a negative response toward unlimited Japanese military operations in China from the United States, Australia, and New Zealand, British Foreign Secretary Edward Grey was anxious to set geographic limits to Japanese military operations.[7] When the British government canceled its request for Japanese military assistance on August 10, Japanese Foreign Minister Kato insisted that British cancellation of its request for Japanese military cooperation would put the Japanese government in an "extremely embarrassing position," because it was public knowledge that the Japanese government was about to declare war on Germany. Two days later, the British government agreed to Japanese military participation, however, with a view to confining Japan's action to as small an area as possible. The British also proposed an Anglo-Japanese joint declaration in which the two not only would guarantee the independence and territorial integrity of China but also the restoration of the territory of Jiaozhou to China.[8]

In the summer of 1914, the Japanese government's attitude toward the question of postwar restoration of German territory to China was vague and evasive. On August 8, the Okuma cabinet decided that should Japan declare war on Germany and occupy Jiaozhou by force, Japan would hold the territory for a while before returning it to China. Japan's ultimatum to Germany expressed Japan's intention to restore Jiaozhou to China if Germany would return it peacefully, but it did not state when and how Japan would do so.[9] In response to the British proposal for an Anglo-Japanese joint declaration to China, the Japanese foreign minister firmly refused to give any assurance for the retrocession of Jiaozhou to China, insisting that any reference to future peace terms should be eliminated from the declaration. However, on August 18, without the consent of the Japanese government, the British Press Bureau published a statement regarding the limits of Japanese military operations. It assured China of the Anglo-Japanese intention to maintain the independence and integrity of China and stated, "It is understood that the action of Japan will not extend to the Pacific Ocean beyond the China seas . . . nor beyond Asiatic waters westward of the China seas, nor to any foreign territory except territory in German occupation on the continent of eastern Asia."[10] Japanese Foreign Minister Kato resented this independent act by the British government and discontinued the negotiation for a joint declaration. Thus, although Japan publicly obtained Britain's consent to a Japanese occupation of German territory in Shandong, it avoided making any specific commitment regarding the restitution of Jiaozhou to China.

The attitude of the United States was a great diplomatic concern for Japan. In the summer of 1914, relations between the two countries were not as good as they had been a decade earlier. The issue of immigration, especially the controversy over the 1913 California Alien Land Law, which banned Japanese immigrants from owning land in the state, strained relations. China was another thorny problem for the two. Since 1899, the United States had maintained a historic interest in China to preserve the Open Door and the territorial and administrative integrity of China. This publicly declared American policy was quietly matched by another equally important policy to maintain the balance of power in East Asia for the protection of American territories in the Pacific. Although the balance of power in East Asia had been preserved by the Western powers and Japan since the Russo-Japanese War through agreements and precedents such as the Root-Takahira agreement of 1908 between the United States and Japan,[11] the outbreak of the First World War was likely to upset this fragile balance of power, as European powers became more and more absorbed by fighting in their homelands. Japan saw clearly that the United States was the only country that could make certain that Japan would strictly observe the Open Door in China and maintain the status quo in the Pacific.

At the outset of the war, the State Department briefly contemplated making a sweeping proposal to neutralize and preserve the status quo in China. The idea originally came from the Chinese government of Yuan Shikai on

August 3, 1914. Because President Wilson was mourning for his wife who had passed away on August 6, Secretary of State William J. Bryan authorized the American Legation at Beijing on August 7 to participate in China's proposal to neutralize its own territories except leased areas. Robert Lansing, the counselor for the State Department, who considered the preservation of the status quo to be "the most important to American interests," made specific proposals to Secretary Bryan on August 8: (1) to obtain the belligerents' pledge to respect the neutrality of Chinese territory except areas leased to belligerent powers; and (2) to obtain from all interested powers an agreement that the status quo of all foreign rights and interests in China should continue until peace in Europe was restored. When Secretary Bryan transmitted Counselor Lansing's suggestion to President Wilson, Bryan, being a pacifist, went even further and proposed "an agreement that hostilities be not extended to the Far East."[12]

However, the American desire to preserve the status quo in China failed to materialize. Upon learning that the Japanese declaration of war on Germany was imminent, Lansing changed his opinion and advised the secretary of state to withhold any action until Japan took a decisive action against Germany. Lansing thought that in the event of Japan's entry into the war the United States would be able to approach all the belligerents simultaneously, without being bound to present the matter to Japan in advance in accordance with the Root-Takahira agreement of 1908. However, after Japan sent an ultimatum to Germany, seemingly having been convinced that Japan and Britain had decided to extend the war to the Pacific and East Asia, President Wilson suspended the whole idea of neutralization of China. On August 17, the president wrote to Secretary Bryan that "things have developed very fast in the East," and that "it is evidently too late to pursue the course suggested."[13]

The Japan government was sensitive to every American move in China, especially after it received the news on August 6 that the Chinese minister in Washington had asked the American government to take the initiative in securing an agreement among the European belligerents to maintain peace in China. On August 10, Foreign Minister Kato asked London to advise the United States not to interfere with the existing situation in East Asia. He ordered Japanese Ambassador Sutemi Chinda, in Washington, to keep him posted on the American attitude toward Japanese participation in the war.[14]

At the same time, Japanese government officials went too far with their efforts to assure the United States of Japan's good intentions in China. They did not seem to be very concerned about the serious consequences that might result from the disparity between their words and their deeds. Discrepancy between stated policy and real objectives was not uncommon among Japanese politicians, whose political culture expected them to use such discrepancy between what one said and what one really intended as part of political maneuvering. When Kato met American Ambassador George W. Guthrie at Tokyo on August 15, and gave him the text of the Japanese ultimatum to Germany, Kato asked the Ambassador to impress on the American government "as strongly as possible" that Japan "would not seek any territorial aggrandizement or selfish advantage in China and would carefully respect all neutral interests."[15] The following day, the Japanese ambassador delivered to the State Department a memorandum which expressed Japan's determination "to exercise utmost care not to injure in any way the interests" of the United States or any other third power. Premier Okuma also made a similar public statement on August 17 in which he declared "Japan's object is to eliminate from the Continent of China the root of the German influence," and that Japan "harbours no design for territorial aggrandizement or entertains no desire to promote any other selfish end."[16]

American government officials interpreted these Japanese statements as a commitment to the eventual restoration of Jiaozhou to China. Sending to President Wilson the text of the Japanese ultimatum and their explanation given on August 16, Secretary of State Bryan noted: "The enclosed is an important document to keep. It contains a definite statement of purpose and a disclaimer of value." Although Bryan had doubts about sending an American reply to Tokyo to confirm Japan's good faith, Wilson, who was determined to practice what he preached, wrote to Bryan: "I think it wise for us to be on the safe side in letting the Japanese Government know what our understanding of the situation is."[17] In the note of August 19 to Japan, the American government expressed its satisfaction with the knowledge that "Japan, in demanding the surrender by Germany of the entire leased territory of Kiaochou, does so with the purpose of restoring that territory to China, and that Japan is seeking no territorial aggrandizement in China in the movement now contemplated."[18] The United States also suggested that should disturbances in China require Japan to take measures to restore order, the Japanese government "will no doubt desire to consult with the American Government" in accordance with the Root-Takahira agreement. This American note was a polite but clear warning against Japanese independent action in China. The Root-Takahira agreement stipulated that should "any event occur threatening the status quo" in the Pacific Ocean or the principle of equal opportunity in China, the Japanese and American governments would discuss possible measures to be taken by both parties.[19]

The American press questioned Japan's official explanation for her entry into the war. The *New York Times* editorial on August 17, 1914, said:

The entrance of Japan upon the conflict between Germany and Great Britain cannot fairly be based on the requirements of the treaty of alliance of 1911. . . . The motive for this sudden and surprising action must be sought in the aims and ambitions of the Japanese Government, and it is impossible to regard these as unselfish. . . . The action of Japan now strengthens the suspicion she had long ago aroused that her desire for aggrandizement only awaited an opportunity for its assertion.

In spite of repeated requests from the Japanese ambassador and consuls in the United States that further explanations should be issued by the Japanese government to clear away American suspicions, Tokyo failed to find an effective way to do so. It soon became apparent that the United States was opposed to Japan's independent action in Shandong, and the two countries were on a collision course in East Asia. Colonel Edward M. House, President Wilson's adviser and intimate friend, wrote to the president on August 22 that he was sorry that Japan had "injected herself into the general melee for it will place an additional strain upon us not to become involved."[20]

Upon declaring war on Germany on August 23, 1914, Japan carried out the occupation of Shandong forcibly against the will of the Chinese. China, which had already declared its neutrality on August 6, wanted the Japanese to confine the war zone to the east of Weixian and not to use the Shandong Railway to transfer Japanese army troops, but Japan demanded that Chinese territory south of the Yellow River should be excluded from the neutral zone and that Chinese soldiers should withdraw from the area along the Shandong Railway between Qingdao and Jinan. The Chinese eventually gave in to Japan's pressure, and on September 3, 1914, the Japanese army landed at Longkou outside the German-leased territory and seized the Shandong Railway.[21] The Japanese were even more high-handed in their negotiations with China regarding the seizure of the railway in Weixian. The Japanese foreign office simply ignored repeated Chinese protests and insisted on the continuation of scheduled military operations. Upon the surrender of the German governor in Qingdao on November 7, a Japanese military administration took control of the entire German-leased territory in Shandong.

Japan was willing to seize the Shandong Railway in spite of Chinese protests because of the railway's diplomatic and military importance. Although the Germans had initiated its construction, the Shandong Railway was under German-Chinese joint management by a private enterprise named the Shandong Railway Company from which Germany received only 5 or 6 percent of the annual benefit. It was not really a part of the German leasehold and a Chinese police force was responsible for its security.[22] Therefore, Japan did not have sound ground in seizing the railway. However, Foreign Minister Kato justified the action by arguing that the Shandong

Railway was the main artery of the German-leased territory and that the Germans were using it to transport military supplies to Qingdao to fight against the Japanese army.[23] Kato's public pronouncements did not mention the significance of the railway for a future peace settlement; however, his confidential telegram to Japanese Minister Eki Hioki in Beijing on September 26 revealed the real purpose behind the seizure of the railway. In case the Japanese government decided to return Jiaozhou to China, Kato intended to keep the railway as part of the compensation for the restoration of Jiaozhou.[24] This became the basis of Group I of the Twenty-one Demands the Japanese government made on China four months later.

In the meantime, by October 5, the Japanese navy had occupied the German islands of the Marshalls and Carolines in the Pacific, although the Okuma cabinet had not decided whether Japan should retain these islands permanently.[25] However, when the Australian minister of defense, without consulting the Japanese government, announced on November 18 that the Australian navy was planning to take over the Marshalls and Carolines until the end of the war, Foreign Minister Kato immediately told the British government that Japan had no intention of handing over the islands to the Australians and requested that the British correct the misunderstanding. In a confidential note to the British ambassador in Tokyo, Kato agreed that the final disposition of all the German territories occupied by the Japanese and British forces must be made at a peace conference after the conclusion of the war. However, Kato added that Japan would "naturally insist on the permanent retention of all the German Islands north of the Equator" and would have to rely on the support of the British government.[26] Thus, in late 1914, the Japanese foreign minister began his diplomatic efforts to secure the allies' consent to Japan's permanent possession of the German Pacific islands north of the equator. However, the British government refused to make any commitment at that time, and negotiations for the Pacific islands were not resumed until the winter of 1917.

In the United States, the majority of government officials were apparently unperturbed by the Japanese occupation of the German islands, but their reticence did not mean that their country acquiesced to the Japanese action. The navy—and some of the major press—expressed uneasiness about possible serious consequences in the Pacific. On October 7, 1914, when news arrived that the Japanese navy had occupied the German island of Jaluit, the chief island of the Marshalls located directly between the Hawaiian Islands and the Philippines, a *New York Times* editorial said that Japan's seizure of Jaluit appeared to be "an act not in harmony" with the reasons Tokyo had given for entering the war. "In our declaration of policy in respect to Japan's ultimatum to Germany," said the *Times*, "we took occasion to say that our understanding of the matter was that Japan would not seek territorial aggrandizement, that she would restore Kiao-chau to China, and she would as a matter of course 'consult the United States before taking any steps beyond the boundaries of the territory of Kiao-chau.' " The American ambassador in Tokyo told Washington, "In reply to inquiry made by the naval attaché of the [American] Embassy, the private secretary of the Minister of Marine stated that he thought it likely that small force had been left on the island but that if there was any occupation it was temporary and for military purposes only."[27] This could hardly be called an official announcement of the Japanese intention, but the *New York Times* of October 8 reported that "definite and positive assurances were given" to the American government by the Japanese government that "the seizure of the Island of Jaluit . . . and the occupation by a Japanese naval force is only temporary and entirely for military purpose." According to the *Times*, the American government was believed to have accepted the statement from Tokyo as sufficient guarantee that the situation in East Asia would not be altered to America's disadvantage. Although President Wilson said that he had not followed the details of the Japanese explanations of the attack on the German islands in the Pacific, he indicated that "nothing had occurred liable to cause concern on the part of the American Government."[28]

In Tokyo, Kato was concerned about various speculations by the American press on Japan's military operations in the Pacific. He instructed Ambassador Chinda in Washington to make no comment on the question whether the Japanese occupation of the German islands should be temporary or permanent.[29]

Thus, during the first year of the great war, Tokyo and Washington began to hold different views of the postwar disposition of the German territories in China and the Pacific. Japanese government officials believed that they successfully avoided giving any specific guarantees that Japan would return Jiaozhou to China. Only a vague statement was made in its ultimatum to Germany to the effect that Japan would declare war on Germany unless Germany handed over the leased territory of Jiaozhou to Japan "with a view to eventual restoration of the same to China." Japan also successfully refrained from making a definite promise that its occupation of the German islands in the Pacific was temporary, for military purposes only. Available Japanese government documents indicate that the Okuma cabinet, in fact, hoped to retain all the German territories Japan had occupied even after the conclusion of the war. The United States government, on the other hand, interpreted the denial of territorial aggrandizement by Japanese government officials as Japan's positive guarantee of the postwar restoration of those territories to the native peoples. The State Department officials and Presi-

dent Wilson thought that the record was on their side and seemed to be confident that should Japan violate American interests in the region, they would be able to rectify the situation through some sort of diplomatic means.

On December 10, 1914, Foreign Minister Kato, in response to a question by a parliamentary member of the lower house, declared that he had never given any guarantee to the United States concerning the German islands in the Pacific or made any promise to Great Britain regarding the retrocession of Jiaozhou.[30] Kato's statement was not false as far as official documents were concerned, but when the State Department received this report from the American ambassador in Tokyo, officials in Washington could have been easily confused or aroused by what appeared to be a two-faced attitude on the part of the government in Tokyo.

The capture of Qingdao on November 7, 1914, completed Japan's military occupation of the German territories in Shandong, and, thereafter, Japanese efforts concentrated on diplomatic maneuvers to make the most of the German rights and concessions then under Japanese control. The first step Japan had to take was to obtain Chinese consent to a Japanese succession to all these German rights. Foreign Minister Kato also saw a long-awaited opportunity to settle other outstanding diplomatic problems with China. The most important issue was the settlement of Sino-Japanese differences regarding the definition of Japan's predominant position in South Manchuria and Eastern Inner Mongolia. Japan's occupation of Jiaozhou allowed Kato to combine the Manchurian issue and the Shandong issue. He intended to use Jiaozhou to draw a favorable deal from China concerning Japanese rights in Manchuria: the formula that he constructed was the Twenty-one Demands.

Foreign Minister Kato had been contemplating possible measures to strengthen Japan's foothold in Manchuria and Eastern Inner Mongolia for over two years. When he was ambassador in London and was about to return to Tokyo in January 1913 to accept the position of foreign minister, Kato met with British Foreign Secretary Grey twice to talk about Japan's plans for Manchuria. On January 3, Kato confided to Grey that the Japanese were determined to hold the Province of Guandong permanently through an extension of the duration of lease in Port Arthur and Dairen (Dalian). Grey showed sympathy for the Japanese attachment to Guandong, saying that the Japanese "planted blood" there, and told Kato that the issue of the Japanese leasehold in Guandong should be settled between Japan and China and that other countries did not need to interfere. A week later, Kato also told Grey that Japan intended to demand an extension of the concession terms of the South Manchurian Railroad and the Andong-Mukden Railroad. This time the British foreign secretary made no comment. On his way home from

London, Kato met the Japanese minister, Motohiko Ijuin, in Beijing and reminded him that the most important task of the minister in Beijing was to
lay the groundwork for a favorable settlement of the terms of Japanese concessions in Manchuria.[31]

On August 26, 1914, three days after Japan declared war on Germany,
the new minister to China, Eki Hioki, telegraphed Kato that "the time was
most opportune for the settlement of the China issue" because the Chinese
were greatly concerned about the Japanese military operation in Shandong
and anxious not to offend Japan. Hioki suggested that Japan should guarantee the restoration of Jiaozhou to China in exchange for her consent to an extension of the terms of the Japanese concessions in Manchuria. However,
Kato did not think that the time was ripe and instructed Hioki to make further efforts to create an atmosphere most favorable to future negotiations.[32]
The idea to exchange Jiaozhou for Chinese concessions was likely to be approved by the British. In the telegram of August 21, 1914, British Foreign
Secretary Grey told the Japanese foreign office that he had "not forgotten"
the previous year's conversation with Kato concerning the Liaodong Peninsula. Recognizing Japan's need to "make a condition" in return for her "expen-
diture of blood and money," Grey said, "We are now prepared to cooperate."[33]

While Kato and other Foreign Ministry officials were contemplating the
terms of the negotiation with China within the realm of legal possibility, focusing on the exchange between the restitution of the sovereignty in Jiaozhou to China and the extension of the duration of Japanese lease in
Manchuria, the Japanese army wanted to demand more from China. From
the outset of the war, the general staff office had a clear intention to use the
Japanese occupation of Shandong as a pretext "to bring China over to Japan's side" through a series of Sino-Japanese agreements reached either by
mutual consent or under duress.[34] As early as August 7, 1914, the general staff
delivered to the foreign office an outline of the proposal for a Sino-Japanese
agreement. It included extensive Japanese demands such as Sino-Japanese
joint defense in case of an extension of the war to East Asia, autonomy for
South Manchuria and Inner Mongolia, and a Japanese trusteeship of military, administrative, and currency reforms in China. In November, War Minister Oka presented a modified and more realistic, but still ambitious proposal. Although the ideas of joint defense, autonomy, and trusteeship were
dropped, the army insisted on Japanese ownership of the railways in South
Manchuria, the right of the Japanese citizens to own land and reside in the
region, and preferential treatment for the Japanese in the development of
mines. The army also demanded that China should consult with Japan before making concessions to or obtaining loans from other foreign countries,
and that China should seek Japan's advice on matters such as military re-

form and construction of arsenals. In addition to those army demands, an influential private organization of hard-liners called the *Kokuryukai* (Black Dragon Society) presented to the chief of the Political Bureau of the Foreign Ministry a far more aggressive proposition—a plan to make China a virtual vassal state of Japan. The proposal not only called for Japan's complete domination over South Manchuria and Inner Mongolia but also for Japanese control over Chinese military and financial affairs.[35]

Apparently, such persistent pressure from the army and the right-wing organization resulted in an array of Japanese proposals that were far more voluminous than Foreign Minister Kato had originally intended. The foreign office and the army settled on at least four common objectives: (1) the extension of the Japanese lease and railway rights in Manchuria; (2) the predominant position of Japan in South Manchuria and Easter Inner Mongolia and the expansion of Japanese residential area in the regions; (3) a special position for the Japanese in Fujian; and (4) Japanese rights to construct railways in southeastern China. Foreign Minister Kato and War Minister Oka also agreed on the fundamental policy concerning the Shandong Peninsula—that is, upon the completion of Japanese occupation of Jiaozhou, Japan would make a set of demands on China in exchange for the retrocession of the sovereignty of Jiaozhou to China. Accordingly, the chief of the Political Bureau, Chozo Koike, in charge of drafting a proposal, incorporated substantial portion of the army demands.[36]

The outcome was the so-called Twenty-one Demands consisting of five groups. The first two groups formed the core of the entire scheme. Group I made clear Japan's position vis-à-vis Shandong. First, to eliminate any possibility of direct restitution of Jiaozhou from Germany to China, Japan demanded that the Chinese government "give full assent to all matters that the Japanese Government may hereafter agree with the German Government respecting the disposition of all the rights, interests, and concessions" Germany possessed in the province of Shandong. Second, to strengthen Japan's position in Shandong, Japan demanded that the Chinese government agree to cede or lease no territory or island in the Province of Shandong to any other country; to allow the Japanese to build a railway connecting Chefoo or Longkou with the Jiaozhou-Jinanfu Railway; and to open certain important cities and towns in Shandong to foreigners for the purposes of trade.[37]

Group II of the Twenty-one Demands was intended to establish Japan's predominant position in South Manchuria and Eastern Inner Mongolia, and therefore was the most important group in terms of long-range Japanese foreign policy in the Asian continent. Here Japan demanded the extension to ninety-nine years of leases covering Port Arthur and Dairen, as well as Japan's rights to the South Manchurian and Andong-Mukden railways. China was to grant to Japanese nationals the right to own or lease land, to conduct mining operations, and to enter, reside, and travel in South Manchuria and Eastern Inner Mongolia. China was also asked to consult Japan if it needed a foreign loan or required political, financial, or military advisers in those areas. Group III demanded that the Hanyeping Company should be made a Sino-Japanese joint concern. Group IV required China not to cede or lease to any other power any harbor, bay, or island along the coast of China.

Group V of the Demands contained seven proposals, which were, according to Foreign Minister Kato's instruction to Minister Hioki, "entirely different in character" from the first four groups. Most of the items were adopted from a series of proposals that the army general staff presented to the Foreign Ministry. Japan asked the Chinese government:

1. to employ influential Japanese as political, financial, and military advisers;
2. to grant to Japanese hospitals, temples and schools in the interior of China the right to own land;
3. to place police in certain areas in China under Sino-Japanese joint administration or to employ Japanese in these police offices;
4. to purchase from Japan a fixed amount of arms or to establish a joint arsenal in China;
5. to grant Japan the right to construct three railways in southeastern China;
6. to consult Japan first in case China needed foreign loans for railway construction, mining, and harbor work in the Province of Fujian;
7. finally to grant the Japanese the right to preach in China.[38]

After securing the cabinet's approval of opening the negotiation for the Twenty-one Demands with China, Kato recalled Ambassador Hioki from Beijing in mid-November 1914 to give him detailed instructions. Kato's instructions to Hioki on December 3 indicate the government's intention to use the restoration of Jiaozhou as a bargaining point. The instructions stated, in part, that if the Chinese government accepted Tokyo's proposals, Japan "may . . . well consider the question with a view to restoring the said territory [Jiaozhou] to China in the event of Japan's being given a free hand in the disposition [of that area] as the result of the coming peace conference between Japan and Germany."[39]

Minister Hioki returned to Beijing and presented the Twenty-one Demands to Chinese President Yuan Shikai on January 18, 1915. He reminded President Yuan that the negotiations required absolute secrecy. Hioki was instructed not to discuss the first four groups of the demands separately but to negotiate them "en bloc." Because Jiaozhou was the only bargaining point of Japan, Kato ordered Hioki to seek further instructions in advance when he felt it necessary to discuss the question of Jiaozhou with the Chinese.[40]

Although the Japanese expected a quick settlement of the matter, the Chinese did not easily surrender. Yuan tried to invite foreign intervention in favor of his country. Because the European countries were preoccupied with the war, the United States was the only country that China could rely on to resist the Japanese demands. Following the advice of American Minister Paul S. Reinsch, the Chinese employed delaying tactics and refused to negotiate the demands en bloc, agreeing to discuss only Groups I and II at first, and later reluctantly agreeing to include Groups III and IV into their discussion. Throughout, the Chinese refused to negotiate Group V.

When Minister Hioki and Chinese Foreign Minister Lu Zhengxiang discussed the question of the restoration of Jiaozhou on the first day of the conference, February 2, 1915, there were great differences between the Japanese and Chinese positions. The Chinese foreign minister suggested that Japan should return Jiaozhou to China and consent to Chinese participation in a future peace conference, and that, in return, China would consent to Japan's succession to German rights in the Province of Shandong except the leasehold in Jiaozhou. Kato in Tokyo responded by saying that the Japanese declaration of war changed the situation and that Japan's intention to restore Jiaozhou to China expressed in its ultimatum to Germany was no longer applicable because Germany failed to surrender Jiaozhou peacefully. Japan had taken over Jiaozhou at the cost of many human lives and a large amount of money. Considering the Chinese desire to attend a peace conference without having participated in the war absurd, Kato said, "We may return Jiaozhou to China in the future, but it will happen only when we feel we can balance the gain against the loss."[41]

The Chinese counterproposal handed to Minister Hioki on February 12, 1915, was totally unacceptable to the Japanese government. China refused to consent to Japan's succession to the German leasehold in Jiaozhou, although it was willing to agree to the transfer of other German possessions in Shandong to Japan. In return for this concession, China wanted Japan's promise to return Jiaozhou to China and to recognize China's right to participate in the German-Japanese negotiations. In addition, the Chinese irritated Japanese officials by demanding compensation for "losses of all kinds" caused by Japan's military operations in Jiaozhou; immediate removal of the military railways and telegraphs constructed for the use of the Japanese troops; and withdrawal of the Japanese forces from Jiaozhou and the surrounding areas at the time of the restoration. As for the other demands, the Chinese excluded Eastern Inner Mongolia from Group II and dismissed Groups IV and V altogether.[42] In response to the Chinese counter proposal,

Tokyo insisted on China's acceptance of the slightly modified Japanese proposal. Kato instructed Minister Hioki to suggest to the Chinese, on his own initiative, that Japan might return Jiaozhou if the Chinese accepted Japan's modified proposals. However, realizing that Jiaozhou was the only bargaining chip Japan had, Kato added that the minister should not even hint at that possibility until an absolutely necessary moment arrived.[43] That moment did not come until late April 1915.

From mid-February to mid-March, there was little progress in the negotiation. The only significant concession Japan obtained from China was the latter's consent to give Japan a free hand in its negotiations with Germany.[44] The foreign office in Tokyo, frustrated by the firm attitude of the Chinese government and pressed by the military at home, began to contemplate the employment of some sort of coercive measure. In late March, the Okuma cabinet allowed the army to add twelve hundred new Japanese troops along the Shandong Railway and six thousand in Manchuria. However, because the foreign office was not ready to use actual military force to settle the differences, Japan's halfway measure only aroused Chinese ill feelings toward Japan and increased bitterness in the negotiations without producing any positive outcome.

By mid-April, the negotiations came to a stalemate. The Japanese primarily focused on Group II in relation to the Japanese rights in Manchuria and Eastern Inner Mongolia, and obtained China's consent to the extension of both the Japanese lease in Manchuria and the rights to the Manchurian and Andong-Mukden railways. However, the Chinese insisted on excluding Eastern Inner Mongolia from Group II. They were even more adamantly opposed to the demands of Group V. When, on April 17, the Chinese foreign minister firmly refused to make any compromise regarding Eastern Inner Mongolia as well as Group V, Minister Hioki reported to Tokyo the increasingly firm attitude of the Chinese government and the difficulty in continuing to negotiate with them. Because there was no settling these Sino-Japanese differences, Hioki asked Tokyo to consider sending China an ultimatum in which Japan offered the most conciliatory terms from its standpoint.[45]

Three months had passed since Japan had handed the Twenty-one Demands to China, but there was no prospect of Japan's settling Groups II, III, and V. Foreign Minster Kato wondered what made the Chinese government stiffen its attitude and instructed Hioki to find out the reason. In response, on April 19, Hioki reported some information he received from Russian Minister Vasilii Nikolaevich Krupenskii in Beijing. According to Krupenskii, American Minister Reinsch, under instruction from his government, had sent a note to the Chinese government on April 16. The note allegedly stated that "the Chinese Government shall not make any concession that would impair in any way the treaty rights of America"; that "the American Government will not recede an iota from the principle of territorial integrity and equal opportunity"; and that "the negotiation may be concluded to mutual satisfaction." The same news was reported in the *Peking-Tientsin Times* of April 19. Hioki was convinced that the American note had encouraged the Chinese government to adopt a firm attitude against Japan.[46]

Wishing to settle the issue peacefully, the Okuma government made one more attempt at negotiations. The most significant concession in Japan's revised "final concession proposals" was a formal overture that Jiaozhou be restored to China in return for a Chinese acceptance of these proposals. Japan also proposed to withdraw or postpone the negotiation of some of the articles in Group V.[47] Japan's final proposals were communicated to the Chinese government by Minister Hioki on April 26, 1915.

To Foreign Minister Kato, Japan's offer of the restoration of Jiaozhou was a trump card. He earnestly, but rather arrogantly, believed that Japan was entitled to determine the destiny of Jiaozhou because the Japanese had expended much blood and money to take over the territory from Germany. The restoration of Jiaozhou was an extremely large concession for Japan to make. Therefore, Kato assumed that China would be sensible enough to appreciate Japan's offer and accept its proposals in return for the former German-leased territory. He repeatedly urged Minister Hioki to use all possible diplomatic means to bring the negotiations to completion, but at the same time, he was prepared to face a worst case scenario. Should the Chinese government reject Tokyo's final proposals, in Kato's opinion, the Japanese government must be resolved to adopt the strongest measure possible to conclude the negotiations.[48]

The Chinese government's reply on May 1 was, in Hioki's words, extremely unsatisfactory. The Chinese government refused to consent to some of the Japanese revised demands in Groups II, III, and IV and rejected all the articles of Group V except the one regarding Fujian. To Japan's surprise, the Chinese government retracted the arrangement made in late February with regard to Shandong and went back to the original position in the beginning of the negotiations, demanding the restoration of Jiaozhou, China's participation in the German-Japanese negotiations regarding the disposition of the German interests in Shandong, and indemnity for all losses caused by Japanese military operation in Shandong.[49]

Japan's response to China was an ultimatum. The Foreign Ministry officials and the Okuma cabinet supported the sending of an ultimatum to China, but the genro who had been unhappy about Foreign Minister Kato's tendency to ignore their advice preferred a more cautious and moderate policy toward China. They were worried about economic consequences and the possible reactions of Great Britain, the United States, and Russia. Yamagata, the most powerful genro, suggested that instead of sending an ultimatum Kato should go to China and talk over the issues directly with President Yuan in order to solve the diplomatic deadlock. However, Kato refused to follow this advice, saying that there was no guarantee that the Chinese attitude would change if he went to China. The genro hesitated to give their consent to the sending of an ultimatum primarily because they wanted Group V to be excluded from it. Yamagata thought that it could have been justifiable for Japan to resort to arms to win the right to stay in Manchuria—Japan's lifeline—but he considered it to be a disgrace for Japan to use force on China to settle such matters of marginal importance in Group V. The cabinet at least decided to drop Group V from the ultimatum.[50]

Although the primary reason for the elimination of Group V from the ultimatum was the genro's objection, Japanese officials were also aware that the British and the American governments were strongly against it. While the Okuma cabinet members were conferring with the genro on May 4, Kato received a telegram from British Foreign Secretary Grey, in which Grey advised that there should not be "rupture between China and Japan" because of Japan's insistence on the appointment of Japanese advisers and the Japanese supply of arms and ammunition in Group V. If it happened, Grey warned, "[I]t would in the eye of public opinion in England be impossible to reconcile the position thus created with the terms of the Anglo-Japanese Alliance."[51] There is no doubt that Secretary Grey's telegram influenced the cabinet decision on Group V. On the same day, the foreign office also received a report from the Japanese ambassador in London regarding an American attempt to obstruct the Japanese demands on China. The vice director of the foreign news department of the *London Times* told the councilor of the Japanese Embassy:

I have reason to believe that malignant attempts are being made in Washington just now to create difficulty between [the] United States and Japan. I do not know whether the intrigue is German or American, but I should rather think [the] latter. Certain sections of American politicians are trying hard to impress administration that Japan is pushing too far her demands upon China. This comes to me privately but from the highest authority in the country. You may draw your own inference from what I told you.[52]

As it will be shown in the next chapter, this information was not entirely misleading.

The tone of the Japanese ultimatum delivered to China on May 7, 1915, was one of fatalism, suggesting that China's unresponsive and obstinate attitude had made the Japanese ultimatum inevitable. It censured the Chinese government for not appreciating Japan's goodwill in respect to the issue of the restoration of Jiaozhou, and concluded that "the last reply of the Chinese Government, taken as a whole, amounts to nothing more than a rejection of the entire Japanese proposals." Japan urged the Chinese government to accept without amendment all items included in Groups I, II, III, and IV, as outlined in Japan's final and modified proposals of April 26. Japan reserved Group V for future discussion except the issue of Fujian Province upon which the two had reached an agreement. The most important sentence came at the very end: "In case the Imperial Government fail to receive from the Chinese Government, before 6 p.m. of May 9, a satisfactory response to their advice, they will take such independent actions as they may deem necessary to meet the situation."[53]

Ironically, the hard attitude of the Chinese government had begun to soften immediately before Japan handed over the ultimatum, but the last minute Chinese concessions came too late and failed to prevent a showdown. President Yuan and Foreign Ministry officials made at least two miscalculations. First, they maintained a firm attitude against Japan because they thought that they could rely on intervention from the Western powers to fend off the Japanese pressure. President Yuan hinted to his Japanese adviser, Rihachiro Banzai, that he was expecting a friendly intervention by the British whose public opinion was becoming sympathetic toward China. The Russian minister in Beijing told Minister Hioki that China was paying special attention to the U.S. government's note given to China on April 16, which declared that the United States would not recede from the principle of territorial integrity and equal opportunity in China. According to the Russian minister, China appeared to cling to the hope that Japan's high-handed policy would arouse American public opinion, which, in turn, would influence the British government and the British would eventually restrain the Japanese.[54] However, the intervention that China expected did not occur. In fact, councils were held daily at the residence of President Yuan from May 1 on, and the ministers of the European Allies "advised the Chinese not to attempt armed resistance to Japan."[55]

The Chinese leaders' disappointment over the Western powers' failure to assist them coincided with their realization that they underestimated the Japanese government's determination to press its demands. According to Hioki, Chinese Vice Foreign Minister Cao Rulin turned pale on May 4 when he learned that Japan was about to deliver an ultimatum. The Chinese Foreign Office either had failed to take the Japanese warning seriously when Japan handed in the final proposal of April 26, or had been unable to foresee the danger of a diplomatic break with Japan when it made the uncompromising reply on May 1. The Chinese vice foreign minister had an interview with Minister Hioki on May 5 and proposed to withdraw China's counterproposal of May 1 and resume the negotiations of the Japanese proposals of April 26. Hioki immediately sought Tokyo's instructions, but Kato ordered Hioki to reject the Chinese offer. Kato wanted China's unconditional acceptance of the Japanese proposals.[56]

The Chinese government attempted to offer one more compromise proposal on May 6, which was more advantageous to Japan than Japan's own proposal. However, by that time in Tokyo the decision to send the ultimatum had already received the genro's approval and imperial sanction. The foreign office had informed the governments of Great Britain, the United States, France, and Russia about the ultimatum. Kato simply ordered Hioki to carry out the original plan. Minister Hioki visited Chinese Foreign Minister Lu and handed over the ultimatum on May 7.[57] The Chinese government made a formal decision to accept the Japanese ultimatum on May 8 and notified Minister Hioki the following day. According to Hioki, as early as the night of May 6, the Chinese government leaders had agreed to accept the Japanese demands to avoid a diplomatic crisis. The Chinese did so because by this time they were convinced that the Japanese were deadly serious and realized that neither Britain nor the United States would stop Japan. They also found the Japanese ultimatum more moderate than the previous proposals. In fact, Minister Reinsch recorded that the Chinese were "astonished and chagrined to find that the demands of Group V were not urged in the ultimatum."[58]

The treaties were signed between Japanese Minister Hioki and Chinese Foreign Minister Lu on May 25, 1915, and thus, the long-protracted negotiation of the Twenty-one Demands came to an end. Japan appeared to have obtained what it wanted. China agreed to accept all the arrangements Japan would make concerning the disposition of the German rights and concessions in Shandong. In other words, Japan obtained a free hand in its negotiations with Germany. Among other treaties and agreements signed on May 25, 1915, Japan's greatest achievement was to solidify Japan's paramount position in South Manchuria. China agreed to the extension of the duration of Japan's lease in Port Arthur and Dairen, as well as the South Manchuria and Andong-Mukden railways to ninety-nine years. The Japanese could now lease land, and enter, travel, reside, and carry on business in South Manchuria. China also agreed to approach Japan first, if a foreign loan was necessary to build railways in South Manchuria and Eastern Inner Mongolia, or if foreign advisers were needed. Group III of the demands was settled by the exchange of notes in which China promised to conclude an agreement for the Hanyeping Company's joint undertaking with Japanese investors in the future. With regard to the coast of Fujian, China declared that it would not allow a foreign country to build a shipyard, military coaling-station, naval bases, or any other military establishment in this area. Moreover, on May 13, 1915, President Yuan issued a mandate declaring that China would not cede or lease any port, bay, or island along the coast of China to any foreign state.[59] Thus, on the surface, Japan appeared successful in its strategic move to secure her footholds in China.

Japan's entry to the First World War was a purposeful act by its government leaders to take advantage of the European powers' distress and expand Japan's political and economic interests in China and Manchuria. Japan seized German-leased territory in Shandong and used it as a springboard to make a far more ambitious demands on China. The Twenty-one Demands revealed the Japanese leaders' intent to depart from the traditional foreign policy of accommodation with the West and venture on a more independent, assertive policy to establish Japan's supremacy in China and act as the dominant power in East Asia. The Sino-Japanese negotiations of the Twenty-one Demands were a harbinger of Japan's regionalist approach to Asian questions. Japanese leaders looked on their demands on China strictly as a matter of concern to Asia and made conscious efforts to leave the Western powers out of their negotiations, although they occasionally consulted or informed the European Allied powers and the United States. These Sino-Japanese negotiations also suggested the further development of a peculiar and ambivalent relationship between Japan and China. The Japanese knew that the establishment of a special relationship with China was the key to the success of Japan's regionalist aspirations, yet they treated China as an inferior partner which needed Japan's protection and guidance. At the same time, the Japanese tried to command China's loyalty by pressuring the Chinese leadership, and, even worse, they exploited China's wealth to augment Japan's national strength. The difficulties Japan faced in the negotiations of the Twenty-one Demands revealed this contradiction in its China policy. However, that was not the only problem Japan encountered in this episode, as unexpected objections came from the other side of the Pacific in the United States.

NOTES

1. Katsumi Usui, *Nihon to chugoku: Taisho jidai* (Japan and China: Taisho era) (Tokyo: Hara shobo, 1972), 41–42.

2. Greene to Kato, August 7, 1914, in the Foreign Ministry of Japan, *Nihon gaiko bunsho* (Documents on Japanese foreign policy), 1914 (Tokyo, 1966), 3: 103. Hereafter cited as *NGB*.

3. Cabinet decision of August 8, 1914, cited by Tatsuo Kobayashi, "Pari heiwa kaigi to nihon no gaiko" (The Paris Peace Conference and Japanese diplomacy)," in Toshio Ueda, ed., *Kindai nihon gaiko-shi no kenkyu* (Studies of modern Japanese diplomatic history) (Tokyo: Yuhikaku, 1956), 368.

4. Masanori Ito, ed., *Kato Takaaki* (Tokyo: Jitsubunkan, 1929), 2: 78–79.

5. "Written Opinion Concerning China Policy" by Aritomo Yamagata, August 1914, in Azusa Oyama, ed., *Yamagata Aritomo ikensho* (Collection of memoranda of Aritomo Yamagata) (Tokyo: Hara shobo, 1966), 339–345. Partial English translation in Ryusaku Tsunoda, Wm. Theodore de Bary, and Donald Keene, eds., *Sources of Japanese Tradition* (New York: Columbia University Press, 1958), 2: 207–209.

6. Shiro Yamamoto, "Sansen, nijuikkajo yokyu to rikugun" (War participation, the Twenty-one Demands and the army), *Shirin* 57 (May 1974): 4–12. The author cites Akashi's letter to Terauchi on July 30, 1914, Akashi's letter to Oka undated, and Kotaro Mochizuki's papers.

7. Edward Grey, *Twenty-five Years 1892–1916* (New York: Frederick A. Stokes Company, 1925), 2: 103–104.

8. Inoue to Kato, August 10, 1914, *NGB*, 1914, 3: 116; Kato to Inoue, August 11, 1914, *NGB*, 1914,3:120; British aide-Memoir, August 12, 1914, *NGB*, 1914, 3: 127; *NGB*, 1914, 3: 143.

9. Japanese ultimatum to Germany, August 15, 1914, *NGB*, 1914, 3: 146.

10. Japanese acting chargé d'affaires at Beijing to Kato, August 18, 1914, *NGB* 1914, 3: 177.

11. The Root-Takahira agreement was signed between Secretary of State Elihu Root and the Japanese ambassador to the United States, Kogoro Takahira, on November 30, 1908. This executive agreement stipulated that the United States and Japan would respect each other's territorial possessions in the Pacific, maintain the status quo in the region, and uphold the principles of the Open Door in China.

12. Bryan to McMurray, August 7, 1914, the U.S. Department of State, *Papers Relating to the Foreign Relations of the United States*, 1914, Supplement (Washington, D.C., 1928), 163. Hereafter cited as *FR*. U.S. Department of State, *Papers Relating to the Foreign Relations of the United States: The Lansing Papers 1914–1920* (Washington, D.C., 1940), 1: 2. Hereafter cited as *FRLP*. Bryan to Wilson, August 8, 1914, in Arthur S. Link, ed., *The Papers of Woodrow Wilson* (Princeton: Princeton University Press, 1966–1994), 30: 363. Hereafter cited as *PWW*.

13. Lansing to Bryan, August 14, 1914, *FRLP*, 1: 4; Wilson to Bryan, August 17, 1914, *FRLP*, 1: 5.

14. Kato to Inoue, August 10, 1914, *NGB*, 1914, 3: 117; Kato to Chinda, August 13, 1914, *NGB*, 1914, 3: 143.

15. Guthrie to Bryan, August 15, 1914, *FR*, 1914, Supplement, 170–171.

16. *PWW* 30: 391; *NGB*, 1914, 3: 186.

17. Bryan to Wilson, August 17, 1914, *PWW*, 30: 390; Wilson to Bryan, August 19, 1914, *PWW*, 30: 402.

18. Bryan to Guthrie, August 19, 1914, *FR*, 1914, Supplement, 171. Guthrie to Kato, August 21, 1914, *NGB*, 1914, 3: 207.

19. Root to Takahira, November 30, 1908, *FR*, 1908, 511–512.

20. House to Wilson, August 22, 1914, *PWW*, 30: 432.

21. Hioki to Kato, August 27, 1914, *NGB*, 1914, 3: 364–365; Hioki to Kato, August 31, 1914, *NGB*, 1914, 3: 375.

22. Masakuma Uchiyama, "Nichi-doku senso to Santo mondai" (The German-Japanese war and the Shandong problem) *Hogaku kenkyu* 33 (February 1960): 275.

23. Kato to Hioki, September 22, 1914, *NGB*, 1914, 3: 399.

24. Kato to Hioki, September 26, 1914, *NGB*, 1914, 3: 410.

25. Cabinet decision, October 2, 1914, *NGB*, 1914, 3: 666.

26. Chinda to Kato, November 9, 1914, *NGB*, 1914, 3: 670. Confidential note from Kato to Greene, December 1, 1914, *NGB*, 1914, 3: 676.

27. Guthrie to Bryan, October 6, 1914, *FR*, 1914, Supplement, 183.

28. *New York Times*, October 9, 1914.

29. Kato to Chinda, October 12, 1914, *NGB*, 1914, 3: 667.

30. Guthrie to Bryan, December 18, 1914, *FR*, 1914, Supplement, 208.

31. Masanori Ito, ed., *Kato Takaaki*, 2: 132–140, 144.

32. Hioki to Kato, August 23, 1914, *NGB*, 1914, 3: 544; Masanori Ito, ed., *Kato Takaaki*, 2: 154.

33. Telegram from Grey, August 21, 1914, *NGB*, 1914, 3: 215.

34. Shiro Yamamoto, "Sansen, nijuikkajo yokyu to rikugun," 13–23.

35. Katsumi Usui, *Nihon to chugoku*, 55–59.

36. Mamoru Shigemitsu, *Sugamo nikki* (Sugamo diary) (Tokyo: Bungeishunju-shinsha, 1953), 406.

37. *NGB*, 1914, 3: 563. English translation in Carnegie Endowment for International Peace, *The Sino-Japanese Negotiations of 1915* (Washington, D.C., 1921), 3.

38. Kato to Hioki, December 3, 1914, *NGB*, 1914, 3: 563–568; Carnegie Endowment, *Sino-Japanese Negotiations of 1915*, 3–8.

39. Kato to Hioki, December 3, 1914, *NGB*, 1914, 3: 561; Carnegie Endowment, *Sino-Japanese Negotiations of 1915*, 2.

40. Kato to Hioki, January 10, 1915, *NGB*, 1915, 3: 111.

41. Hioki to Kato, February 3, 1915, *NGB*, 1915, 3: 128; February 10, 1915, *NGB*, 1915, 3: 150.

42. *NGB*, 1915, 3:157. Carnegie Endowment, *Sino-Japanese Negotiations of 1915*, 8.

43. Kato to Hioki, February 16, 1915, *NGB*, 1915, 3: 164–167.

44. Hioki to Kato, February 23, 1915, *NGB*, 1915, 3: 182.

45. Hioki to Kato, April 15, 1915, *NGB*, 1915, 3:322; Hioki to Kato, April 17, 1915, *NGB*, 1915, 3: 329–332.

46. Kato to Hioki, April 18, 1915, *NGB*, 1915, 3: 332; Hioki to Kato, April 19, 1915, *NGB*, 1915, 3: 333; Hioki to Kato, April 19, 1915, *NGB*, 1915, 3: 335.

47. Kato to Hioki, April 22, 1915, *NGB*, 1915, 3: 337–339.

48. Kato to Hioki, April 24, 1915, *NGB*, 1915, 3: 342.

49. Hioki to Kato, May 1 and 2, 1915, *NGB*,1915, 3: 358–361.

50. Takeo Horikawa, *Kyokuto kokusai seiji-shi josetsu: 21–kajo yokyu no kenkyu* (An introduction to the history of Far Eastern international politics: A study of the Twenty-one Demands) (Tokyo: Yuhikaku, 1958), 257, 259–260.

51. Telegram from Grey, May 3, 1915, *NGB*, 1915, 3: 729–730.

52. Inoue to Kato, May 4, 1915, *NGB*, 1915, 3: 717.

53. Kato to Hioki, May 6, 1915, *NGB*, 1915, 3: 379–381. Carnegie Endowment, *Sino-Japanese Negotiations of 1915*, 31–36.

54. Hioki to Kato, May 4, 1915, *NGB*, 1915, 3: 366.

55. Paul S. Reinsch, *An American Diplomat in China* (Garden City, N.Y.: Doubleday, Page & Company, 1922), 145.

56. *NGB*, 1915, 3: 367–374.

57. *NGB*, 1915, 3: 390–392.

58. Hioki to Kato, May 8, 1915, *NGB*, 1915, 3: 414–415. Reinsch to Bryan, May 17, 1915, *FR*, 1915, 149.

59. English, Japanese, and Chinese texts of the treaty of May 25, 1915, are printed in *NGB*, 1915, 3: 486–528. The English text is also printed in Carnegie Endowment, *Sino-Japanese Negotiations of 1915*, 39–63.

CHAPTER 2

American Response to the Twenty-one Demands

The Twenty-one Demands, despite Japan's apparent territorial and commercial gains, was hardly a sweeping diplomatic victory for Tokyo. In fact, these gains came at a very high price. The whole episode, as it unfolded, became a turning point in Japanese-American relations, as the United States became more and more apprehensive about Japanese intentions in China. President Wilson called the Twenty-one Demands a "suspicious business" and emerged as a self-proclaimed protector of the Open Door and the territorial integrity of China against its selfish neighbor. Chinese efforts to invite the Western powers' intervention in its favor helped create the popular American image of Japan as an aggressor, and further aroused American suspicion of Japan. At the same time, Tokyo's response to such foreign apprehension and criticism was ineffective. However misguided the means adopted by the Okuma cabinet to attain its objectives were, the government's main problem with the United States was its inability to articulate Japan's incipient regionalism.

This chapter examines how and why Japanese relations with the United States became strained during the Sino-Japanese negotiations of the Twenty-one Demands. Paul S. Reinsch, American minister in Beijing, observed in retrospect: "[The Japanese] made two fundamental mistakes. The first was in their disingenuous denials and misrepresentation of the true character of the demands; the second, in the actual use of an ultimatum threatening force."[1] With regard to Reinsch's latter point on the Japanese ultimatum, as the first chapter describes, China's last-minute concessions to avert the ultimatum made Japan's action appear unnecessarily harsh in the eyes of foreigners. Contrary to Japanese expectations, the ultimatum against China not only rallied anti-Japanese sentiments in China but also allowed the Chinese delegates at the peace conference in 1919 to argue that the treaties of 1915 were signed under duress and thus should be abrogated. The evidence indicates that the ultimatum was an injudicious decision on the part of Japan. As for Reinsch's reference to Japanese secrecy or misrepresentation of the demands, obviously, the Japanese government prevaricated regarding the Twenty-one Demands in its explanations to the U.S. government, fearing America's interference in its negotiations with Beijing. But, when we take a closer look at the interactions among Japan, China, the United States, and to some degree Great Britain, we see that the circumstances which created the image of the infamous Twenty-one Demands were far more complex than Minister Reinsch believed. This chapter looks into gaps of perception and differences in position between American and Japanese government leaders regarding their respective role in shaping the future of East Asia, especially of China.

The Japanese government was determined to try to keep the Demands secret from the Western powers to avoid any interference in Sino-Japanese negotiations. The only exception was Tokyo's confidential disclosure of the contents of the Demands to the British government (not including Group V). Foreign Minister Kato counted on Foreign Secretary Grey's telegram supporting Japanese intentions in the Liaodong Peninsula. When Grey was informed of the Japanese Demands by the Japanese ambassador, he promised to confine the information within his government. Grey expressed his sympathy for the Demands regarding Shandong, South Manchuria, and Eastern Inner Mongolia, but he reserved his opinion on the issue of the Hanyeping Company.[2] Hoping that secret negotiations with China would lead to a speedy conclusion of an agreement, Tokyo did not give the American government an official list of the Demands until it was forced to do so on February 8, 1915.

Tokyo's attempt to keep the Sino-Japanese negotiations of the Demands secret from the United States to avoid its interference, however, backfired and aroused apprehension in the Wilson administration. Minister Reinsch in Beijing, who learned about the Demands from Chinese government officials, informed the State Department of "the astonishing nature of the Japanese proposal" on January 22. Reinsch, a former political science professor at the University of Wisconsin, was the embodiment of Wilsonian universal idealism and unilateralist internationalism. He shared Wilson's conviction regarding the universality of American institution and values, and he sincerely believed that the United States would provide a model for a democratic, federal commonwealth and that America's peaceful Open Door economic expansion in China, as opposed to other great powers' predatory imperialism and formal colonialism, would bring both material improvement and moral regeneration to the Chinese people. Reinsch was eager to test his ideas in the real world, and President Wilson could not have found a more enthusiastic advocate for his mission in China. Clearly seeing the grave implications of the Japanese Demands, Reinsch immediately "impressed it on the Chinese that, since the subjects under discussion intimately affected American rights in China," he should be kept informed in order that his government could take "necessary steps to safeguard its interests." Thus, Reinsch and Chinese officials kept up their frequent informal conversations during the negotiation.[3] Reinsch warned Washington on January 23 that the Japanese Demands "are stated to be such as could not be granted without abandoning entirely the open-door policy as well as independence in political and industrial matters." He added, "It is feared that refusal to comply will be met by causing trouble to China through instigation of revolutionary movements which would offer pretext for military occupation."[4] The reports Reinsch sent to Washington during the following days were increasingly alarming, warning that the Demands "would effectively work the exclusion of American participation in economic and industrial development of China." Some of Reinsch's reports, however, contained inaccurate information, exaggerating the extent of the Japanese Demands. For instance, he informed Washington that Japan allegedly demanded "administrative powers in South Manchuria" and "special rights respecting the nationalized iron deposits throughout China."[5]

The initial reaction of the Wilson administration was to avoid an open conflict with Japan, while standing firmly to protect the principles of the Open Door and territorial integrity of China, as well as American interests in that country. After a meeting with Wilson and State Department Counselor Robert Lansing on January 25, 1915, Colonel House wrote in his diary, "Trouble may grow out of this and I advised great caution. [Because of the Great War] we are not at present in a position to war with Japan over the 'open door' in China."[6] Wilson, nevertheless, was disturbed by the possibility of Japanese violation of the Open Door in China. For example, when Secretary of State Bryan brought up the issue of the Japanese status in the United States in relation to the California land legislation controversy, Wilson acknowledged the desirability of the settlement of the immigration issue, but he was not willing to separate it from the other issue of Japanese behavior in China. He wrote to Bryan that "there are many things to consider first: among the rest her present attitude and intentions in China and her willingness or unwillingness to live up to the open door in the East." He asked Bryan to have State Counselor Lansing study Japanese obligations in complying with the Open Door.[7]

From Beijing, Minister Reinsch repeatedly urged his government to act in behalf of China either independently or in cooperation with Great Britain. On January 26, he advised the State Department to make representations to the British government on the desirability of jointly obtaining from Japan a full statement of all the Twenty-one Demands. Again on February 1, Reinsch repeated the necessity of "an understanding with Great Britain for the purpose of influencing Japan towards a course of moderation and equity," saying that "the British Government holds the key of the situation." In addition to calling Washington's attention to the Japanese refusal to disclose the demands on China, Reinsch also expressed his opinion that the Chinese government would readily disregard the injunction for secrecy and make public the Japanese demands if the United States assured the Chinese that the American government "would assume moral and consequent political responsibility for insistence upon the disclosure of matters affecting its rights."[8]

Before the State Department's inquiry into the Japanese Demands bore any fruit, the Japanese government itself decided to inform the American, Russian, and French governments of the contents of the Demands. Significantly, however, Group V was excluded from the Japanese communication. Frequent Russian inquiries about the Demands and adverse international publicity persuaded Foreign Minister Kato that it would be better to let the great powers know the Demands before inaccurate information became widespread. Kato's instructions on February 4 to the ambassadors in the United States, Russia, and France asked them to deliver the lists of the Demands but Kato did not mention Group V. It seems likely that the ambassadors were not aware of the existence of Group V, for there is no record in the foreign office indicating that Tokyo informed them of Group V. At the same time, Premier Okuma assured American Ambassador Guthrie in Tokyo that "Japan's interest in China was to preserve peace and China's territorial integrity and that it was Japan's intention to adhere to the policy of the open door and equal opportunity."[9] Ambassador Chinda in Washington, who later became the most outspoken Japanese delegate at the Paris peace conference of 1919, handed the English translation of the demands to Secretary Bryan on February 8. It consisted of an abridged version of the first four groups of the Demands. Chinda reported to Tokyo that the secretary of state did not make any objections to the Demands, merely insisting that his government be reassured that the Japanese Demands regarding mining rights and the employment of Japanese advisers applied strictly to South Manchuria and Eastern Inner Mongolia. Chinda observed that "judging from the

Secretary's way of talking and behavior, he did not appear to be surprised at or have suspicions about all the demands."[10]

President Wilson's "personal and confidential" letter to Minister Reinsch on February 8 clearly shows his sympathy toward China, but it also indicates an initially cautious response to the crisis in China. "[I] have been doing what I could indirectly to work in the interests of China," Wilson wrote. But he believed that watchful waiting, and counseling the British to restrain their Japanese ally, were the best moves for the moment, until at least the situation might require the United States to intervene. He thought that "any direct advice to China or direct intervention on her behalf in the present negotiations would really do her more harm than good, inasmuch as it would very likely provoke the jealousy and excite the hostility of Japan, which would first be manifested against China herself." He told Reinsch, "For the present, I am watching the situation very carefully indeed, ready to step in at any point where it is wise to do so."[11] As far as Shandong, South Manchuria, and Eastern Inner Mongolia were concerned, neither President Wilson nor Secretary Bryan at that time were willing to take action to oppose the Japanese Demands, although they now had nearly the full extent of information regarding these areas.

In mid-February 1915, however, the manner in which the existence and contents of Group V were disclosed to Americans made the Wilson administration increasingly suspicious of Japanese motives and honesty, and eventually prompted Wilson to "step in." Two days after Ambassador Chinda delivered the summary of the Demands excluding Group V to Secretary Bryan, Ambassador Guthrie in Tokyo telegraphed Washington that the statement given to the United States did not contain all of Japan's Demands. From Beijing, Minister Reinsch also repeatedly reported the objectionable character of the Demands which were omitted from the Japanese memorandum. He said he believed that the list of demands delivered to the United States was "a minimum" which the Japanese government wanted from China.[12] In the meantime, in late January, the Chinese press began to discuss the demands publicly. Around February 10, hoping to win over British and American public opinion, Chinese government officials revealed the substance of the Demands to the Beijing correspondents of the *London Times* and the Associated Press. The Associated Press in the United States did not publish the telegram from Beijing because the Japanese Ambassador denied it, but the *Washington Post* printed it on February 11. Later the *Peking Gazette* of February 17 reported that the Japanese government actually made twenty-one demands but told the great powers only about eleven of them. This news was published in the American newspapers on February 18. The next day, the *Chicago Herald* and the *New York Times* printed the full text of the Demands, including Group V, which had been obtained by the *Chicago Herald* through Chinese sources. Although there were some exaggerations, the text was mostly accurate.

At the same time, the Chinese government instructed its ministers abroad to communicate confidentially the full text of the Japanese demands to their respective host-country governments. By February 18, the State Department in Washington received the memorandum from the Chinese minister. The somewhat exaggerated wording of the Chinese version of Group V was to the disadvantage of Japan. For example, with regard to Chinese-Japanese joint police administration, the Japanese Demand actually read, "In view of the fact that police incidents between the Japanese and the Chinese are increasing and causing annoying disputes, the police *in localities where such arrangements are necessary* is to be placed under joint Japanese and Chinese administration, or *many* Japanese are to be employed *in police offices in such localities*." However, the Chinese version given to State Department officials said, "China and Japan shall jointly police the *important places* in China, or employ *a majority of* Japanese in *the police department of China*." In regard to the purchase of arms, Japan asked China "to obtain *a certain amount of arms supply (say half of the Chinese need)* or to establish a Japanese-Chinese joint arsenal *in China* to be supplied with technical experts and materials from Japan." However, the Chinese version said, "China shall purchase from Japan *at least half* the arms and ammunition used in the whole country or establish jointly *in Japan* factories for the manufacture of arms."[13]

Secretary Bryan's initial response to the disclosure of Group V was cautious and did not lay any blame upon the Japanese. Bryan appeared to be operating on the basis that there might have been a misunderstanding. He instructed Ambassador Guthrie in Tokyo to make an inquiry at the Japanese foreign office, telling Guthrie that Group V "may have been informally discussed and having met with opposition from China, abandoned before the shorter memorandum was sent to us." In the telegram sent to the Japanese government on February 19, Bryan quoted Group V in press dispatches which, if presented, "would have menaced the political integrity and independence of China and would have materially discriminated against other nations which are entitled to equal treatment." He said, "We were very much relieved to receive the memorandum delivered by the Japanese Ambassador . . . for this memorandum is a complete denial of the press reports above quoted and gives assurance that Japan has no such intention as the press reports would have indicated."[14]

The Japanese government was now placed in the embarrassing position of having to explain why Group V was excluded from the Japanese memorandum of February 8. After meeting with Foreign Minister Kato on February 20, Guthrie reported to Secretary Bryan that, according to Kato, the statement handed to the United States was, indeed, the complete list of the "demands" upon which Japan would insist. Guthrie added, "In addition to these demands several matters had been presented to China as 'requests' or wishes [on] which friendly consideration was desired." Kato admitted that, although press reports were exaggerated and distorted, these requests were mostly accurate. Guthrie wrote that Kato was "particularly anxious" to persuade the Wilson administration that he did not mention Group V because the items in it were "requests" and were so designated when presented to China.[15]

Kato's explanation must have sounded like a shabby excuse to "friends" of China, such as Minister Reinsch who spoke of the foreign minister's "disingenuous denials and misrepresentation of the true character of the demands." But Kato may not, in fact, have been as "disingenuous" as Reinsch believed he was. As Kato explained to Ambassador Guthrie on February 20, he had made a distinction between the first four groups of the demands and Group V in his original instruction to Minister Hioki on December 3, 1914, which read:

The matters contained in Group V are entirely different in character and, on this occasion, China is to be advised to fulfill them. Since an adjustment of all these matters, some of which have been pending between the two countries, is urgent to advance the friendly relations between Japan and China and to protect our common interests, you are requested to do your best to have our wishes fulfilled.[16]

It is true that Kato several times asked Minister Hioki to do his best to negotiate Group V with the Chinese and did not abandon these instructions totally until the very end of the negotiations; it is also true that the issues in Group V were no more than a group of subordinate issues added piecemeal. Facing China's firm refusal to discuss Group V, Tokyo began to deemphasize Group V issues. On February 16, 1915, three days before Group V was made public in the United States, Kato communicated to Minister Hioki the maximum concessions that Japan was prepared to make regarding Group V. First, the proposal for the Japanese and Chinese joint police administration would be withdrawn. Second, as to the employment of Japanese political, financial, and military advisers, Japan would simply declare that it would earnestly advise China to employ them. Third, the proposal for the arms purchase would also be withdrawn, and if China should not agree to establish a joint arsenal in China, Japan would be satisfied with the Chinese promise to discuss this matter in the future. Fourth, if the Chinese should not agree to the railway concessions, Japan would extend a loan so that China could construct the railways. Fifth, as for the nonalienation declaration on Fujian, Japan would be satisfied with the conclusion of a secret agreement with China on the matter. Finally, the rest of the items of Group V were to be postponed if China would promise to consider them in the future.[17] Thus, by mid-February the Japanese government had been prepared to change the infamous Group V into a virtual declaration of wishes.

Whether Group V issues were called requests or demands, the fact that Japan would broach these issues at all made both the United States and Great Britain realize that Japan might violate the Open Door and the territorial integrity of China and infringe their own treaty rights in China if the opportunity should arise. Upon receiving the English translation of Group V from the Japanese ambassador, British Foreign Secretary Grey sent a diplomatic note to Tokyo with a view to protecting British interests in China, as well as saving his government's face toward the United States regarding the Open Door. He advised Tokyo to discuss the "wishes" of Group V "freely" with his government should any of them be found to "conflict with the commercial interests of Great Britain." Grey added, "I am very anxious that the Japanese Government should refrain from advancing any demands which could reasonably be considered to impair the integrity or independence of China."[18] The British government, however, did not make further objections to specific provisions of Group V, with the exception of a Japanese request for the right to construct three railways in southern China, which conflicted with a prior British agreement with the Chinese government. In fact, Grey implied British acquiescence to most of Group V when he frankly admitted during the conversation with the Japanese ambassador on March 8 that "the increase of Japan's share of development of China" was natural.[19]

Having been fully introduced to the contents of Group V, the American government also formulated its own policy toward Japan. Although President Wilson was closely watching the development in Asia, for the moment, Secretary of State Bryan's policy of compromise and mediation prevailed. On February 22, Bryan made a proposal to Wilson regarding America's official response to Group V. He told the president that the five requests among Group V—namely, the requests for advisers, police, arms, railways, and territory in Fujian—were objectionable on the grounds that they would threaten the political integrity of China and interfere with the agreement for the equal treatment of all nations. Bryan also suggested a skillful way to file the American objections with the Japanese. He said, "We can follow the plan adopted in the last telegram [of February 19, 1915] and express gratification that these are not made as demands but merely presented as requests, and, thus, our discussion of them upon their merits will not be objectionable."[20] President Wilson was more eager to make clear where the United States stood concerning the fundamental China policy than his secretary of state. Wilson replied to Bryan, "I fully approve of taking advantage of the opening to present to Japan very frankly our views on her 'suggestions' or 'requests.' I think those views can be made very weighty and conclusive. We shall not have uttered a more important state paper." Wishing to have the message sent quickly, Wilson added, "It is evident that things are pressed at Peking. It would be wise to let Tokyo have our views by cable."[21]

Despite the president's anxiety, the American note to Japan was delayed because advisers in the State Department were considering a somewhat different "reciprocal understanding" or "bargain" with Japan. On February 26, Edward T. Williams, chief of the Division of Far Eastern Affairs, who had been against the entire package of Japanese Demands from the beginning, suggested to Secretary Bryan that he should consider obtaining a quid pro quo before the State Department finalized the decision to make no objections to the Japanese Demands as distinguished from the requests. Developing his idea from a Japanese memorandum, which former Secretary of State Philander Knox received in September 1912 regarding the possible effect that the Japanese settlement in Manchuria might have on Japanese emigration to America, Williams wrote, "The diversion of the tide of Japanese emigration towards Manchuria may somewhat relieve the situation on our Pacific Coast." Therefore, if the United States acquiesced in the Japanese demands as to Manchuria and did not protest against the Japanese actions in Manchuria or in Shandong, he suggested, "Possibly a better understanding with respect to the California land question might be brought about."[22] Counselor Lansing supported the suggestion of Williams and developed it into a substantial proposal. In his letter to Bryan on March 1, Lansing suggested that the United States refrain from "urging its undoubted treaty rights relative to South Manchuria and Shan Tung" in exchange for a Japanese declaration that the Japanese government:

(1) Will make no further complaint in regard to legislation affecting land tenures in the United States unless such legislation is confiscatory in character, or materially affects vested rights;

(2) Will reaffirm explicitly the principle of the 'Open Door', making it particularly applicable to the territories affected by the demands;

(3) And will prevent any monopolization by Japanese subjects of particular trades in these territories, and any preferential rates or treatment by Japanese railways or other transportation concerns for the benefit of Japanese subjects or their merchandise.[23]

Lansing advised Bryan to wait until this proposal could be considered before sending a memorandum on the issue of the Japanese requests.

The idea of making a "reciprocal understanding" failed because President Wilson and probably Secretary Bryan opposed it. The idea of striking a bargain with Japan at the expense of helpless China was morally repugnant to Wilson. He wrote to Bryan on March 4, "My judgment is against this, as yours is. It would seem like bargaining away some of the rights of China in exchange for relief from some of our own difficulties. I think we ought to go straight at the matter of the requests, in the way you and I agreed." A few days later, Wilson received news from Beijing that Japan was dissatisfied with the slow progress in negotiations with China and might resort to means outside of diplomacy. Responding to this, the president wrote to Bryan on March 10, "I am anxious to know whether our note to Japan about the 'requests' she made on China has gone forward or not."[24]

The U.S. government's note of March 13, 1915, which was delivered to the Japanese ambassador in Washington on March 15, was, as Wilson had said, an important state paper with significance for the future. The note stated at the beginning that "[t]he American Government is glad to learn . . . that the 'requests' were not presented to China as 'demands' but that they were but 'wishes.' " The note continued, "The American Government understands . . . that the latter are not to be pressed if the Chinese Government should decline to consider them." Reviewing both the long-standing American tradition of the Open Door in China since the days of Secretary of State John Hay, and the Sino-American treaties which guaranteed "broad and extensive" rights and privileges for Americans in China, the note declared that the American policy was "directed to the maintenance of the independence, integrity and commercial freedom of China and the preservation of legitimate American rights and interests in that Republic." The note also pointed out the Japanese commitment to the same principles in various treaties, including the Root-Takahira agreement of 1908. Then, the Americans noted their objections to Group IV (regarding the nonalienation of the Chinese coast) and to four items in Group V (the requests for advisers, arms purchase, joint police, and territory in Fujian province). The assertion of U.S. interests and involvement was unmistakable: "These proposals, if accepted by China, while not infringing the territorial integrity of the Republic, are clearly derogatory to the political independence and administrative entity of that country. . . . The United States, therefore could not regard with indifference the assumption of political, military or economic domination over China by a foreign Power." However, the United States did make significant concessions to Japan regarding Manchuria and Shandong. The note stated that although the United States, in view of a series of Sino-American treaties, had grounds for raising objections to the Japanese Demands relative to Shandong, South Manchuria, and Eastern Mongolia, "the United States frankly recognizes that territorial contiguity creates special relations between Japan and these districts." Therefore, the note continued, "[The American government] is disposed to raise no question, at this time," to Group I demands regarding Shandong or to Group II demands regarding South Manchuria and Eastern Inner Mongolia.[25]

Thus, in the note of March 13, 1915, strongly enunciating its policy of the open door and the territorial and administrative integrity of China, the United States demonstrated that it was willing to "step into" the Sino-Japanese negotiations. At the same time the United States made no objections to Japanese demands on Manchuria and Shandong, and recognized that "territorial contiguity" created Japan's "special relations" with both Shandong and South Manchuria. Although at first the State Department did not seem to realize the far-reaching implication of these concessions, Japanese leaders immediately saw the chance to strengthen their country's footing in China. As we see in the following chapters, the Japanese government would use the argument of "territorial contiguity" to urge the Americans to recognize Japan's special position in China.

On March 22, Ambassador Chinda in Washington presented Japan's reply to Secretary Bryan orally and in the form of an unofficial memorandum. In the beginning, Chinda expressed Tokyo's gratitude for the U.S. government, which "in frank recognition of Japan's special position in South Manchuria, Eastern Mongolia and Shantung," raised no question regarding the Japanese proposals relating to those regions. Then Chinda explained Japan's position regarding the four "requests" to which the United States made objections. First, the Japanese government disclaimed "any attempt to coerce China to accept the proposal" on the employment of Japanese advisers. Second, the Japanese government regarded the proposal for purchasing a fixed amount of arms as "a pure and simple business proposition." Chinda added that Germany and Austria-Hungary had been furnishing China with a "greater portion of her arms and ammunition" and were contemplating the establishment of an arsenal in China. Third, the proposal for joint policing "is to have its practical application nowhere except Manchuria and possibly Mongolia in certain contingency." Finally, Chinda provided a long explanation for the nonalienation proposal of Fujian. In view of the geographic propinquity to Taiwan, a Japanese colony, "any intrusion of foreign influence in Fukien would lead the people of Japan to entertain fear that the defense of Taiwan would thereby be directly or indirectly menaced." To support this point, Kato relayed the Japanese people's great concern about American activities in Fujian. For instance, Kato earlier had mentioned to Guthrie former Secretary of State John Hay's suggestion that the United States desired to improve a harbor in Fujian for a naval coaling station. Other examples were recent reports that the Bethlehem Steel Company was negotiating a contract with China for the Fujian harbor's improvement. In the memorandum, the Japanese government suggested that it might withdraw the request on Fujian if the American government entered into "an engagement to make the citizens of the United States refrain from any undertaking in Fukien which may directly or indirectly cause the above-indicated fear on the part of the Japanese people."[26]

Bryan took the Japanese government's explanation at face value and responded with a sympathetic attitude toward its position. He wrote President Wilson on March 22 that if Japan disclaimed any attempt to coerce China to accept the proposal for advisers, "there is no objection to the offering of such a suggestion." He believed that the request for arms purchase could be substituted for the Chinese pledge that "Japan shall not be discriminated against in the purchase of arms," and that the police proposal could apply only to Manchuria and Mongolia. As to Fujian, Bryan suggested that the problem should be solved by the exchange of notes between the United States and Japan in which the American government stated that it had no desire to secure a coaling station on the border of Fujian.[27]

The issue of Fujian was quickly settled between Japan and the United States. Upon receiving full approval from President Wilson, Ambassador Guthrie met Kato on March 29 and gave the American consent to a nonalienation agreement between Japan and China. The ambassador showed Kato the telegram from Washington, which stated that the U.S. government had no objection to any Sino-Japanese arrangement to withhold "any concession to any foreign Power which contemplates the improvement of any harbor on the coast of Fukien or the establishment of a coaling station or naval base along said coast by any foreign Power."[28] Consequently, the Japanese and Chinese negotiated the issue of Fujian along the line indicated by the United States, and notes were exchanged between the two governments on the occasion of the signing of other treaties in May.

As for the other three Japanese requests, President Wilson had more misgivings about Japanese intentions than Bryan. To Wilson, any degree of violation of the Open Door principles was unacceptable. On March 22, he told Bryan that the explanations of these requests offered by the Japanese were not convincing. Although he could understand the Japanese motives that were disclosed, he said, "I think that the remedies and safeguards proposed in the 'requests' go too far. Whatever the intention, they do, in effect constitute a serious limitation upon China's independence of action, and a very definite preference of Japan before other nations, to whom the door was to be kept open."[29] Bryan's reply to the president reflected the current political realities: "As Japan and China must remain neighbors it is of vital importance that they should be neighborly, and a neighborly spirit cannot be expected if Japan demands too much, or if China concedes too little."[30] Bryan proposed compromises on those three requests: China would promise not to discriminate against Japan when employing advisers or purchasing arms, and the joint policing should be limited to Manchuria, Eastern Mongolia, or other places which had a considerable percentage of Japanese subjects. Wilson approved of Bryan's idea,[31] and Ambassador Guthrie presented this message orally to Foreign Minister Kato on March 29. The same statement in written form was handed to Ambassador Chinda at Kato's request.

The mediation effort of Bryan appeared to be going to work well at that time, but as Arthur S. Link says, "Rarely has a diplomatic effort so well meant turned out so badly in the end."[32] Bryan's compromise suggestion unintentionally encouraged the Japanese to go ahead with their requests without significant changes. When Kato heard about the American compromise proposal from Ambassador Guthrie on March 29, Kato believed that the Wilson administration was not strongly opposed to those items of Group V which were in question. The next day, Kato wrote Minister Hioki at Beijing that the United States would not make objections to China's employment of Japanese advisers or to China's purchase of Japanese arms if both were limited to certain numbers. He also wrote that Americans would not oppose joint Sino-Japanese policing in a certain area in Manchuria and Mongolia where a large number of Japanese resided. Kato concluded, "I don't think that the American government is attaching importance to the above issues."[33] Therefore, Minister Hioki began to press the Chinese to negotiate on some of the items of Group V, despite the constant Chinese refusal to consider them.

There was an unfortunate chain of events. Because of Japan's strategy to negotiate the groups sequentially, the issues of Group V came at the end and had not been seriously discussed. However, on March 27, the Japanese were now ready to concentrate on this group. Hioki, who devoted himself to the task of negotiating the Demands, was personally determined to fulfill his mission. However, the Chinese foreign minister's firm resistance to Hioki's pressure forced him to admit in his letter to Kato on April 14 that there was little possibility of persuading the Chinese to accept the items of Group V. Bryan's conciliatory communication led Tokyo to assume that the United States would not make serious objections, and, thus, the Japanese continued strenuously but unsuccessfully to press the Chinese to accept Group V.[34]

Meanwhile, Minister Reinsch in Beijing, who was eager to spoil the entire Japanese scheme, raised a forthright objection against Bryan's compromise suggestion of March 28. In his telegram of March 30, Reinsch told Bryan that should the Chinese become aware that the American government favored

an adjustment by which China would forego its freedom to choose advisers whom it trusts, to buy munitions according to its needs and without foreign supervision of its military organization and to exercise police functions independently in the territory still under its sovereignty, I fear that such knowledge would produce in the minds of the Chinese a conviction that United States had betrayed its historic friendship and its moral responsibility in respect to principles of China's administrative integrity and the Open Door.[35]

Reinsch urged Bryan not to offer a compromise suggestions to the Japanese government. However, there was little Bryan could do to change the course of events by the time Reinsch's telegram reached Washington, for the substance of the proposal had been already communicated to the Japanese foreign minister, and Bryan himself had handed a copy of the proposal to Ambassador Chinda on March 30. Bryan replied to Reinsch that the suggestions were made "for the purpose of removing the friction between the two countries" in a spirit of friendliness and that they were "no more binding upon China than upon Japan." Nevertheless, Reinsch's objection disturbed President Wilson, who wrote Bryan that "I had read Reinsch's message . . . and it had given me a good deal of concern. I sincerely hope that this [Bryan's] telegram will set the matter in the right light alike in Reinsch's mind and in the mind of the Chinese, when they learn of our interchange of views with Japan."[36]

Minister Reinsch continued to send disquieting news from Beijing which would discredit the Japanese. He reported that the Japanese were adopting "an attitude of uncompromising exigence" and that "an ultimatum backed by force is momentarily expected." On April 5, Reinsch reported that when the Japanese government presented the demands on January 18, 1915, no distinction was made between the alleged requests and the Demands, nor had the Japanese minister in his negotiations with the Chinese foreign office "ever placed these matters in a different category from the rest of the demands." Reinsch also informed the State Department on April 7 that Japan insisted on "the demand concerning purchase of one-half of all war materials from Japan," and on April 9 that the Japanese minister made additional demands in regard to Fujian, namely, the concession of coal mines at Anxi.[37]

However, as we shall see, these reports were not necessarily accurate and turned out to have a very unfortunate effect on Japanese-American relations at this critical moment. Reinsch was transmitting information to Washington, relying solely on the Chinese sources, and although those reports conveyed the tense atmosphere of Beijing, as well as the high-handed policy of Japan, they were not accurate except for the Japanese proposal on coal mines at Anxi in Fujian. These Chinese accusations and complaints concerning Japan's unreasonable attitude, as communicated by Minister Reinsch, were apparently interpreted by President Wilson and the State Department as examples of bad faith on the part of the Japanese government.

President Wilson also became uneasy about the twenty-page telegram which was sent to him as a petition by seven American religious and educational leaders in China. On April 12, Wilson wrote to Bryan, "I shall be very much interested to learn what you think of it." The telegram strongly denounced alleged Japanese imperialism and militarism and compared the struggle in East Asia to the war in Europe, namely, the conflict to decide whether militarism would dominate or be subdued. The petition urged that the United States, possibly in cooperation with Great Britain and other European powers, or by itself, claim to participate in a conference between China and Japan to discuss the Japanese demands. Later it was revealed that the Chinese government financed both the expense of the missionary's telegram to Wilson, which was more than $7,000, and the charge for the United Press, which published the summary of this telegram.[38]

The Chinese government, which depended on sympathetic foreigners and pressure groups, as in the case of the missionary's petition to President Wilson, was, to some degree, successful in its efforts to pit one power against another. Even Minister Reinsch once acknowledged the problem arising from the fact that the Chinese had high expectations of American intervention in their favor. He wrote to Bryan that "there has been some difficulty in preserving an attitude of friendliness while carefully avoiding to give an encouragement to the idea that the United States might actively intervene in behalf of China for the sake of friendship and in the cause of international justice."[39]

The most startling news from Minister Reinsch reached Washington on April 14. According to "trustworthy sources" (in his words), while the Japanese minister was discussing the issue of Fujian with a Chinese official, he took occasion "to make disparaging reference to the alleged complaisance of the Government of the United States and the futility of China's basing any hopes upon American support." Reinsch quoted as evidence of "the success of Japanese efforts to alienate Chinese confidence in the United States" an article of the *Tientsin Times*, which reported that "a prominent Japanese" publicly declared "the absurdity of anticipating any action by the United State[s] in opposition to Japanese policy since the Secretary of State is so much under the influence of Baron Chinda that he is not saying a word against the wishes of Japan." The newspaper commented bitterly that "the facts seem to warrant this view inasmuch as the American Government seems to have abandoned its championship of the open-door policy." Reinsch feared that unless the American government dissociated itself from "the appearance of acquiescence in the unconscionable demands of Japan," its misrepresentations would inflame Chinese public opinion against the United States. Therefore, Reinsch requested that he be authorized to give informal publicity "to the view that the American Government has not abandoned either its material interests or its moral obligations in respect to China," and that "it may be expected to take appropriate action if that belief should prove likely to be disappointed."[40]

Reinsch's telegram was so disconcerting that Bryan decided to communicate with the Chinese to correct their misunderstanding of the American position. Although he did not seem to forget his note of March 13 to Japan in which the United States made no objections to most of the Japanese Demands, he apparently realized that it was necessary for the United States government to assert its position clearly. He drew up a draft of a statement to the Chinese government similar to the language Reinsch suggested. After getting Wilson's approval, Bryan authorized Reinsch on April 15 to tell the Chinese government "informally and unofficially" that "the American Government has not surrendered any of its treaty rights in China or abated one iota of its friendly interests in all that concerns the industrial and political welfare of China." Bryan added that his government was "awaiting the results of the present negotiations in the confident expectation that the rights and obligations of the United States will not be affected or interests impaired."[41]

The news of the distorted publicity of the American position allegedly by the Japanese further deepened President Wilson's suspicion of Japan. He finally decided to put an end to the policy of accommodation which had been initiated by Bryan and adopted an uncompromising policy for the defense of the Open Door in China. In reply to Bryan's inquiry on the American communication to China, Wilson wrote to Bryan, "I am very uneasy about what is going on as reported by Mr. Reinsch, and must frankly admit that I do not credit the assurances the Japanese have sought to give us." He asked Bryan to convey to the Japanese ambassador his "grave concern" about the rumor about Tokyo's insistence upon China's acquiescence in Group V. He emphatically stated that "we should be as active as the circumstances permit in showing ourselves to be champions of the sovereign rights of China, now as always, though with no thought of seeking any special advantages or privileges for ourselves."[42] Thus, the crisis in East Asia transformed Wilson from a "prudent friend" of China into a "champion" of the Open Door and sovereign rights of China, and the United States assumed a posture of forthright opposition to the Japanese Demands.

In the same memorandum to Bryan, Wilson asked, "Has Reinsch been told definitely that it is not true that we have acquiesced in any of Japan's demands? Count Okuma has been quoted in the newspaper despatch as saying that we had acquiesced." Apparently there was a misunderstanding between Wilson and Okuma. Premier Okuma's remark on the American consent to the Japanese demands was made a few days after the vital American note of March 13 was sent to Japan. In an interview with a Japanese newspaperman on a train during his election campaign tour, Okuma was quoted as saying, "As we sent friendly explanations to the Western powers, they all understood our intention and even the United States went so far as to express her general consent to us."[43] The *Osaka Asahi* printed this interview on March 18, which was later cited by a Chinese newspaper. Certainly, Premier Okuma was careless and irresponsible when he made such a categorical statement for domestic consumption without considering its implications on diplomatic relations. But President Wilson also seems to have either forgotten or misunderstood the concessions implied in Secretary Bryan's note of March 13 to Japan. As Arthur Link observes, "Obviously, he was ready to begin anew, as if the preceding negotiations with Japan had not occurred."[44] This action by Wilson indicates either his indifference to or his inexperience with the reality of East Asia in which the European great powers, Japan, and China had been maintaining some sort of order in diplomatic relations.

Wilson no longer hesitated to use strong language when the State Department found "some discrepancy" between the Japanese explanation of the demands and the full text of the demands sent by Minister Reinsch regarding the joint ownership proposal of the Hanyeping Company. Upon learning that Japan was insisting on the company's exclusive right to the mines in its neighborhood, Wilson wrote Bryan that he was convinced that "we shall have to try in every practicable way to defend China." He continued, "We shall have to be very chary hereafter about seeming to concede the reasonableness of any of Japan's demands or requests either, until we get the whole of the situation in our minds by hearing from Peking as well as from Tokyo."[45] Japan's diplomacy of the Twenty-one Demands made a permanently negative impression on Wilson. In view of Wilson's dealings with Japan during the next four years of the war and at the peace conference in 1919, his statement carries significant implications. Wilson's loss of trust in the leaders of Japan in the spring of 1915 was so deep that it seemed almost irrecoverable. His tendency to make a moralistic judgment on a nation's behavior based on his religious and cultural background and his sense of mission to protect underdogs from un-American abuses no doubt helped shape his image of Japan as an untrustworthy, predatory nation.

In the meantime, on April 16, Minister Reinsch gave an unofficial note to the Chinese government in which the United States declared that it would neither surrender any of its treaty rights in China nor retreat one iota from the principle of territorial integrity and equal opportunity. As has been described in the previous chapter, the Japanese foreign office believed that this American note suddenly made the Chinese attitude stiffen on April 17. Consequently, the Japanese government made the "final concession" proposal on April 26.

In an attempt to break the stalemate in the Sino-Japanese negotiations in China's favor, Reinsch recommended to Washington, on April 24, a more serious way of intervening in the controversy. He suggested that an American circular note asking all the powers to reassert their pledge to support the principles of the Open Door and the territorial integrity of China might get favorable response from the British and the French. Reinsch was under the impression that "the British Government might welcome such a proposal as a means of determining the disposition and intention of Japan with respect to the [Anglo-Japanese] alliance."[46] Before the United States went directly to the European powers, Secretary Bryan drafted a note of warning to Japan. It expressed the grave concern of the United States regarding several issues: (1) the increase of the Japanese troops in China; (2) Japan's failure to make clear the distinctions between the demands and the requests to the Chinese government; and (3) Japan's particular demand concerning joint control of the Hanyeping Company. The note ended with an important warning that if Japan and the United States failed to have "a perfectly clear and cordial relationship of mutual understanding," the United States might have to make a public announcement to avoid misrepresentation of the American position by other countries. This warning was initially suggested by President Wilson. In fact, he wanted to go even further and warn the Japanese ambassador of the possibility of sending a joint note among the Western great powers. Wilson wrote to Bryan, "I think . . . that it would be wise to say to the Japanese Ambassador that our position with regard to these important matters . . . has been so generally misunderstood and so misleadingly speculated about that we feel that it may become immediately necessary to make our views public, *perhaps* in conjunction with other nations whose interests and sympathies are equally involved." Bryan, however, was reluctant to include the phrase following the word "perhaps," saying that "[n]one of the Allies are in position to join us in anything we say or do and of course we could not invite Germany to join us. . . . I am inclined to think that any suggestion of union with them would divert attention from the course which we desire

them to consider." Wilson agreed with Bryan and simply asked him to intimate the possibility of a circular note to Ambassador Chinda.[47] Bryan
showed the note of warning to Chinda on April 29. After reading the note,
Chinda asked Bryan to withhold it until he finished decoding the text of the
new Japanese concession proposals to China that had just arrived from Tokyo. Bryan was relieved and became somewhat optimistic about the Japanese attitude when he saw the Japanese revised demands Chinda handed to
him on April 30. He wrote to Wilson, "Considering the concessions which
Japan made, I think we are justified in believing that she will modify such of
the demands as are still unreasonable, and that we ought to so change the
letter that we wrote as to call attention to these points."[48]

On May 4, while Bryan was redrafting a note to the Japanese ambassador, alarming news came from Beijing. According to Minister Reinsch,
"The Chinese Government has been advised that tonight or tomorrow it will
receive from Japan an ultimatum requiring absolute compliance with the revised demands." Bryan informed Wilson that he was going to tell the Japanese ambassador that "there is every reason why the doctrine that 'Nothing
is final between friends' should be applied to this situation." Ambassador
Chinda, however, did not mention Bryan's concern about the possibility of a
Japanese ultimatum in his report to Tokyo. He merely reported the U.S.
government's intention to make a public statement regarding the East Asian
crisis in order to avoid misrepresentation of its position. Because Chinda
knew that the tension between China and Japan was increasing after the
Chinese reply of May 1, he persuaded Bryan to postpone the issue of a public statement until the afternoon of May 6, saying that Tokyo might also
have something to announce.[49] On May 6, as scheduled, Secretary Bryan
made a statement to the press regarding the American no-concession policy
toward Japan. He stated that the Japanese government, at the beginning of
its negotiations with China, confidentially assured the U.S. government that
Japan would not interfere with either the Open Door or the political and territorial integrity of China. The U.S. government, declared Bryan, had no
thought of surrendering any of its treaty rights with China. He concluded,
"There is no abatement of its interest in the welfare and progress of China
and its sole interest in the present negotiations is that they may be concluded
in a manner satisfactory to both nations."[50]

However, this public statement and Bryan's painstaking note to Ambassador Chinda were too late to change the outcome of the Sino-Japanese crisis. The Japanese government had already decided to send an ultimatum by
the time Chinda transmitted Secretary Bryan's note to Tokyo. Japan was to
withdraw the controversial Group V and would demand China's unconditional acceptance of the rest of Japan's April 26 concession proposals.

By this time, that is, the day before Japan delivered the ultimatum to China, events were moving rapidly on both sides of the Pacific. In Tokyo, Foreign Minister Kato was busy consulting with the Japanese minister in Beijing regarding the best way to deal with the Chinese. At the same time, Kato instructed the ambassadors in Great Britain, the United States, and Russia to notify their respective host-country governments of the Japanese decision to send the ultimatum to China. Kato also met the ambassadors of the great powers in Tokyo in an attempt to explain his government's decision.

Kato's interview with American Chargé Post Wheeler revealed that Kato was irritated by news that the Americans had been encouraging China since mid-April to resist the Japanese pressure. Kato asked Wheeler to relay the following point to Bryan: "There is no room for concession on the part of my Government. We have made all concessions we could possibly make. Whatever may happen, we cannot go any further in the way of concessions." Kato also told Wheeler that China had been making concessions up to mid-April, but at that point had taken a rigid position and had suddenly told the Japanese that there was no room for discussion. Kato added that some people were blaming this on the United States. It was highly likely, Kato said, that China relied too heavily on certain American communications and believed that it would receive substantial help from the United States.[51]

In Washington, Bryan prepared three more notes on May 6, trying to prevent an armed conflict between Japan and China, and with Wilson's full approval, he dispatched them immediately. First, he sent a personal message to Premier Okuma in which Bryan said, "I take the liberty of appealing to you personally and unofficially to use your great influence with your Government to have it deal with China in the spirit of patience." Second, Bryan instructed Minister Reinsch to urge the Chinese foreign office to negotiate with Japan "in a spirit of patience and friendliness" until an amicable solution was found. Third, Bryan sent identical notes to London, Paris, and Petrograd asking whether they would join the United States in "a friendly but earnest appeal to Japan and China to continue their negotiations in the spirit of patience and friendship until a satisfactory conclusion is reached."[52]

However, all these appeals by the United States on the eve of the Japanese ultimatum had disappointing outcomes. The State Department soon learned that the controversy was anesthetized, at least for the moment, between China and Japan after some important British counseling. American lobbying for peace at best annoyed, and at worst antagonized, Japanese officials. Bryan's personal appeal to Premier Okuma was delayed because of a problem in the cable transmission system and reached Tokyo the day after the ultimatum had been delivered. In his reply to Bryan, the Japanese premier guaranteed a peaceful intention of his government, but he repeated Japan's determination to conclude the negotiations on its own terms. The premier said that the Chinese government, which had been using provocative methods to invite foreign intervention, would realize its false position and want to come to terms if it was left alone. He warned, "It is most desirable to avoid any action which might be interpreted by the Chinese Government as giving them encouragement for hope of securing outside assistance." Thus, it is clear from the tone that the Japanese premier did not appreciate Bryan's message. When he wrote this reply, the American call for a joint note among the European powers may have been on his mind. Japanese leaders were genuinely concerned that the American appeal to other great powers might encourage China to reject the ultimatum.

Meanwhile, in Washington, Ambassador Chinda asked Bryan to reconsider the proposal on a joint note, warning that the American action might bolster the Chinese position and make a settlement of the issues difficult. Chinda added that such a joint note might be regarded as American intervention into Sino-Japanese negotiations and might thus affect Japanese-American relations. In response, Bryan asserted that it was impossible to reconsider the matter of a joint note because the president regarded it as extremely important. On May 8, Chinda met Bryan again and made a formal protest against the American proposal for the joint note. He told Bryan that the proposed action might disrupt negotiations at the critical moment when China was about to accept Japan's final, modified proposals. After a moment of silence, Bryan stated that his government would withhold the action for the moment.[53]

The American appeal to the European powers to present a joint diplomatic note did not have the desired effect. While France and Russia failed to respond, Britain took action into its own hands at this pivotal moment. British Foreign Secretary Grey warned Tokyo that his government was "very much concerned at the prospect of a war between China and Japan," which might "imperil the independence and integrity of China." He urged Japanese leaders to settle the matter peacefully. At the same time, upon learning that the Japanese ultimatum was relatively conciliatory, Grey urged the Chinese minister in London to accept it to avert the crisis. In response to American Ambassador Walter H. Pages's inquiry of the proposed joint note, Grey simply informed the ambassador that his office had already taken action.[54]

Colonel House, who had a conversation with Secretary Grey on May 7, sent Wilson a telegram which succinctly summarized the British perspective of the crisis in East Asia.

[Grey] said after getting at the bottom of the matter, China seemed to be acting in a very stupid and foolish way diplomatically. That she said, at one time, she was

willing to accept the terms which Japan had offered with exception of Clause 5. . . .
After Japan agreed to eliminate Clau[s]e 5, then China raised trivial objections.

Sir Edward told the [Japanese] Ambassador that England was very desirous that
good relations between China and Japan should be maintained, and that she would
view with concern any rupture between them. . . .

The feeling here is that Japan is taking advantage of the war to further her own
ends. She sees clearly that Europe was in no position to object, and that we are not
much better off.

Sir Edward said he felt there was some excuse for Japan wanting an outlet in
Manchuria for the reason that North and South America, Africa and the British
Colonies were closed against her citizens.[55]

There was a general sense of relief in Washington after May 8. Reinsch
reported from Beijing that "[i]t is surprising that these demands were presented in the form of an ultimatum, being in fact almost identical with those
conceded by China as reported in my telegram of May 3 . . . and on the surface less exigent than those which this Government informally offered to
concede yesterday." Bryan must have realized that the American peace appeals to the European powers and to Japan had not been successful nor necessary, but he seemed unconcerned, writing to the president on May 8 that
he had "no doubt that the despatch [to the powers] had its influence in Japan
in helping to reduce the severity of the demands." What neither Wilson nor
Bryan seemed to understand fully was the negative effect the American attempt to intervene in the Sino-Japanese negotiations had upon Tokyo.
Pleased with Japan's withdrawal of Group V, Bryan told Wilson that "the
matter is now all settled." Significantly, he added that it was "a great relief at
such a time as this."[56] Bryan had many other problems—the day before, the
Lusitania had been sunk by a German submarine, with the loss of more than
one thousand lives. This incident precipitated a diplomatic crisis in the Atlantic, which eventually led to Bryan's resignation as secretary of state.

President Wilson, too, was inclined to consider the crisis of the Twenty-
one Demands settled for the moment, but he felt it necessary to make clear
where the United States stood with regard to China policy. On May 10, Wilson told Bryan that "the whole suspicious business has lost for the time being its critical character." However, he asked Bryan to file a caveat reserving
full American rights in China. Wilson called the Open Door principles "the
solemn understandings of the nations with regard to China," and he did not
want Japanese leaders to have the impression that the United States seemed
to "acquiesce in any part of the Japanese plan which violates the solemn understandings." He hoped that the American caveat might pressure "the
Japanese official mind" to postpone the discussion on Group V "for a very
long time." Wilson apparently did not realize that after days of unpleasant

diplomatic exchanges Japanese leaders resented America's attempt to intervene in a matter they considered strictly between China and Japan. The Japanese were by now adamant about trying to keep the United States out of the matter.

The idea of filing a caveat was originally suggested by Lansing on May 7 as an alternative, in case the Allied powers refused to issue a joint note to Japan. According to Lansing, its purpose was to "constitute a complete reservation of all possible rights affecting American interests and Chinese interests as well, so that any agreement forced upon China at the present time could properly become the subject of discussion in the future when the conditions are more propitious." President Wilson liked the idea of postponing the settlement of the issue until peace was restored in Europe.[57]

The outcome was the American caveat of May 11 dispatched by Secretary Bryan to Tokyo and Beijing. It declared that the government of the United States "cannot recognize any agreement or undertaking which has been entered into or which may be entered into between the Governments of Japan and China, impairing the treaty rights of the United States and its citizens in China, the political or territorial integrity of the Republic of China, or the international policy relative to China commonly known as the open door policy."[58]

The wording of the American note puzzled the Japanese leaders. When Foreign Minister Kato asked Chargé Wheeler what motivated the American government to send this note, Wheeler simply replied that it was his government's intention to keep it on record. Kato hurriedly instructed Ambassador Chinda in Washington to find out the true intentions of the Wilson administration. On the same day Chinda met Bryan and asked whether the American government was planning to make objections to any particular points. Bryan answered that the president wished to keep the record straight and that his government merely stated its position as a "precaution." Kato did not make any formal reply to the American note. He thought that the document lacked specificity; besides there was nothing he could do about the American nonrecognition of the facts his government had already established. Kato was said to have observed, not without sarcasm, that since the departure of John Bassett Moore from the State Department, no one was able to handle diplomatic matters skillfully.[59]

The American note was vague enough to have several implications. First, obviously Wilson wanted to issue a warning to prevent Japan from ever reviving Group V. Second, the note might be interpreted as a repudiation of the American concessions made on March 13, 1915, regarding Japan's special relations with Shandong, South Manchuria, and Eastern Inner Mongolia. Third, the note could be taken as a statement of attitude in which the

United States committed itself to opposition against any future Japanese encroachments on China.[60] Yet, in the eyes of the American and Japanese leaders at that time, the implications of the American caveat were not so clear as they are from a retrospective viewpoint. As events unfolded, the significance of the American caveat increased, and by the time of the peace settlement, it would become clear. The Chinese delegates at the Paris Peace Conference, supported by President Wilson, would challenge the validity of the Sino-Japanese treaty of 1915, with regard to Japan's succession to the German rights and concessions in Shandong, on the ground that the treaty was signed under duress.

In conclusion, the controversy over the Twenty-one Demands became the turning point in Japanese-American relations. The incident had imprinted on the American official mind an irrevocable distrust of Japanese intentions in China. President Wilson called upon the principles of the Open Door and independence of China to forestall Japan's attempt to expand its influence over China. The evocation of the Open Door principles by the Wilson administration, however, sowed the seeds of future Japanese-American confrontation in East Asia. As shown in this chapter, inadequate representation of the positions of both governments, inconsistency in the positions they assumed, miscommunication between the governments, and misunderstandings caused by distorted information, all made the American and Japanese governments excessively suspicious of each other. Consequently, relations between the two powers chilled rapidly. This chain of unfortunate circumstances contributed to the bitter feelings Japan and the United States held toward each other throughout the First World War.

NOTES

1. Paul S. Reinsch, *An American Diplomat in China* (Garden City, N.Y.: Doubleday, Page & Company, 1922), 146.

2. Inoue to Kato, January 22, 1915, in the Foreign Ministry of Japan, *Nihon gaiko bunsho* (Documents on Japanese foreign policy), 1915 (Tokyo, 1966), 3: 541–542. Hereafter cited as *NGB*.

3. Paul S. Reinsch, *An American Diplomat in China*, 130.

4. Reinsch to Bryan, January 23, 1915, in U.S. Department of State, *Papers Relating to the Foreign Relations of the United States*, 1915 (Washington, D.C., 1924), 79. Hereafter cited as *FR*.

5. Reinsch to Bryan, January 26 and 27, 1915, *FR*, 1915, 80.

6. House Diary, January 25, 1915, in Arthur S. Link, ed., *The Papers of Woodrow Wilson* (Princeton: Princeton University Press, 1966–1994), 32: 120. Hereafter cited as *PWW*.

7. Wilson to Bryan, January 27, 1915, *PWW*, 32: 139.

8. Telegram from Reinsch, January 26, 1915, *PWW*, 32: 137–138; Reinsch to Bryan, February 1, 1915, *PWW*, 32:170.

9. Kato to Motono and Chinda, February 2, 1915, *NGB*, 1915, 3: 549–550. Guthrie to Bryan, February 6, 1915, *FR*, 1915, 558.

10. Chinda to Kato, February 11, 1915, *NGB*, 1915, 3: 558.

11. Wilson to Reinsch, February 8, 1915, *PWW*, 32: 197.

12. Guthrie to Bryan, February 11, 1915; Reinsch to Bryan, February 15, 1915, *NGB*, 1915, 87–89.

13. Japanese version in Kato to Hioki, December 3, 1914, *NGB*, 1914, 3: 567; italics mine. English version communicated by the Chinese minister to Bryan, not dated, *FR*, 1915, 95; italics mine.

14. Bryan to Wilson, enclosure II, February 18, 1915, *PWW*, 32: 247; Bryan to Guthrie, February 19, 1915, *FR*, 1915, 93.

15. Guthrie to Bryan, February 21, 1915, *FR*, 1915, 96.

16. Kato to Hioki, December 3, 1914, *NGB*, 1914, 3: 562–563.

17. Kato to Hioki, February 16, 1915, *NGB*, 1915, 3: 166–167.

18. *NGB*, 1915, 3: 561–562. Note from British Embassy, February 22, 1915, *NGB*, 1915, 3: 590.

19. Inoue to Kato, March 3, 1915, *NGB*, 1915, 3: 607; British Embassy, March 10, 1915, *NGB*, 1915, 3: 609. The railways in question were one connecting Wuchang with the Jiujiang-Nanchang line, and the railways between Nanchang and Hangzhou and between Nanchang and Chaozhou.

20. Bryan to Wilson, February 22, 1915, *PWW*, 32:270–271; U.S. Department of State, *Papers Relating to the Foreign Relations of the United States: The Lansing Papers 1914–1920* (Washington, D.C., 1940), 2: 406–407. Hereafter cited as *FRLP*.

21. Wilson to Bryan, February 25, 1915, *PWW*, 32: 287; *FRLP*, 2: 407.

22. William to Bryan, February 26, 1915, *PWW*, 32: 319–322.

23. Lansing to Bryan, March 1, 1915, *FRLP*, 2: 408.

24. Wilson to Bryan, March 4, 1915, *PWW*, 32: 319; Wilson to Bryan, March 10, 1915, *PWW*, 32: 353; *FRLP*, 2: 409.

25. Bryan to Chinda, March 13, 1915, *FR*, 1915, 105–111.

26. Guthrie to Bryan, February 21, 1915, *NGB*, 1915, 113–114; *PWW*, 32: 416–421. *NGB*, 1915, 3: 658–664.

27. Bryan to Wilson, March 22, 1915, *FRLP*, 2: 409–411; *PWW*, 32: 414–416.

28. Bryan to Guthrie, March 26, 1915, *FR*, 1915, 117.

29. Wilson to Bryan, March 24, 1915, *PWW*, 32: 426; *FRLP*, 2: 411.

30. Bryan to Wilson, March 25, 1915, *PWW*, 32: 434; *FRLP*, 2: 413.

31. Wilson to Bryan, March 25, 1915, *PWW*, 32: 436.

32. Arthur S. Link, *Wilson: The Struggle for Neutrality 1914–1915* (Princeton: Princeton University Press, 1960), 288.

33. Kato to Hioki, March 30, 1915, *NGB*, 1915, 3: 269.

34. Hioki to Kato, April 10, 11, and 14, 1915, *NGB*, 1915, 3: 307, 309, 322.

35. Reinsch's telegram, March 30, 1915, *PWW*, 32: 459–460.

36. Bryan to Wilson, Enclosure II, March 31, 1915; Wilson to Bryan, March 31, 1915, *PWW*, 32: 460–461.

37. Reinsch to Bryan, March 31, April 5, 7, 9, 1915; *FR*, 1915, 118, 119, 124, 125.

38. Wilson to Bryan, April 12, 1915, *PWW*, 32: 508, 508–509 n1; Roy W. Curry, *Woodrow Wilson and Far Eastern Policy 1913–1921* (New York: Bookman Associates, 1957), 122.

39. Reinsch to Bryan, April 5, 1915, *FR*, 1915, 122.

40. Reinsch, April 14, 1915, *PWW*, 32: 519–520.

41. Bryan to Reinsch, April 15, 1915, *PWW*, 32: 520; *FRLP*, 2:417.

42. Wilson to Bryan, April 14, 1915, *PWW*, 32: 520–521; *FRLP*, 2: 416–417.

43. Kato to Chinda, March 21, 1915, *NGB*, 1915, 3: 652.

44. Arthur S. Link, *Wilson: The Struggle for Neutrality 1914–1915*, 294.

45. Wilson to Bryan, April 16, 1915, *PWW*, 32: 531.

46. Arthur S. Link, *Wilson: The Struggle for Neutrality 1914–1915*, 295.

47. Bryan to Chinda, April 27, 1915, *PWW*, 33: 84; Wilson to Bryan, April 27, 1915, *PWW*, 33: 81; *FRLP*, 2:417; Bryan to Wilson, April 28, 1915, *PWW*, 33: 82.

48. Bryan to Wilson, May 3, 1915, *PWW*, 33: 95–99; *FRLP*, 2:418–422.

49. Reinsch to Bryan, May 4, 1915, *PWW*, 33: 104–105; Bryan to Wilson, May 4, 1915, *PWW*, 33: 101.

50. Bryan to Reinsch, May 6, 1915, *FR*, 1915, 143.

51. May 6, 1915, *NGB*, 1915, 3:737.

52. Bryan to Wilson, May 6, 1915, *PWW*, 33: 113–115; *FRLP*, 2: 422–423.

53. Kato to Chinda, May 8, 1915; Chinda to Kato, May 7, 1915; Chinda to Kato, May 8, 1915, *NGB*, 1915, 3: 775, 766–767, 778.

54. Page to Bryan, May 7, 1915, *FR*, 1915, 144.

55. House to Wilson, May 7, 1915, *PWW*, 33: 121–122.

56. Reinsch to Bryan, May 7, 1915, *FR*, 1915, 144; Bryan to Wilson, May 8, 1915, *PWW*, 33:131.

57. Wilson to Bryan, May 10, 1915, *PWW*, 33: 139–140; Lansing to Bryan, May 7, 1915, *PWW*, 33: 140.

58. Bryan to Guthrie, May 11, 1915, *FR*, 146.

59. Chinda to Kato, May 13, 1915, *NGB*, 1915, 3: 795; *NGB*, 1915, 3: 798; Russell H. Fifield, *Woodrow Wilson and the Far East: The Diplomacy of the Shantung Question* (1952; reprint, Hamden, Conn.: Archon Books, 1965), 48.

60. Arthur S. Link, *Wilson: The Struggle for Neutrality 1914–1915*, 308.

CHAPTER 3

Who Should Lead China into the War?

America's severance of diplomatic relations with Berlin in February 1917 and subsequent declaration of war against Germany two months later had a profound impact on the situation in East Asia. President Wilson's symbolic appeal to all neutral states to follow America's example in breaking diplomatic relations with Germany prompted Japanese-American rivalry over who should take the initiative in leading China, itself divided, into the Great War. The examination of how Japan and the United States dealt with the issue of China's participation in the war is important, for China's entry into the war had major consequences for international politics in East Asia both during and after the war. First, China's entry marked the beginning of negotiations for various Japanese loans to China and for a Sino-Japanese military alliance; second, it led the United States and Japan to negotiate the Lansing-Ishii agreement on China; and third, it created the basis for Sino-American opposition to the Japanese claim for German rights in Shandong at the Paris Peace Conference in 1919.

However, Japanese-American tensions over China's entry into the war did not spring up simply as a result of the two countries' disagreements over the Twenty-one Demands. As this chapter shows, Japanese-American rivalry could be seen as a contest between President Wilson's universalist aspiration to serve as a mentor to a young and deeply troubled republic in China on the one hand, and regionalist aspirations of the new Japanese government under Premier Masatake Terauchi on the other. Terauchi wanted to establish Japan's supremacy in China through paternalistic financial assistance in a manner that was, as Japanese leaders saw it, not so different from

America's role in the Western Hemisphere in the tradition of the Monroe Doctrine.

On the eve of the U.S. decision to enter the war against Germany, leaders on both sides of the Pacific were aware of the grave prospect of interracial rivalry—or even a race war—between the white and yellow races. While the Wilson administration was debating whether the United States should break off diplomatic relations with Germany in response to Germany's unrestricted submarine warfare, President Wilson could not overlook the grim consequences the American decision might have on the fragile situation in East Asia. Although "deeply incensed at Germany's insolent notice," the president told Secretary Lansing that "he had been more and more impressed with the idea that 'white civilization' and its domination over the world rested largely on our ability to keep this country intact, as we would have to build up the nations ravaged by the war," and that "he was willing to go to any lengths rather than to have the nation actually involved in the conflict."[1] When the cabinet members met on February 2, 1917, according to Secretary of Agriculture David Houston, President Wilson asked, "Shall I break off diplomatic relations with Germany?" The president answered his own question "with a somewhat startling statement." Houston wrote that the president "frankly" said that "in order to keep the white race or part of it strong to meet yellow race—Japan, for instance . . . [if he felt that] it was wise to do nothing, he would do nothing, and would submit to anything and any imputation of weakness or cowardice."[2] These statements not only indicate Wilson's strong interest in keeping Japanese activities in check during the war, but also his apprehension or even fear of the spread of the alien civilization that the Japanese represented, which he considered to be an antithesis of American Christian democracy.

Premier Terauchi and his advisers in Japan were equally haunted by the specter of interracial rivalry, and their regionalist aspiration to put East Asia under Japan's guidance stemmed in large part from their distrust of rival powers in the West. Terauchi shared the fears of his mentor, genro Aritomo Yamagata, concerning postwar competition between the "white and yellow races" over the domination of East Asia. The Asian continent, especially China, with plenty of natural resources and population but without a great regional power to protect it from foreign encroachment, would naturally become the arena for imperial competition—unlike Latin America where the United States upheld the Monroe Doctrine to ward off European intervention. To survive a future war between the white and yellow races, Yamagata argued, Japan must assume a regionalist stance of "Asia for Asians" and pursue a policy of Sino-Japanese cooperation and "coexistence and co-prosperity."[3] Genro Masayoshi Matsukata also advised Terauchi that his government should pursue a policy of Sino-Japanese cooperation as Japan's means of self-defense in the face of intensifying interracial competitions and act as "the leader of the yellow race." Terauchi himself admitted, as early as the summer of 1914, that because the government in Beijing was unable to maintain order and unity even within its country, Japan must assume the responsibility of preserving peace and stability in East Asia. Anticipating the relative increase in American influence over China during the war in Europe, he expressed his determination to outbid the Americans.[4]

When Terauchi became premier in October 1916, his perception of the international environment, especially his concern about a possible interracial rivalry and competition between the East and the West, aroused his aspiration to achieve a vertically integrated regionalism in Asia under Japan's leadership. The first official decision on the China policy adopted by the Terauchi cabinet on January 9, 1917, clearly demonstrated its intent to pursue the regionalist policy. The government's ultimate goal was to establish Japan's supremacy over China and make the Western great powers recognize that they must consult with Japan concerning their activities in China. First, the cabinet resolution stated, "In order to make China carry out political reform necessary to maintain her independence and territorial integrity, the empire shall guide and educate the Chinese with sincerity and attempt to promote amity between the two countries." However, the decision also contained a statement to the effect that Japan must take appropriate action in case China became suspicious of Japan's friendly intent and obstructed Japan's activities in China. It reflected Japanese leaders' view of China as an inferior partner and implied that Tokyo would not hesitate to take unilateral action contrary to the Chinese wishes if disagreements should arise between the two countries. Second, the resolution expressed the cabinet's intention of obtaining the Western powers' recognition of Japan's "paramount position in China." Even though recognizing the necessity of acting in concert with the Western powers, the Terauchi government was determined to prevent the Western powers from launching any activities of a political nature in China without first seeking Japan's initiative or approval.[5]

Although Japan's policy of Sino-Japanese cooperation through economic assistance was part of its efforts to assume the leadership role in East Asian politics, there was also a clear causal relationship between Japanese-American rivalry over the issue of China's participation in the war against Germany and the Terauchi cabinet's decision to accelerate the extension of the Nishihara Loans to the government of Duan Qirui in Beijing. The rest of this chapter examines how and why President Wilson's idealistic and universalistic appeal to all neutral countries unwittingly stimulated Japan's regionalist aspiration and hardened the Terauchi government's determination to establish Japan's predominant position in China through economic assistance.

On February 3, when the United States declared to sever diplomatic relations with Germany, President Wilson appealed to all neutral countries, including China, to follow the American example. Wilson's message not only conveyed his determination to use American national power to protect American citizens from German assaults, but also expressed a belief that "it will make for the peace of the world if the other neutral powers can find it possible to take similar action."[6] This was his attempt to mobilize international cooperation by appealing to the moralistic sentiment of neutral states.

Minister Reinsch in Beijing enthusiastically received his government's instruction. Considering the American invitation to the neutrals as "more than a pious wish," Reinsch believed that his duty was "to prevail upon China to associate herself with the American action." He immediately began to persuade the Chinese government to follow the American leadership in severing the relations with Germany, but the Chinese government could not afford to do so without getting some quid pro quo. The Chinese asked Reinsch whether, in the event of China's being drawn into the war, the United States could give assurances that "Chinese arsenals and military forces would not come under foreign control," and that "China would be admitted to full membership in the peace conference." Regarding the first point, China further suggested that the U.S. government loan China ten million dollars to improve arsenals and agree to the funding of the American portion of the Boxer indemnity in long-term bonds.[7]

Reinsch was eager to obtain a favorable decision from China before other influences, particularly that of Japan, could be interposed, and went a little too far in giving American assurances on financial assistance. Without instructions from Washington, Reinsch gave the Chinese his assurances on the loan and the Boxer indemnity. On February 7, he told Chinese Premier Duan Qirui and his foreign office that although he could not guarantee his government's "definite commitments," he felt warranted "in assuming the responsibility of assuring" that "adequate means will be developed to enable China to fulfill the responsibilities consequent upon associating itself with the action of the United States." Behind Reinsch's hasty action, there was the specter of Japan. The Chinese officials convinced him that without American financial assistance and guidance the Chinese were deterred from taking the proposed action because of "the fear that evident necessity for more adequate military organization might lead the Japanese Government to seek from the Allies mandate to supervise such organization."[8]

Six hours after Reinsch gave his personal assurances on the loan and the indemnity, the Chinese government informed Reinsch that it would send a protest against the German submarine policy. The next day, on February 8, Beijing delivered the protest to the German government. At the same time, the Chinese government made a formal reply to the American invitation of February 3, stating that it firmly associated itself with the American government. China also confidentially informed Reinsch by a *note verbale*: "In case an act should be performed by the German Government which should be considered by the American Government as sufficient cause for declaration of war between the United States and Germany, the Chinese Government should [at] least break its diplomatic relations with Germany." Upon receiving the above communication, Reinsch wrote to Washington that to bring about the Chinese diplomatic severance with Germany, he found it "imperatively necessary to give the assurances" that he had previously suggested. "The strongest exertion of influence and persuasion was necessary," Reinsch added. He also said that the Chinese government had "committed itself to the leadership of the United States in this momentous matter." Thus, China moved one step toward the diplomatic severance with Germany upon the invitation of the United States. The Chinese leaders in Beijing counted on the assurances Reinsch gave on his own initiative, while Reinsch kept pressing Washington to authorize those assurances.[9]

In the meantime, the State Department also received another report from Reinsch regarding the question of China's position at a future peace conference. According to Reinsch's conversations with the Chinese officials on January 10, the Chinese government felt that China should be represented at the final settlement because the territorial right of Qingdao belonged to China. Reinsch reported that Japan had already hinted that it would represent the interests of China at a peace conference and might admit a Chinese attaché to the Japanese delegation. He recognized that the "weakness" of China's claim to be represented in the peace conference arose from the fact that the Chinese government had already agreed in 1915 "to sanction any transfer" of the German rights in Shandong to Japan that might be decided at the conclusion of the war. Nevertheless, Reinsch said, "[T]he high officials of the Government have repeatedly expressed to me their confidence that they may count on the assistance of the American Government in aiding them to prevent any development during, or at the end of, the war which would make of China a field of 'compensations.'" Reinsch needed instructions from the State Department on this matter as well.[10]

President Wilson was deeply disturbed by the developments in China. Having read four telegrams sent by Minister Reinsch between February 6 and 8, the president wrote to Secretary of State Lansing on February 9:

"These and earlier telegrams about the possible action of China make my conscience uneasy. We may be leading China to risk her doom." He foresaw the difficulty in providing financial assistance to China:

It seems to me that if we suffer China to follow us in what we are now doing we ought to be ready to assist and stand by her in every possible way consistent with her and our engagements in the East. What she has asked through Reinsch has not been unreasonable, but can we count on the Senate and on our bankers to fulfill any expectations we may arouse in China?

Secretary Lansing, as well as President Wilson, understood the dilemma that China must face in the event of its being drawn into the war, and neither of them wanted China to take a risk. Lansing believed that if China should be involved in the war as a result of its diplomatic break with Germany, "the fears of the Chinese Government would be only too sure to be realized, for if China attempted to improve its defense, Japan would probably consider any strengthening of China's military forces a menace that would justify Japan in demanding control of arsenals and command of the troops." Lansing thought that, although it would be of immense advantage to China as well as to the United States to create a Chinese army of sufficient size to defend itself and put an end to foreign encroachments, "if we encourage such an effort I feel confident we shall have to be prepared to meet Japanese opposition."[11]

On February 10, President Wilson approved of a message to Reinsch which stated that the American government was not able to give any assurances to the Chinese government at that moment. Wilson's suggestion for "a few changes and additions" to the text of the message well indicates that he was placed in a frustrating situation. Wilson added the underlined words and deleted the words in angle brackets.

The American Government highly appreciates disposition of China but does not wish to lead it into danger. It regrets practical inability to give any present assurances. Unwillingness of any other important neutral to follow American example ought <perhaps> to be very gravely considered by China, who should in prudence avoid isolated action. The Chinese Government, therefore, <might> would do well to consult its representatives in the allied countries. Ignorance of Japan's attitude also suggests caution.

When Wilson returned the draft telegram to Lansing, he wrote, "I think that it would be well to let Reinsch tell the Government of China how sincerely we desire to help China and that we are constantly trying to shield her against the selfishness of her neighbor."[12] This was a candid expression of President Wilson's sentiment.

Reinsch tried in vain to persuade his government to change its position. He insisted that "[o]ur national security demands that there should be no surrender of Chinese sovereign rights of military control through admissions." He even wrote a letter directly to the president, arguing that "the opportunity is at hand for the solving of the Chinese problem for a long time to come in a manner consistent with our national safety and the fundamental rights of China without coming in direct conflict with the position and legitimate interests of other nations."[13] Lansing, however, responded to Reinsch with a warning not to exceed the department's instructions and told him that "China should not, unless compelled by extraordinary circumstances, do more than break off diplomatic relations with Germany until the definite decision of this Government in the premises is communicated to it." As for the issue of China's participation in a future peace conference, Lansing expressed the desirability of China's representation in any conference that might affect Chinese territory. However, Lansing made it clear that, for the time being, the United States "is not disposed, in the event of hostilities between the United States and Germany, to urge China to declare war also on Germany," because evidently the United States would not be able to give China the proposed assistance "if serious opposition should be offered to such assistance." He pointed out that "[a]n attempt to override that opposition might precipitate the very aggression which China fears."[14]

Disappointed at the attitude of Washington, Reinsch warned what would become of China. According to Reinsch, "Japan is bringing strong pressure to bear to force China to join the Allies. The Vice President, the Premier, and other influential leaders, partly from fear of Japan and partly to advance their political ambitions, are disposed to fall into line." He, therefore, warned that without some American assurances to maintain China's independence, it would be impossible for the Chinese president, Li Yuanhong, to resist the "tendency to forego reliance on the United States and accept the inevitable alternative of entering the war [as] protégé of Japan."[15] Reinsch was eager to outbid the Japanese.

The State Department, nonetheless, refused to change its attitude of watchful waiting. Lansing learned from the French ambassador that China had made overtures to join the Allies on condition that the latter would secure a consortium loan, agree to revise the tariff, remit the indemnity, and revise the protocol of 1901. He wrote to Reinsch, "The [Chinese] Foreign Office has not told you the whole situation. There is nothing in the situation to hasten China's entrance into the war under the Entente leadership." In fact, on February 13, Lu Zhengxiang, under instruction from Premier Duan, visited the Allied representatives at Beijing to request that the Allies accept those conditions referred to by the French ambassador in exchange for China's diplomatic severance with Germany.[16]

China made a decision to break off diplomatic relations with Germany on March 12, but the State Department had no intention of taking any action. Reinsch sourly telegraphed Washington that because the United States had failed to give any general assurances to the Chinese, those who had confidence in American leadership "have no cogent alternative to offer to those won over to Japan and have to let the decision go by default." In reply, Lansing, although repeating the desirability of China's having a voice in a possible peace conference, stated that the American government "is not bidding against the Entente for adherence of China to American course of action." Significantly, however, Lansing's instruction to withdraw Reinsch's assurances of American assistance to China was omitted from the note actually sent to Reinsch. This omission was suggested by Counselor Frank Polk and approved by President Wilson so as not to shut the door entirely against China who was, in Polk's words, "taking this opportunity to play a little international politics with a view to making friends here and in Europe who would be useful in its relations with Japan." Polk wrote to President Wilson, "While the chances of giving any assurances are remote, yet if we flatly say so at this time we would not be consulted further by the Chinese." Therefore, the Wilson administration by no means lost interest in having a voice in China; on the contrary, it intended to prevent China from placing itself in a position that might invite foreign encroachments on its territory. Lansing wrote to Reinsch on March 12: "For your guidance it is important to bear in mind that the American Government is disposed to regard as inadvisable a declaration of war in China upon Germany at this time, if such declaration would mean the control of China's military resources by a foreign power."[17]

Thus, the United States began by encouraging the Chinese to sever diplomatic relations with Germany, but eventually opposed China's participation in the war against Germany. Although Minister Reinsch and his superiors in Washington disagreed as to what action China should take and how the United States should help China, they all shared the same concern about the expansion of Japanese influence over China. The Japan that Washington saw, mostly through the eyes of Minister Reinsch, was an aggressive state waiting to seize every opportunity to increase its control over China's political and military organizations. The Americans were determined to try "to shield" China, as Wilson put it, "against the selfishness of her neighbor."

By the irony of circumstances, however, the American initial attempt to encourage China to sever diplomatic relations with Germany invited the very Japanese counteraction that the American government was most anxious to avoid. It indeed became the turning point in the Terauchi cabinet's decision to support China's entry into the war. Ever since November 1915, when the European Allies suggested the desirability of China's participation in the war on their side, the Okuma cabinet had resisted the idea. The Japanese government claimed that China's entry into the war at the time of domestic political unrest involving Yuan Shikai's attempt at an imperial restoration would only accelerate internal disruption and make it difficult for the Chinese people to restore the domestic peace and unity that they really needed.[18] However, by the end of 1916, half a year after Yuan's death, members of the Terauchi cabinet, who were engaged in the negotiations for a loan to the Chinese Communications Bank, became receptive to the idea of China's entry into the war. Kamezo Nishihara, a private agent of Premier Terauchi who was negotiating a loan with the key Chinese officials through informal channels, began to persuade Tokyo in late December that the Allies should agree to revise the unfair Chinese tariff in exchange for China's participation in the war because the unfair tariff was the greatest hindrance to political and economic reform in China.[19] Upon learning about the American note inviting China to sever diplomatic relations with Germany from the British minister, Japanese Chargé Kenkichi Yoshizawa, in Beijing, pointed out to Tokyo the advantages of Japan's taking the initiative in drawing China into the Allied side before the European Allies took any action. Yoshizawa believed that if the Japanese government acted prudently, after the elimination of German influence from China the Chinese government might employ a large number of Japanese as successors to the German officials at the customs service, the postal service, and so forth. Yoshizawa also reported that the majority of Chinese government officials were inclined to accept the American invitation. Because the Chinese were trying to sound out the attitude of the Japanese Legation, Yoshizawa requested Tokyo's instructions.[20] On February 9, the Terauchi cabinet decided to support China's diplomatic break with Germany because it did not see any harm to Japan in supporting the American proposition.

On the same day, however, Tokyo learned that the Chinese government had already sent a protest against the German submarine operation without consulting Tokyo. The fact that China acted independently in its important foreign policy decision before Japan offered any advice upset the Terauchi government officials and drove them to interfere more actively in China's foreign policy. Foreign Minister Ichiro Motono complained to the Chinese minister in Tokyo on February 10 that China did not sincerely respect Japan's opinion and asked for it only after the action had already been taken. Motono reminded China that his government expected China to consult with it every time China planned to take a new step.[21]

Premier Duan, placed in a difficult position to deal with both Japan and the United States, within the same day sent a note to Tokyo, in which he expressed China's willingness to cooperate closely with Japan in case China should break off diplomatic relations with Germany and requested Japanese advice on this subject. The next day, Chargé Yoshizawa met Premier Duan and conveyed that his government desired China to sever diplomatic relations with Germany. Yoshizawa also repeated Tokyo's grievance on China's failure to consult with Japan when it issued the warning to Germany. Duan told Yoshizawa that it was too early for his government to decide whether to break off relations with Germany because his government had not heard from Germany, but Duan promised to confer with Japan in advance on this matter. Several Chinese officials close to Premier Duan had conversations with Yoshizawa and were relieved to hear that Japan was in favor of China's break with Germany and committed themselves to close association with Japan.[22] These Chinese words seemed to ease Tokyo's mind. Thus, while the Duan government was gradually losing hope for the American financial support, it was developing closer ties with Japan, promising that it would confer with Japan concerning China's policy toward Germany.

Premier Terauchi sent Nishihara to Beijing on February 13 for the purpose of explaining the Japanese position, finding out the real intention of the Chinese officials through informal channels, and, if possible, persuading the Duan government to join the war against Germany. Although Nishihara held no official post in the government, he had been instrumental in contracting large loans to China in 1916. Sending Nishihara to Beijing at this juncture conveyed to the Duan government a strong message of the possibility of a new Japanese loan to China as compensation for China's acceptance of Tokyo's initiative in taking action against Germany. Nishihara met Cao Rulin and Liang Qichao, his two most important contacts in the Duan government, and urged China to declare war on Germany on its own initiative. In return, Nishihara suggested the following conditions: (1) the postponement of the Boxer indemnity payments to the Allies; (2) the cancellation of the same to Germany and Austria; (3) the increase of Chinese customs tariff; (4) noninterference in China's domestic politics; and (5) support of Chinese industrial development and political unity.[23] Meanwhile in Tokyo, the Chinese minister informed Foreign Minister Motono of the Chinese government's decision to sever diplomatic relations with Germany and requested Japan to consider the revision of the Chinese tariff and the postponement of the indemnity payment. Motono promised to give the Chinese proposal serious consideration, and, at the same time, he emphasized the advisability of China's going further and joining the Allies.[24]

The Japanese government's efforts to draw China into the war became more conspicuous after Japan obtained a promise from the European Allies to support Japanese claims for Shandong at a future peace conference. Tokyo secured a secret agreement on this subject from Britain on February 16 in exchange for Japanese naval assistance in the Mediterranean and the South Atlantic. The agreement stipulated that the British government "will support Japan's claims in regard to disposal of Germany's rights in Shantung and possessions in Islands North of Equator on occasion of Peace Conference, it being understood that the Japanese Government will, . . . treat in same spirit Great Britain's claims to German Islands South of Equator."[25] This British guarantee meant that Japan's succession to German rights and concessions was more firmly secured even if China entered the war against Germany. On March 1, Japan secured from France a similar promise to support Japan's claims for Shandong and the German islands north of the equator at the future peace conference in return for Japan's offering "all the desirable extended support" to the French efforts to obtain from China "the rupture of her diplomatic relations with Germany."[26] Russia accepted a similar deal on March 5. In the meantime, Foreign Minister Motono, who had already emphasized the advisability of China's joining the Allies during his meeting with the Chinese minister on February 15, further pressed the Chinese minister on February 17 to declare war on Germany. Motono intended to reward China by agreeing to the revision of the tariff and the postponement of the indemnity payment.[27]

In Beijing, once Premier Duan made up his mind to lead his country into the war under Japanese guidance, Nishihara began secret negotiations with the Chinese liaison to Duan concerning the details of the conditions for China's entry into the war. During his meeting with Nishihara on February 21, Premier Duan expressed his gratitude for the Japanese overtures and repeated his determination to enter the war. He told Nishihara that he decided to use this opportunity to carry out administrative reforms with the help of Japan, which meant that he intended to eliminate his political enemies and unite China under his influence. The same day, Cao Rulin, the managing director of the government-operated Bank of Communications, requested a second Japanese loan of twenty million yen for the purpose of securing weapons, training officers and military technicians in preparation for the war against Germany, as well as for the prevention of "domestic insurrections." In the meantime, Liang Qichao, the president of the Progressive Party and well-known intellectual leader who would later join the Duan cabinet as minister of finance in July, continued to emphasize the need for the revision of unfair Chinese tariff. Ignoring President Li Yuanhong's adamant insistence on China's maintaining neutrality, the Duan cabinet sought a joint recommendation of the Allied powers for China's entry into the war. Being reluctant to take a high-handed measure, the Allies merely sent a friendly note expressing the advisability of China's diplomatic rupture with Germany on February 28. On the same day, Nishihara received news from Tokyo that the Japanese minister of finance had informally agreed to support the plan for a twenty million yen loan to the Communications Bank. Apparently, these developments prompted the Chinese council of state affairs to make the decision to join the Allies on that day.[28]

The debate over China's entry into the war, however, deeply divided Chinese leaders and further threatened the disintegration of China from within. The real reason for the split was the continuing power struggle between Premier Duan and his clique on the one hand and President Li and his Guomindang followers on the other. According to a Chinese historian, Madeleine Chi, "the bone of contention" between the two factions "was a question of how and where funds were to be distributed."[29] President Li was determined to block Duan from using war funds to eliminate his political enemies. Duan was equally determined to overcome the opposition of the president and the Guomindang-dominated parliament against China's declaration of war on Germany. This intensified the antagonism between the two factions. Duan managed to extract the president's consent and severed diplomatic relations with Germany on March 14, but he had yet to lead the country to war because China's declaration of war was prerequisite for Allied, especially Japanese, financial assistance. His government's use of force to impel the parliament to accept the decision for war in May led to the dismissal of Duan himself by President Li; this action further heightened the tension between Duan's clique and the president. However, Duan was given a second chance by an unexpected coup d'état attempt to restore the Manchu dynasty by General Zhang Xun, who had been cooperating with President Li up to that point. After the president reappointed Duan as premier and commander-in-chief, the president took refuge in the Japanese legation. Duan defeated Zhang's forces in Beijing on July 12, and three days later, he formed a new cabinet.

During this political turmoil in China, the Terauchi cabinet continued to support Duan with the intention of guiding the Duan government to the war under Japan's auspices. Premier Terauchi did not want to interfere openly in China's internal power struggle, but his government quietly extended moral and financial support to Duan and his followers on at least three occasions.[30] First, on April 29, Duan's confident, Cao Rulin, visited Japanese Minister Hayashi and asked whether Japan could give "moral support," if not an open intervention, in favor of the Duan government in case it should resort to "extreme measures" to overcome the obstructions by President Li and his supporters in the parliament. On May 3, under instruction from To-kyo, Hayashi tried to persuade President Li to agree to a declaration of war, but the president did not change his position.[31] When Chinese Minister Zhang Zongxian in Tokyo met Nishihara and asked about the possibility of a twenty million yen loan to the Communications Bank on May 7, neither the minister for foreign affairs nor the minister of finance saw any problem in continuing its negotiation, as long as its objective was domestic reform, and not the removal of the president by coup d'état.[32]

The second occasion that the Duan faction asked for Japan's assistance was when President Li dismissed Premier Duan. On May 27, Cao asked Nishihara for a loan to start a counter–coup d'état against General Zhang Xun who was then cooperating with the president. Nishihara was person-ally sympathetic toward Cao's plea, for he thought that Japan's assistance to Duan's efforts to eliminate his opponents might provide Japan with a chance to expand its influence over China. However, Premier Terauchi op-posed the idea of naked intervention in China's internal power struggle. Nishihara decided to go to China anyway. Once in Beijing, he found Presi-dent Li and his supporters working to make Li Jingyi the new premier, and, more important, Nishihara was convinced that American Minister Reinsch was behind this move. Determined to counteract U.S. interference, Nishi-hara sought an alternative financial source to assist Duan's counter–coup d'état. Somehow he persuaded the Bank of Korea to extend a five million yen loan for that purpose.[33]

Third, on July 1, as soon as Zhang Xun proclaimed the restoration of the Manchu Dynasty, Cao contacted Nishihara and requested a two million yen loan to raise an army to defeat General Zhang's forces. The two men worked out a plan to extend a loan from a private company, Mitsubishi. Premier Terauchi again opposed the plan on the ground of noninterference in do-mestic conflicts in China. However, strong pleas from Nishihara, as well as from the Japanese diplomats from Beijing and Tianjin, persuaded Tokyo to allow an extension of a private loan. Consequently, on July 12, Mitsubishi and the province of Zhili (Hebei) signed a contract for a one million yen loan.[34] Thus, although the Japanese government never openly intervened on behalf of Duan, it remained friendly to the Duan faction throughout the political unrest in China and extended financial assistance through informal channels.

Upon the establishment of the new Duan government in mid-July, the Terauchi government made an official commitment to a pro-Duan policy and aggressively enlisted China into the war. The resolution reached by the cabinet on July 27 declared that it would extend friendly assistance, both fi-nancial and military, to the Duan government so as to restore political stability in China and settle various problems existing between China and Japan. The Terauchi cabinet did not consider Tokyo's assistance to the Duan regime as interference in domestic affairs of China because the government in Beijing was the only legitimate one recognized by the Western powers as representing China. The resolution stated that in view of Japan's responsibility to maintain peace in East Asia, it was essential for the Japanese government to render support to the legitimate government in China. However, the resolution also declared that Japan would not intervene in political conflicts between the north and the south in China.[35]

The Beijing government declared war on Germany and Austria-Hungary on August 14, soon after it received the Allied consent to a small increase in the Chinese customs tariff and the postponement of the Boxer indemnity payment for five years. Later at the peace conference, the Chinese delegation demanded the direct restitution of German rights and concessions in Shandong on the ground that China's declaration of war on Germany had abrogated all the treaties of whatever nature between China and Germany. However, in August 1917, the Japanese government was not very alarmed by China's abrogation of all the treaties and agreements with Germany because Japan relied on the Sino-Japanese treaty of May 1915, in which China promised to consent to all arrangements made between Japan and Germany concerning Shandong. Moreover, the Terauchi government intended to guide the Duan government in war-related matters and hoped to bring the Chinese over to Japan's side at a future peace conference by extending both financial and military assistance. With this expectation presumably in mind, the Japanese government extended a series of loans to the Duan government in rapid succession during the rest of 1917: a reform loan of ten million yen in August, a loan of twenty million yen to the Communications Bank in September, a railway loan of six and a half million yen in October, and a loan for arms amounted to seventeen million yen in December. At least nine more loans followed the next year.[36]

In this way, the rivalry between Japan and the United States over the issue of China's entry into the war against Germany provided the Terauchi government with an opportunity to assert Japan's special position in China and to experiment with the idea of a Japanese-led vertical regionalism in East Asia through Sino-Japanese cooperation based on an unequal partnership. Premier Terauchi and his government's initial attempt to lead China into the war under Japan's guidance appeared to have produced some desired outcomes for the moment. In the face of China's internal division and the specter of U.S. interference, the Terauchi cabinet found itself in a marriage of convenience with the Duan government, which came to depend on Japanese financial assistance, the Nishihara loans in particular.

NOTES

1. Robert Lansing, *War Memoirs of Robert Lansing* (Indianapolis, Ind.: Bobbs-Merrill Company, 1935), 212.

2. David F. Houston, *Eight Years with Wilson's Cabinet 1913 to 1920* (Garden City, N.Y.: Doubleday, Page & Company, 1926), 1: 229.

3. Azusa Oyama, ed., *Yamagata Aritomo Ikensho* (Collection of memoranda of Aritomo Yamagata) (Tokyo: Hara shobo, 1966), 339–348.

4. Terauchi's letter to Shinpei Goto, August 7, 1914, quoted in Shinichi Kitaoka, *Nihon rikugun to tairiku seisaku, 1906–1918 nen* (Japanese army and its continental policy, 1906–1918) (Tokyo: Tokyo daigaku shuppankai, 1978), 164.

5. Gaimusho (Foreign Ministry of Japan), *Nihon gaiko nenpyo Narabi ni shuyo bunsho* (A chronology and major documents of Japanese foreign policy) (Tokyo: Hara shobo, 1965), 1: 424–426.

6. Lansing to the diplomatic representatives in neutral countries, February 3, 1917, in U.S. Department of State, *Papers Relating to the Foreign Relations of the United States*, 1917, Supplement (Washington, D.C., 1931), 1: 108. Hereafter cited as *FR*.

7. Paul Reinsch, *An American Diplomat in China* (Garden City, N.Y.: Doubleday, Page & Company, 1922), 241–242; Reinsch to Lansing, February 6, 1917, *FR*, 1917, Supplement 1: 401–402.

8. Reinsch to Lansing, February 7, 1917, *FR*, 1917, Supplement 1: 403–404.

9. Reinsch to Lansing, February 8, 9, 1917, *FR*, 1917, Supplement 1: 404, 407–408. Reinsch to Lansing, February 10, 1917, in Arthur S. Link, ed., *The Papers of Woodrow Wilson* (Princeton: Princeton University Press, 1966–1994), 41: 195. Hereafter cited as *PWW*.

10. Reinsch to Lansing, January 10, 1917, *FR*, 1917, Supplement 1: 404–407.

11. Wilson to Lansing, February 9, 1917, *PWW*, 41: 175; Lansing to Wilson, February 10, 1917, *PWW*, 41: 185–186.

12. Wilson to Lansing, February 10, 1917, *PWW*, 41: 186–187.

13. Reinsch to Lansing, February 12, 1917, *FR*, 1917, Supplement 1: 409; Reinsch to Wilson, February 14, 1917, *PWW*, 41: 229.

14. Lansing to Reinsch, February 17, 26, 1917, *FR*, 1917, Supplement 1: 410–411.

15. Reinsch to Lansing, February 28, 1917, *FR*, 1917, Supplement 1: 412.

16. Lansing to Reinsch, March 2, 1917, *FR*, 1917, Supplement 1:412; Reinsch to Lansing, April 13, 1917, *FR*, 1917, Supplement 1: 441–442.

17. Reinsch to Lansing, March 12, 1917, *FR*, 1917, Supplement 1: 418; Lansing to Reinsch, March 12, 1917, *FR*, 1917, Supplement 1: 419; Polk to Wilson, March 10, 1917, *PWW*, 41: 382–383; Lansing to Reinsch, March 13, 1917, *PWW*, 41: 401–402.

18. Shidehara heiwa zaidan, *Shidehara Kijuro* (The biography of Kiguro Shidehara) (Tokyo: Shidehara heiwa zaidan, 1955), 102.

19. Shiro Yamamoto, ed., *Nishihara Kamezo nikki* (Diary of Kamezo Nishihara) (Kyoto: Kyoto joshi daigaku, 1983), 163.

20. Yoshizawa to Motono, February 6, 7, 8, 9, 1917, in the Foreign Ministry of Japan, *Nihon gaiko bunsho* (Documents on Japanese foreign policy), 1917 (Tokyo, 1968), 3: 220–222, 223–225. Hereafter cited as *NGB*.

21. Obata-Chinese Minister talk, February 9, 1917; Yoshizawa to Motono, February 9, 1917; Motono to Yoshizawa, February 10, 1917, *NGB*, 1917, 3: 227–228, 232–233.

22. Chinese Minister to the Japanese Foreign Ministry, February 10, 1917; Yoshizawa to Motono, February 12, 1917, *NGB*, 1917, 3: 238, 240.

23. Seiji Saito, "Terauchi naikaku to Nishihara Kamezo" (The Terauchi cabinet and Kamezo Nishihara) *Kokusai seiji* 75 (October 1983): 20–21.

24. Motono to Chinda, Uchida, and Yoshizawa, February 15, 1917, *NGB*, 1917, 3: 257.

25. Green to Motono, February 16, 1917, *NGB*, 1917, 3: 644.

26. French Ambassador to the Japanese Foreign Ministry, March 1, 1917, *NGB*, 1917, 3: 656–657.

27. Motono to Chinda, Uchida, and Yoshizawa, February 15, 1917, *NGB*, 1917, 3: 257. Motono to Yoshizawa, February 18, 1917, *NGB*, 1917, 3: 265.

28. Yoshizawa to Motono, February 21, 28, March 1, 1917, *NGB*, 1917, 3: 273, 302–303, 311; Shiro Yamamoto, ed., *Nishihara Kamezo nikki*, 189.

29. Madeleine Chi, *China Diplomacy, 1914–1918* (Cambridge: Harvard University Press, 1970), 123.

30. Seiji Saito, "Terauchi naikaku ni okeru endan seisaku kakuritsu no keii" (The circumstances under which the Terauchi cabinet adopted the policy to assist Duan), *Kokusai seiji* 83 (October 1986): 157.

31. Motono to Hayashi, April 30, 1917; Hayashi to Motono, May 3, 1917, *NGB*, 1917, 3: 464, 466.

32. Shiro Yamamoto, ed., *Nishihara Kamezo nikki*, 200.

33. Ibid., 203–205; Nishihara to Shoda, June 10, 1917; Nishihara to Kimura, June 25, 26, 1917; Minobe to Nishihara, June 28, 1917, *NGB*, 1917, 2: 665–668, 679–680, 683.

34. Seiji Saito, "Terauchi naikaku ni okeru endan seisaku kakuritsu no keii," 154–155.

35. Foreign Ministry of Japan, *Nihon gaiko nenpyo narabi ni shuyo bunsho*, Cabinet decision, July 20, 1917, 1: 437–438. The cabinet decision is dated July 20, 1917, but Kitaoka and Saito consider the diary of Den Kenjiro to be the most reliable source on the date of decision and argue that the decision was made on July 27. Shinichi Kitaoka, *Nihon rikugun to tairiku seisaku*, 203.

36. Katsumi Usui, "Chugoku no taisen sanka to nihon no tachiba" (China's participation in the great war and Japan's position), *Rekishi kyoiku* 8 (1960): 27.

CHAPTER 4

The Lansing-Ishii Agreement

On November 2, 1917, Secretary of State Robert Lansing and Japanese Ambassador Extraordinary and Plenipotentiary Kikujiro Ishii signed an executive agreement concerning China. As some historians have pointed out, the agreement was "largely window dressing," intended to create an appearance of harmony as part of a wartime measure; in reality, it did little to resolve the fundamental differences regarding China that existed between the Wilson administration and the Terauchi government.[1] The agreement was obviously a declaration of divergent objectives, consisting of two incompatible ideas, namely, recognition of "Japan's special interests in China" and adherence to the principles of the Open Door and the territorial and administrative integrity of China. As soon as the agreement was made public, Tokyo emphasized the first part of the agreement, and Washington stressed the latter.

How and why did the two countries conclude such an ambiguous agreement which was susceptible to contradictory interpretations? As discussed in the previous chapter, both the Japanese and American governments tried to influence China's decision to sever diplomatic relations with Germany in early February 1917. This chapter demonstrates that the negotiation for the Lansing-Ishii agreement was prompted by the ongoing Japanese-American rivalry over who should take the initiative in leading or not leading China into the war against Germany. Behind this rivalry was the fundamental question of whether Japan should be allowed to establish a paramount position in China. The Terauchi government, in pursuit of the regionalist objective through Japanese financial assistance to the Duan government in

Beijing, used the U.S.-Japanese controversy over China's declaration of war as an opportunity to press the Wilson administration to recognize Japan's special position in China. Japanese leaders were also aware of the implication that this controversy might have about Japan's claims to Shandong at a future peace settlement, because U.S. entry into the war brought the strong possibility of America's having an influential voice in the peace conference. However, as the examination of the negotiations over the Lansing-Ishii agreement reveals in this chapter, President Wilson had no sympathy for Japan's regionalist aspiration. He refused to sacrifice the principles of the Open Door and the territorial and administrative integrity of China. Moreover, as wartime expediency, the Wilson administration was interested in binding Japan to the principles of equal opportunity and the independence of China for the duration of the war, so that the United States could concentrate on its war efforts in Europe.

The two countries' positional difference regarding China and their deep-seated suspicions and rivalry made it difficult for them to reach an understanding. Ambassador Ishii and Secretary Lansing undertook the strenuous task of reconciling the diametrically opposed views of their respective governments, only to find that neither side was willing to concede. In order to show publicly the evidence of accord, and to avoid projecting the image of ill-coordinated allies working at cross-purposes, the negotiators took pains to make an amalgam of the two incompatible ideas.

In the spring of 1917, the most noticeable pattern in America's diplomatic correspondence on East Asia was the sequence of warnings from Minister Reinsch in Beijing about the Japanese scheme to seize political control over China. On March 12, 1917, Reinsch wrote Lansing, "I have reason to believe . . . that he [Premier Duan] and an important faction have become thoroughly identified with Japanese intrigue and that the Japanese have furnished money and promised further assistance to be used in fortifying the position of those concerned." Two days after China's diplomatic break with Germany, Reinsch urged the State Department to give a favorable response to the Chinese request for assistance, reporting that Premier Duan had told him that "should the American Government now abandon interest in China [sic], the Chinese Government would be driven into the arms of Japan." On March 26, Reinsch cabled, "General dissatisfaction prevails partly because of unprecedented official corruption, lack of policy and authority; partly because of great influence of Japanese clique over the Government." He suggested to Washington that the situation would improve only if China followed the American lead without other entanglements when the United States declared war on Germany.[2]

Moreover, the highly publicized Zimmermann telegram startled the American people, and the fear of a German-Japanese military coalition began to haunt the American official mind. The telegram of the German secretary of state for foreign affairs proposed an alliance with Mexico and possibly with Japan in the event of a war between Germany and the United States. Japanese Foreign Minister Motono publicly dismissed the German attempt, stating that "he considered such an idea ridiculous, it being based on the outrageous presumption that Japan would abandon her allies."[3]

After the United States declared war on Germany on April 6, the confrontation between Premier Duan and President Li in Beijing over the issue of China's declaration of war intensified. The violence at parliament on May 11 caused Minister Reinsch deep concern about the possibility of Japanese intervention into China's domestic affairs. Lindsay Russell, the president of the Japan America Society in New York, who happened to be visiting Beijing at that time, presumably after having conferred with Reinsch, suggested to Japanese Minister Hayashi that Japan and the United States should declare that, excepting Manchuria and Shandong, they would adopt a policy of "conciliation and peaceful participation in the development of China through special enterprises without territorial aggression or claiming exclusive special influence."[4] On May 11, Reinsch visited Hayashi and proposed that the above statement should also be made by Britain and France. Reinsch again visited Hayashi on May 16, after having obtained approval from Secretary Lansing, as well as from the British and French representatives at Beijing, and this time he presented a new proposal for the four powers' joint note to China. The draft note declared that the nations at war with Germany would guarantee "the independence of China and the integrity of Chinese territory" and deny their intentions "to seek in China, either singly or jointly, advantages of [the] nature of territorial or preferential rights, whether local or general."[5] It seems logical to conclude that the note was intended to hold back Japan from taking advantage of China's internal conflict during the war.

Foreign Minister Motono strongly opposed Reinsch's proposal. In the international climate of that time, Motono concluded that if Japan made a joint statement with Britain and France on the initiative of the United States, it would appear as if the United States had manipulated them all. Motono was afraid that this might increase America's prestige in Chinese eyes. He sent a note of flat refusal to Minister Hayashi at Beijing,[6] but before his instruction reached Beijing, however, the May 23 dismissal of Premier Duan, and the following political unrest in China, prevented the American legation from taking any further action.

In the meantime in Washington, Secretary Lansing met with Japanese Ambassador Aimaro Sato on May 12 and suggested that the visit of a Japanese war mission to the United States might contribute to better diplomatic relations between the two countries. Besides discussion of wartime cooperation, Lansing told Sato that he would have no objection if delegates and hosts should exchange views on East Asian questions—but he wanted Sato to propose this consultation to the Japanese government as his own idea. Although Lansing declined to make an official commitment to the idea of discussing East Asian questions in such a forum, a few days later at Sato's request, he officially stated, "If [Japanese] commissioners should come, they would be at liberty of course to take up other matters." The Japanese government assumed that the American government had no objection to using this opportunity to discuss Japanese-American differences over China policy. The Japanese government responded to these overtures, and on May 22 decided to send a war mission to the United States, in the expectation that the two countries would use this opportunity to reach some sort of understanding regarding China policy.[7]

When Chinese President Li and the northern military governors had a showdown and the split between the north and the south seemed imminent, the Wilson administration decided to appeal to Chinese leaders to restore peace and political unity. On June 2, Minister Reinsch reported, "Should the military succeed in overthrowing the President, the South will undoubtedly fight and a division of China will result." Reinsch suggested that only "a united mediation of the powers" might be able to save the situation. This idea received the full support of the secretary of state. Anticipating that the spread of internal chaos would invite further Japanese encroachments on Chinese sovereignty, Lansing had already reached the conclusion by mid-May that "the action by this government which would be most helpful to China would be to obtain a joint identic reassertion by the United States and the principal Allied Powers of China's political and territorial integrity." On June 4, the U.S. government sent a note to the Beijing government, urging the conflicting factions to restore peace and political unity in China. The note warned: "The entry of China into war with Germany, or the continuance of the *status quo* of her relations with that Government, are matters of secondary consideration. The principal necessity for China is to resume and continue her political entity and to proceed along the road of national development on which she has made such marked progress." At the same time, the State Department proposed to Britain, France, and Japan that they make an identical representation to China, urging that the question of its entry into the war should be secondary to the question of the internal peace and unity of China.[8]

This American attempt not only failed but actually produced exactly the opposite effect. The Allies, who were desperate to encourage China's participation in the war, refused to support the American proposal. On the contrary, the American note to Beijing on June 4 provoked a new controversy between Japan and the United States because Japan perceived this gesture as yet more interference into Sino-Japanese affairs. Moreover, the Terauchi cabinet seized this opportunity to press the United States to recognize Japan's "paramount" position in China.

The Japanese foreign office, which began to suspect Americans of obstructing Japanese activities in China, was upset by the way the American government presented the June 4 note to China. When Japanese officials received America's proposal for a joint note on June 6, they assumed that the State Department would not take any action until Tokyo's approval. The Japanese government was surprised by the news that Minister Reinsch had already communicated the sense of the proposed joint representation to the Chinese government. Vice Foreign Minister Kijuro Shidehara hurriedly met the American chargé and expressed his surprise that Reinsch had acted before Japan responded. Foreign Minister Motono instructed Ambassador Sato in Washington to suggest to Secretary Lansing that Japan could not ignore American interference in Chinese domestic affairs. When Sato met Lansing shortly thereafter, the latter told Sato "frankly that the United States has as much rights as Japan had to express its opinion to the Chinese Government," and that the Japanese government "had no monopoly on giving friendly advice to Peking."[9]

The Japanese press severely criticized the U.S. independent communication to China as interference in Chinese internal affairs. An inaccurate text of the American note, which first appeared in the highly influential *Tokyo Asahi*, intensified Japanese resentment, and the American embassy had to request the *Tokyo Asahi* to publish the correct text. However, the most important issue to the Japanese was not the contents of the text but the fact that the United States sent a note of a political nature to China without consulting Japan. The semiofficial *Japan Times* said, "The Foreign Office officials must obtain from the United States an assurance that it will not repeat its action in interfering with domestic affairs in China, completely ignoring the existence and position of Japan." The foreign office, said the *Times*, had stated that Japan was ready to make a frank declaration that its instinct for national existence compelled it to guard its special position in China. The *Times* declared that "Japan should seek America's recognition of Japan's special position in China in order to prevent future misunderstandings."[10] It turned out that this was exactly what the Japanese government intended to do.

The Japanese government not only intended to use the American note of June 4 as a pretext for pressing the United States to recognize Japan's paramount position in China, but also to use the Japanese war mission to Washington to negotiate some sort of formal understanding on the Japanese position in China. On June 13, the Japanese government took a series of actions to improve its bargaining position. First, the Terauchi cabinet appointed Viscount Kikujiro Ishii, former minister for foreign affairs and a distinguished diplomat, as ambassador extraordinary and plenipotentiary empowered to negotiate and sign a formal agreement. Ishii's main task was to solve two problems: status of Japanese nationals in the United States and definition of Japan's special relations to China and the reconciliation of the Japanese and American activities in China.[11]

Second, when Foreign Minister Motono directed Ambassador Sato to inform the State Department of the above appointment, he also instructed the ambassador to deliver the Japanese formal reply to the American proposal of June 4 concerning China. The last paragraph of the Japanese memorandum started with a contentious statement that "Japan possesses paramount interests both political and economic in China and she would no doubt suffer more than any other country should the turn of events there present a grave aspect." Nevertheless, the memorandum expressed Japanese unwillingness to join the proposed representation to China on the ground that such an action was against Japan's "avowed policy of non-interference in the essentially domestic affairs of China."[12]

Third, and finally, the Japanese foreign office simultaneously instructed Ambassador Sato to carry out a tactful maneuver to obtain the American recognition of Japan's special relations with China. Sato was ordered to read to Secretary Lansing an "oral communication," which started with the statement "[t]hat Japan has special and close relations, political as well as economic, with China, is well and has been understood by the American government." Sato was to call Lansing's attention to former Secretary of State Bryan's note of March 13, 1915, which declared that "the United States frankly recognized that territorial contiguity creates special relations between Japan" and Shandong, South Manchuria, and Eastern Inner Mongolia. Then he was to suggest that the U.S. government should see "its way by some appropriate means to confirming the statement made by Mr. Bryan and clearly reasserting its friendly attitude toward Japan in respect of Chinese problems."[13]

These three instructions indicate that before the Ishii mission was sent to Washington, the Terauchi government was anxious to know to what extent the Wilson administration would concede Japan's "paramount" or special interests, political as well as economic, in China. Apparently, Japan this time meant its paramount position in all of China, not only in Shandong, South Manchuria, and Eastern Inner Mongolia as Bryan's note of March 1915 had specified. On June 15, Ambassador Sato met Secretary Lansing and read the messages from Tokyo to him.

The two memoranda from the Japanese government, one written and one oral, confused the Americans and complicated communication between Tokyo and Washington. It took the State Department some time to understand the Japanese maneuver. Paying little attention to the last paragraph of the Japanese formal reply to the American proposal of June 4, Secretary Lansing made no objection to the expression "Japan possesses paramount interests both political and economic in China." According to Sato, Lansing "expressed himself as quite in accord with the deep sense of the memorandum" and no longer saw the necessity of presenting a joint note to China. After listening to Sato's "oral communication," Lansing expressed his understanding of Japan's desire and promised to consider an appropriate handling of the matter. Lansing's favorable response to the Japanese memorandum led Tokyo to believe that the United States had tacitly admitted Japan's paramount interests in China. Hurriedly, Vice Foreign Minister Kijuro Shidehara went to the American embassy and delivered a copy of the Japanese memorandum which Sato handed to Lansing on June 15, telling Chargé Wheeler that the secretary of state was in full accord with this memorandum. On June 19, Foreign Minister Motono instructed Sato to "see the Secretary of State at the earliest opportunity and to assure him of the deep sense of gratitude which the Japanese Government feels upon learning that its frank and sincere expression of views has been received by Mr. Lansing." Because Lansing failed to make any comments on the sentence "Japan possesses paramount interests both political and economic in China," Wheeler had to telegraph Lansing from Tokyo to call his attention to Japan's use of the words "paramount interests."[14]

Lansing who did not understand that the copy handed to Wheeler was a copy of Sato's "oral communication" later commented erroneously, and somewhat bitterly, on the Japanese maneuver:

On June eighteenth the Japanese Minister of Foreign Affairs handed to our Chargé at Tokyo what purported to be a copy of the memorandum which Ambassador Sato had read to me. It was not a copy, for the memorandum delivered to Mr. Wheeler began with the words "Japan possesses paramount interests . . . in China." I would call particular attention to the attempt to make "special and close relations" synonymous with "paramount interests," an attempt which was renewed in connection with the negotiation of the Lansing-Ishii Agreement. Whether this variation in the language of the two documents, which purported to be the same, was or was not intentional, I do not know.[15]

Lansing realized that he must renounce Japan's claim of paramount interests in China. He drew up a draft reply to the Japanese memoranda and asked for President Wilson's approval. On July 3, the president wrote to Lansing that he entirely approved of the draft. He also added: "I hope that you will re-read the latter portion of it, however, with a view to making the idea of Japan's *political* influence over China a little more prominent as the thing we have *not* assented to in the sense she evidently has in mind."[16] In the American formal reply dated July 6, Lansing rejected Japan's contention that Bryan had recognized Japan's "special and close relations, political as well as economic with China as a whole," arguing that "Mr. Bryan merely said that the United States recognized that territorial contiguity created special relations between Japan and the districts of Shantung, South Manchuria and East Mongolia." Lansing also said, "I had no intention in our conversation of June 15 to convey the impression that this Government recognized that Japan possessed in China a paramount interest." He declared that the United States could not be indifferent to matters affecting America's "historic interest in the welfare of the Chinese people" and the territorial and administrative integrity of China.[17]

The foreign office in Tokyo, upon receiving Ambassador Sato's brief telegram regarding the American reply, realized that it had failed in its diplomatic maneuver to obtain America's recognition of Japan's paramount interests in China. With a view to developing a response to the American rebuff, the foreign minister instructed Sato to ask the State Department whether Elihu Root, who was then visiting Russia as head of the special American mission, could arrange to visit Japan on his way home. Because Root had been known to the Japanese as a sympathetic friend, the foreign minister evidently hoped to discuss the Chinese question with him or at least to lay the groundwork for the Ishii mission. However, Secretary Lansing, and apparently President Wilson, had no intention of letting Root discuss East Asian problems with the Japanese. As early as July 5, Lansing wrote to the president that "it would be unwise for Mr. Root or any of the Diplomatic Mission with him to stop in Japan. . . . The present unrest in the Far East and the possible divergence of views of Mr. Root as to the policy of the Administration in regard to that region seems to me to make it unwise for him to represent the Government."[18] Root returned to the United States directly from Vladivostok. Therefore, the Japanese government was unable to obtain any favorable results from preliminary communications with the American government before the departure of the Ishii mission.

The last instructions that Ishii received in Tokyo consisted of four parts: (1) to express Japan's cordial sentiments to the American people who declared war on Germany; (2) to discuss the measures of wartime cooperation; (3) to exchange frank views concerning Japanese-American problems, that is, the problems of American activities in China and the problem of the unjust and discriminatory treatment of Japanese nationals in the United States; and (4) to suggest to responsible American officials that Japan had secured agreements from Britain, France, and Russia guaranteeing the cession of all German islands in the Pacific north of the equator to Japan.[19]

The Terauchi cabinet was clearly most interested in the Chinese questions, for this was the only issue that included additional instructions. The instructions to Ishii provided the rationale for Japan's special position in China, both political and economic. They reflected the consensus among the most influential statesmen and were never to be changed throughout the two-month negotiations between Lansing and Ishii. They justified Japan's special position in China on the grounds of the geopolitical necessity to protect Japan's national security and its close economic ties with the Asian continent. Part of the instructions read as follows:

The interests of the United States in China are chiefly economic, and in no case are they of such importance as to affect the security of the home country. On the other hand, in Japan's relations with China, economically speaking, the amount of our capital investment and the volume of our trade are incomparably greater than those of the United States, while in the political field Japan's interests far outweigh those of the United States and the European Powers, being of special and vital nature closely linked to the security and future welfare of our country. Consequently, should any Power attempt to establish political influence in China in disregard of, or in a manner harmful to, Japan's position, Japan would as a matter of course be compelled to resort to measures of self-defense.

In the eyes of the Japanese leaders, the door of economic opportunities were open in China, as long as the United States respected Japan's special position as the regional power in East Asia.[20]

Having received the complete text of the American note of July 6 several days after Ambassador Ishii sailed for the United States on July 28, Foreign Minister Motono realized that the American government did not accept the Japanese position on the Chinese question. He had no choice but to leave the matter in the hands of Ishii. He directed Ambassador Sato in Washington to ask the secretary of state to "exchange frank opinions unofficially" with Ishii on his arrival "to promote a better understanding between the two governments." There seems to have been curious optimism on the part of the Japanese foreign office that if the United States "fully understood the situation and real intention of the Japanese government" in China, the Japanese-American differences over the region would be solved. Ishii, in the meantime, was instructed to find out what the American government wanted and to keep in close telegraphic communication with Tokyo for further instructions.[21]

By the time the Ishii mission arrived in the United States, the State Department had determined the importance the Japanese were giving to the discussion of Japanese-American problems. As early as June 27, Chargé Wheeler in Tokyo reported to Lansing that he had been "confidentially informed" by a Japanese foreign office official that Ishii "will broach the matter of the undesirable treatment of Japanese who are lawfully in the United States and that of economic cooperation of the United States and Japan in China."[22]

Apparently, the American government's primary objective in receiving the Japanese mission was to discuss how best the two countries could cooperate, both in an economic and a military sense, in carrying on the war. Zimmermann's telegram proposing Mexico's mediation between Japan and Germany made Washington apprehensive about a separate peace between Japan and Germany. State Department officials such as Secretary Lansing and Edward Williams, chief of the Division of Far Eastern Affairs, were concerned about the possibility of Japan's joining with Germany in case the United States openly confronted Japan concerning the Chinese question.[23] They felt that they might have to discuss a compromise, if necessary, on East Asian policy with the Ishii mission so as to assure the two countries' cooperation in the war. At the same time, however, President Wilson refused to sacrifice American idealistic principles of the Open Door and territorial and administrative integrity of China. In his view, the principles were universal and must be observed by all the powers who were interested in China, especially China's "selfish neighbor," Japan. To him, Japan's regionalist rhetoric was merely an excuse to justify its selfish territorial ambition in China.

Upon the arrival of the Japanese mission in San Francisco on August 13, newspapers of the Pacific Coast almost unanimously reported that the Japanese mission was prepared to discuss the Chinese question. The *San Francisco Chronicle* reported that of all the matters that the Japanese were going to take up "none, in Japanese eyes, attain the rank and dignity of the Chinese question; and no man who has carefully studied the march of events in the Far East since August 15, 1914, when Japan served her Kiaochow ultimatum on Germany . . . can doubt that it is this issue which will provide in Washington the critical diplomatic turning point."[24]

The city of San Francisco received the Japanese mission warmly, but because of the recent controversy over the alien land legislation in the state of California, one editorial observer noted, "A certain reserved cordiality, prompted seemingly by a sense of 'safety first,' is noticeable in the welcome." The Japanese immigrants were unpopular in California, and before the mission landed, there had been some uneasiness as to the sort of reception it might receive. Elaborate precautions were taken by the city. A military escort of three thousand troops, the largest in the history of San Francisco, was provided. The cavalry troops formed a hollow square about the Japanese who were riding in automobiles. It was reportedly the first time in the history of the United States that such a formation had been used except for presidential inaugural parades in Washington.[25]

On the East Coast, the Japanese mission was received with more enthusiasm. The State Department tried to deemphasize the Ishii mission's interest in discussing Japanese-American differences in China policy. Following the official explanation, the *New York Times* said that "the most important problem to be discussed is that of the disposition of the Japanese shipping, with the view to making it of the greatest assistance in the conduct of the war." The press, however, did not fail to warn of Japanese intentions. The *New Republic* asserted, "Japan has one chief interest, and one only. All other questions are subordinate, and all policies are shaped with a view to one end. That end is China." The periodical warned that the Ishii mission would be wise to discount in advance its accomplishments because China was vital to Japan, but to the United States it was important to have a just understanding both to Japan and China.[26]

Surrounded by press speculations, the Japanese mission was invited to the White House on August 23, and Ishii had an interview with President Wilson. According to Ishii, the president broached the problem of China "in a roundabout way," and then said, "America desired nothing more than the faithful observation in China of the Open Door and equal opportunity principles." He continued to say that "it was a source of regret to him that the powers had actually set up spheres of influence here and there in China and were threatening the free operation of these principles." When Ishii agreed with the president, saying that his country had never failed to uphold in Manchuria the principle of the Open Door and equal opportunity, the president showed "much interest in the conversation" and suggested that Ishii discuss the Chinese problem with Secretary Lansing. Thus the stage was set for the Lansing-Ishii talks on China.[27]

Secretary Lansing and Ambassador Ishii had their first serious conversation on September 6. After discussing how the two countries could cooperate fully in the prosecution of the war, they moved to other and more controversial questions. First of all, Ishii disclosed Japan's intention to retain the German Islands in the Pacific as "souvenirs" of the war. Although Ishii did not mention Japan's secret arrangements made in early 1917 with the European Allies, he told Lansing that Edward Grey had practically consented to the retention of the German Islands north of the equator by Japan and those south of the equator by Great Britain. However, Ishii did not reveal any understanding with the Allies concerning the German territory in Shandong. Lansing expressed a general appreciation for Ishii's frankness in giving him the information, but Lansing made no specific comment on this matter.[28]

Next, Lansing and Ishii moved to the question of China. When Lansing asked Ishii what further questions he wished to discuss, Ishii inquired, "Have you anything to propose in regard to China?" Lansing proposed the abolition of the spheres of influence in China as the manifestation of the two countries' "full agreement on complete territorial integrity, the Open Door, and equal opportunity in China." Ishii responded that Japan in China, especially in the regions adjacent to Japan, had interests more important than those of any other countries, in the same way as the United States in the western hemisphere had interests greater than those of other nations. He said that "while . . . [Japan's] desire was to have China open and free to all countries, he felt there might be criticism [within Japan] if there was a bare declaration of the 'Open Door' policy without some mention of Japan's special interests." He added that he was not sure whether it would be a real advantage to reaffirm the Open Door. Lansing pointed out that it would be advantageous for Japan to renounce spheres of influence because Japan's geographic position and industrial condition provided it with strong competitive power in the Chinese markets. Lansing asked Ishii to consider the above matter carefully and be prepared to discuss it at the next meeting.[29]

Ishii, who had already been favorably impressed by President Wilson's desire to put an end to spheres of influence in China, was further convinced during the first conference with Lansing that should the United States be satisfied on the matter of spheres of influence, it might agree with Japan on other issues—above all, on the question of Japan's special position in China. Ishii sent a cable to Tokyo, supporting the American argument on the question of spheres of influence. He said, "I believe that Japan might be able to gain advantages from the renunciation of spheres of influence, for Japan's trade in China is bound to outdistance the trade of other powers and occupy a predominant position as long as the Open Door and equal opportunity are effectively maintained." Ishii asked for Tokyo's permission to propose to Lansing a Japanese-American joint declaration containing three articles: (1) the reaffirmation of their adherence to the principle of the Open Door and the independence of China; (2) the renunciation of Japan's sphere of influence in China provided that all other powers would equally renounce theirs; and (3) the United States recognition of Japan's special position in China on the ground of "propinquity."[30]

Receiving this unexpected conciliatory proposal from Ishii, Foreign Minister Motono was unable to respond immediately because of the complex and peculiar decision-making process of the Japanese imperial government. Motono, who had spent a long period of time in France and Russia, was politically isolated in the Terauchi cabinet. He merely represented the voice of the Foreign Ministry. Even Premier Terauchi, though a protégé of genro Yamagata, was not able to make a prompt decision on his own. He not only needed to consult the genro, but also needed the consent of the major political party leaders because he did not represent any of the powerful political parties who often held the government's foreign policy hostage of partisan politics. The decision-making process was further complicated by the establishment of the Advisory Council on Foreign Relations (*gaiko chosakai*) on June 6, 1917. The original purpose of creating the council was to free foreign policy from partisan politics as well as from the personal influence of the genro. It was placed directly under the emperor's command and functioned as the highest advisory organ for Japan's foreign policy from June 1917 through September 1922.[31] Therefore, throughout the Lansing-Ishii negotiations Foreign Minister Motono not only had to submit the matter to the cabinet but also to the Advisory Council on Foreign Relations.

While Ishii was waiting for instructions from Tokyo, Secretary Lansing also attempted to obtain President Wilson's approval of his proposal for a realistic deal with Japan. Ever since the crisis of the Japanese Twenty-one Demands, Lansing had cherished the idea that the United States should publicly recognize Japan's special interests in South Manchuria, Eastern Inner Mongolia, and Shandong Province, and that Japan in return should make no further complaint regarding alien land legislation in the United States, reaffirm the principle of the Open Door, and promise not to discriminate against any foreign commercial activities in the areas where Japan's special interests were recognized.[32] Although by November 1916 Lansing had dropped the province of Shandong from the prospective areas of Japan's special interests, he still believed that the Ishii mission provided another opportunity to strike a bargain with Japan along the lines of his idea.

Lansing, however, had to approach President Wilson carefully because of the president's reservation about Lansing's judgment on certain critical issues. Wilson's confidence in Lansing was shaken when the latter published the "verge of war" speech in an effort to sabotage the president's peace effort in December 1916. According to Colonel Edward House, Wilson almost decided to ask for Lansing's resignation. Later in March 1917, Wilson again complained that Lansing was the most inadequate member in his cabinet, possessing "no imagination, no constructive ability, and but little real ability of any kind." Even during the Lansing-Ishii negotiations, on September 9, Wilson talked to House about the desirability of Lansing's resignation. House wrote in his diary, "Every time he [Wilson] wrote a note, or put out a statement, Lansing followed it with a conservative construction. Then when the President objected, he would correct it, thereby making endless confusion and largely nullifying the effect of the note."[33]

Lansing, who was fully aware of the differences between himself and his superior, chose to use Colonel House, whose mind Lansing thought to be like a "sponge," as a channel to convey his idea to the president—an idea that the president might not have accepted if it had come directly from the secretary of state. As early as March 1917, Lansing began to persuade House of his idea's advantages. Lansing now added another item. He discussed with House the desirability of transferring the Philippines to Japan. He even wrote directly to Wilson that the Philippines was reminiscent of Theodore Roosevelt and that "[I]f we could only let go, what a blessing it would be."[34]

Colonel House, who had a conciliatory attitude toward Japan even before Lansing approached him, agreed in most respects to the line presented by Lansing. Looking at East Asian policy from a realist perspective, House had sympathy with Japan's regionalist aspirations to establish its supremacy in Manchuria and expressed his hope to avoid a direct confrontation with Japan over the issue of the Open Door in China. By the spring of 1917, He had been "pretty well saturated," in his words, concerning Japan and Japanese feeling, and East Asia became one of his main considerations. He once told his friend that he had thought of going to Japan, China, and Russia, but he could not do so because he felt that he was needed in Washington. He was discussing the possibility of Japanese-American financial cooperation in China with such visitors as Japanese Ambassador Sato and Willard Straight. As to the transfer of the Philippines, House thought that "it might be done, provided safeguards be thrown around the Islands for their protection and for their political independence," but he did not bring up this matter either in his letter to or during his conversation with President Wilson.[35]

House began to put forward the Chinese question to President Wilson by using the reports of Richard Washburn Child, author, diplomat, and lawyer, who was traveling in China and Japan at that time and keeping close contact with House. In early June, House forwarded to Wilson a letter he had received from Child. Child reported that poverty, fear, and corruption, and instability in politics, were making the Chinese situation so much worse than it appeared on the surface to American diplomats and businessmen. Child urged that the United States should stay very close to Japan in order to help China's internal development. "Before we are misled by anti-Japanese agitation," said Child, "we must realize: 1) That Japan must have arable land, coal and iron or die; we must count upon her desperateness, 2) That her presence in any territory she occupied in China will be a godsend to the people. . . . There is a wide and growing Chinese agitation to throw open the door to Japan." After returning from Japan to the United States on the same ship as Ambassador Ishii, Child visited House in New York on August 30 to discuss Chinese problems. Impressed and encouraged by Child's suggestions, House asked him to put the substance of their conversation in a memorandum so that House could use it in the way he considered best. On that day House wrote in his diary: "I am eager to have Washington take a more sympathetic view of the Far Eastern situation than they now do, and to give it the attention it deserves. It only needs a little thought to bring a seemingly chaotic condition into a well ordered policy."[36]

Based on Child's report, House advised Wilson on September 6 to consider the idea that China should be administered by three trustees. House wrote to the president:

I think it is generally admitted that China is in a deplorable condition. The prevalence of disease, the lack of sanitation, a near system of slavery, infanticide, and other brutal and degenerate practices make the nation as a whole a menace to civilization. There is no administration of justice worthy of the name, and the intercommunication is wholly inadequate because of the lack of railroads, roads etc. . . .

Child proposes as a solution the administration of China by three trustees. One selected by China, one by Japan and one by the other powers who would subscribe to this plan. He does not advocate the plan being carried out without China's consent, but he believes China would consent if she were properly approached. . . .

This trusteeship to last for an agreed upon number of years, but long enough to put China in order, develop a civilization and purchasing power, and take her out of the backward nations and make her a blessing rather than a menace to the world.

In view of the Japanese Mission I thought these comments might be of service.[37]

House also discussed the issue with Roland Morris, who was ready to leave for Japan as the newly appointed ambassador. When House outlined his idea of East Asian policy along the same line proposed to the president, Morris, who had just seen Theodore Roosevelt, told him that Roosevelt's view and that of House were almost identical. It is important to note that House's letter to Wilson after his meeting with Ambassador Morris not only urged the president to adopt a conciliatory policy toward Japan but also suggested that the United States should recognize Japan as a leading regional power in East Asia. His letter read in part as follows:

I had a talk with Roland Morris today. I hope you will see him for ten or fifteen minutes before he leaves for Japan . . . in order to give him your viewpoint as to Far

Eastern questions. I think he has the right view himself and, if you agree with it, he will understand in what direction to proceed.

We cannot meet Japan in her desires as to land and immigration, and unless we make some concessions in regard to her sphere of influence in the East, trouble is sure, sooner or later to come. Japan is barred from all the undeveloped places of the earth, and if her influence in the East is not recognized as in some degree superior to that of the Western powers, there will be a reckoning.

A policy can be formulated which will leave the open door, rehabilitate China, and satisfy Japan. Morris sees this clearly but needs your sanction, if, indeed such a policy has your sanction.

Seemingly unimpressed by the letter of House, however, Wilson did not give Morris any instructions on that matter when he saw him on September 24. By this time, it was obvious that the attempts of Lansing and House to persuade the president into a realistic East Asian policy based on compromises had not had the desired effect.[38]

On the other side of the Pacific, the members of the Advisory Council on Foreign Relations met on September 15 to discuss Ishii's proposal for renouncing spheres of influence. It provoked somewhat heated discussion. Takashi Hara, the president of the Seiyukai (the largest party occupying 160 out of 381 seats in the Diet), thought that Ishii's proposal was out of the question. Some of the members who strongly opposed Ishii's idea suggested that the government break off the negotiations for an agreement on China. Premier Terauchi, however, somehow persuaded the members to allow Ishii to continue to talk to the Wilson administration. Although Hara gave his consent to the premier's suggestion, he added that Ishii's primary task was to make the United States understand Japan's policy toward China and that Ishii could leave other tasks in the hands of Ambassador Sato in Washington. All the members agreed. Thus, the Japanese leaders were unwilling to grant as much of a concession as Ishii had suggested.[39]

On September 18, the foreign minister instructed Ishii that the Japanese government could not accept the proposal for renouncing spheres of influence because of its great impact on Japan's future. He also pointed out that Japan could not declare the abolition of its sphere of influence without consulting the European powers. The foreign minister told Ishii that the most desirable thing was to obtain the American recognition of Japan's special position in China without referring to spheres of influence.[40] In the meantime, during the conversation with Ishii on September 8, the British ambassador in Washington had taken issue with the renunciation of spheres of influence. Therefore, by the time of the next meeting with Lansing on September 22, Ishii had to abandon his attempt to use the renunciation of spheres of influence as a means to make a better bargain.

When Lansing and Ishii held a conference on September 22, the fundamental differences in the positions of both governments became obvious. Ishii told Lansing that his government did not wish to change the status quo in China and that it was difficult to find grounds for an agreement on the subject of spheres of influence. Lansing replied that Japan and the United States were the only countries which could invest in China at that moment and that "if we permitted the gradual restoration of the policy of 'sphere of influence,' the Allied Governments would look upon us as seeking to monopolize the opportunities." He suggested that a redeclaration of the Open Door would dispel the Allied suspicion and gain their gratitude and confidence. Although Ishii understood Lansing's opinion, he asserted that the Japanese government did not think it wise to repeat the Open Door principles, and that "the Japanese people would be likely to blame the Government if there was nothing said about Japan's 'special interest' in China."[41]

Despite the differences in their positions, Lansing and Ishii tried to avoid a public appearance of discord. They were aware that the American and Japanese public expected some manifestation of cordial relationship. The two negotiators resorted to ambiguity and ambiguity created misunderstandings. The memoranda Lansing and Ishii sent to their respective superiors immediately after the conference of September 22 provide conflicting accounts on how they agreed to employ the words "Japan's special interests in China." This suggests that from that moment Lansing and Ishii began to use the words "special interests" with different meanings.

According to Lansing's memorandum of September 22, when Ishii argued for Japan's special interests in China, Lansing responded to Ishii as follows, "If he meant by 'special interest' 'paramount interest' I could not see my way clear to discuss the matter further; but, if he meant a special interest based upon geographical position, I was not unwilling to take the matter into consideration." Showing his understanding of Ishii's difficulty which pertained to the political situation in Japan, Lansing offered to find "some formula to satisfy the wishes of his people in case a re-declaration of the 'Open Door' policy could be agreed upon in principle." According to Lansing, Ishii asked him to prepare "such a formula" for consideration. In his *War Memoirs*, Lansing repeated the point that if Ishii had used "special interest" as a synonym for "paramount interest," he would not have discussed the matter further with Ishii. He insisted that Ishii understood fully that any reference to "Japan's special interest was based on geographical position and pertained to commercial interests." As far as Lansing was concerned, "the idea of paramount interest applying to political affairs was entirely eliminated from the negotiation."[42]

Ishii, however, presented a different case both at the time and in later years. According to Ishii's telegram to Foreign Minister Motono dated September 23, after Lansing told Ishii that the United States could recognize Japan's economic special interests in China but not the paramount interests of Japan, the two proceeded to exchange their views on the meaning of paramount interests. Ishii claimed that Japan had paramount interests in China in the same way as the United States had paramount interests in Mexico, and that these interests did not run counter to the Open Door policy in China. Lansing explained that the United States had special interests, but not paramount interests, in Mexico. Ishii replied:

Japan would be content with the recognition of Japan's "special interests" in China, if not "paramount interests." However, in order to avoid misunderstanding, I would like to explain the meaning of special interests. Internal disturbances or disaster in China would have no direct consequences for the Western nations, but to Japan, it would be a matter of life and death. Internal disturbances in China would have an immediate effect upon Japan. Japan cannot feel secure in her own defense unless China is well governed in defense and public order. Therefore, Japan deems it its duty to counsel China in administrative reform and to send instructors to assist China within the limits set by the necessity of maintaining its independence.

Lansing argued that in case China needed foreign instructors, Britain, France, and the United States, as well as Japan, should share in providing them and that a monopoly by Japan on sending instructors to China would be against the principle of equal opportunity. Ishii replied that if the Chinese government clearly lacked administrative capability and was on the verge of collapse, it was natural for the neighboring country to give counsel and assistance. The principle of equal opportunity, said Ishii, could not be applied to the matters of defense and politics when China's survival was at stake. Ishii added that the recognition of Japan's special position in China by other powers seemed to be a matter of their trust in Japan's good faith. Finally, the conversation closed with the following words by Lansing: "I understand the intentions of the Japanese Government and shall prepare a draft containing a paragraph which amounts to recognizing Japan's special interest, and will present it to you after obtaining the approval of the President. To issue a declaration now is necessary in order to make Germany realize that there in no chance of alienating Japan from the United States." Thus, toward the end of the conversation Ishii was convinced that Lansing had recognized that "special interests" were related to matters of a mainly political character.[43]

It should be noted that, Ishii, with extensive prior experience as a diplomat in Europe, had a clear idea of what the words "special interests" meant in the standard international practices at that time. These terms had been already used in the treaty of Anglo-Japanese alliance (January 1902), the Franco-Japanese convention (June 1907), and the Russo-Japanese agreement (July 1907). In all these agreements the European powers recognized Japan's special interests in China either in clear writing or by implication. Clearly Ishii knew that established diplomatic usage gave the phrase "special interests" political connotation in the eyes of European powers as well as China.[44]

It is hard to assess the reliability of the two contradictory testimonies, but it should also be noted that the discussion of the meaning of "paramount interests" described by Ishii in his telegram to Tokyo is missing in Lansing's accounts. Whatever the truth was, it remains that the chief executive of each side had no choice but to rely on the reports of his own negotiator. Premier Terauchi and the foreign office in Tokyo assumed that the United States agreed to recognize Japan's special interests, political as well as economic, in China, and interpreted the words "special interests" in the broadest sense. President Wilson and his administration, on the other hand, assumed that Japan's geographic position granted its economic special interests in China, but not its political interests.

Accounts of the Lansing-Ishii talk on September 22 also reveal that the United States and Japan held different notions of the Open Door. For the Americans, the principle of equal opportunity not only was an economic principle but also a political one. The Japanese, however, thought that the equal opportunity principle was primarily concerned with economic activities. They did not believe that, as far as Chinese internal political affairs were concerned, the United States was in the same position as Japan. But neither Ishii nor Lansing was willing to discuss these delicate matters thoroughly. Although Ishii attempted to compare Japan's dominant role in East Asia to that of the United States in the Western Hemisphere in the tradition of Theodore Roosevelt's corollary to the Monroe Doctrine, Lansing simply dismissed the analogy.

Lansing drew up a draft of an agreement and submitted it to President Wilson on September 25, enclosing his memoranda of the two previous conferences of September 6 and 22. Wilson fully supported Lansing's draft and wrote back to him, "I spent half an hour with Viscount Ishii. I did most of the talking (to let him see my *full* thought) and he seemed to agree throughout in *principle*." According to Ishii, during the interview, Wilson illustrated his general ideas of the Chinese problem and the matters of the postwar world.[45] It is not known whether Wilson touched upon the issue of Japan's special interests in China.

On September 26, Lansing and Ishii discussed the draft of an agreement and made several changes in language. The most significant change was made in the following sentence: the "United States Government recognizes that Japan has a special relation to China." Ishii suggested that the phrase "a special relation to China" should be changed to "paramount" or "preeminent interests in China," but Lansing refused to accept it. They decided to employ the phrase "special interests in China." Later, Lansing commented that he did not like the term "relation" because "it seemed to convey the idea of political influence." He was satisfied with the selection of the word "interest" because it was "broader and less used in matters political" in his opinion.[46]

Ishii was also satisfied with this change. He planned to cable the amended text to Tokyo and leave for New York on the next day. Both Lansing and Ishii, believing that the negotiations had been almost completed, exchanged friendly words which they hoped to be the last. Lansing wrote to Wilson on that day, "He leaves tomorrow morning for New York and probably will not return to Washington." Ishii asked Foreign Minister Motono to allow him to return directly from New York to Japan. He urged his government to accept the entire text of the telegraphed draft, saying that the American commitment was firm and could not be changed.[47]

Ishii's journey to New York was triumphal. The *New York Times* reported that "every voice of the thousands gave cordial greeting; flags flew from every building, and from every window men and women waved a colorful welcome." Certainly, the general feeling of the people of the East Coast toward the Japanese was far more cordial than that of the people of the Pacific Coast; but at the same time Ishii's public speeches, which had been widely printed in the press, had done much to strengthen the friendly feeling between Japan and America and to make the association of the two nations against Germany a real thing. The *New York Times* of September 28, 1917, reported: "If we cared to consider the public utterance, so sympathetic and so noble, of Viscount Ishii at Mount Vernon and elsewhere, we might say that no friendly nation has been more fortunate in its spokesman here. Something French in its lucidity, something of EDMUND BURKE in its philosophical eloquence, the student of Viscount Ishii's speeches in this country can discern." Ishii himself was fully aware of the influence of the press in the United States. He later wrote that in the United States, "where state policies are determined by the drift of public opinion, it is frequently necessary for a foreign envoy . . . to win the understanding of the people, so that the authorities, influenced by the wishes of the people, might more readily come around to his way of thinking." He was quite successful in his attempt to explain to the American public that German agents in China sowed distrust between the Japanese and the Americans. Moreover, seemingly encouraged by the result of the negotiations with Lansing, at the municipal banquet for dignitaries in New York, Ishii enunciated the idea that the press later labeled the "Asiatic Monroe Doctrine," in which he declared Japan's intention to respect the principles of the Open Door and independence of China.[48]

Lansing and Ishii, however, could not conclude an agreement quite so early as they wished. In reply to the American draft agreement, Foreign Minister Motono ordered Ishii, then in New York, to postpone his departure for Japan and to continue his negotiation efforts with the State Department, for the government in Tokyo thought that there were many unclear points in the draft. Ishii repeatedly requested the foreign minister to allow him to leave the United States, explaining that prolonged negotiations might make the American people suspicious of the good faith of Japan. In Tokyo, however, the members of the Advisory Council on Foreign Relations were eager to push the United States further to recognize Japan's superior position in China. Following the advice of the council, the foreign minister instructed Ishii, who now returned to Washington, to propose five changes in phraseology. There were two main points: to change the words "Japan has special interests in China" into "Japan has special interests and influence in China"; and to remove the sentence "they [the governments of Japan and the United States] will not take advantage of the present conditions to seek special rights or privileges in China which would abridge the rights of the subjects or citizens of other friendly states."[49]

When Ishii met Lansing on October 8, he failed to propose the insertion of the word "influence." Ishii later explained to Tokyo that President Wilson, who was disappointed at Japan's refusal to renounce spheres of influence in China, was not pleased with the agreement Lansing and he had reached. Ishii was also convinced that the secretary of state would make no more concessions, for, according to his American aide, the concession made by the president and the secretary of state surprised the State Department. Therefore, Ishii believed that should Japan suggest the changes of words which seemed to reaffirm its sphere of influence, the American government might doubt Japan's intentions and that it might lead to the breakdown of the negotiations. However, Motono, without the authority to change the decision of the Advisory Council on Foreign Relations, replied to Ishii that "I urge you to concentrate on carrying out your instructions, since they have been decided upon by the government after careful deliberation."[50]

The Lansing-Ishii negotiations got bogged down in trivial details in the final stage. From October 8 to November 2, Lansing and Ishii met at least eleven times to discuss the changes of phraseology proposed by the Japanese government. As early as October 13, Ishii reported that the American government had reached the limit of its conciliation, and urged Tokyo to accept the pending draft. Ishii's telegram of that day also reveals the difficult position of each negotiator, whose voice could hardly change the mind of his own superior. Both Lansing and Ishii realized this fact and tried in vain to negotiate directly with the chief executive of the other party. Ishii's telegram well describes their respective plight:

I observe that the Secretary of State has changed his attitude and stood firm since I proposed the addition of the word "influence" on twelfth, and I felt difficulties in continuing conversation. I thought that I might come to an understanding with the President if I should talk to him, and I asked the Secretary about its possibility. He replied that the President would not discuss diplomatic problems with a foreign ambassador, and it was, therefore, impossible for me to see the President.

The Secretary of State also stated that he could not meet each and every wish of Japan because of the public opinion of his own country and asked me whether he could explain the circumstances to the Imperial Government through Ambassador Sato. I simply asserted that he should explain the circumstances of the American Government only through me so long as I was in charge of the negotiations.

At any rate, the attitude of the United States Government has changed. Since the President is undoubtedly more stubborn than the Secretary of State, and since the President has stood firm as usual, the Secretary appears to be unable to make any further concession.

The game is about over. I beg a final instruction. If we lose this chance, it will be difficult to reach a settlement of the problem pertaining to China between Japan and the United States. Therefore, it would probably be best to decide to exchange formal notes now even if it is not entirely satisfactory.[51]

Lansing, till the end, successfully resisted Tokyo's pressure to insert the words "and influence" in the clause "Japan has special interests in China." The other controversial pledge "not [to] take advantage of the present conditions" of the European war, upon Tokyo's insistence, was removed from the agreement and retained in a secret protocol. In return, Lansing persuaded the Japanese to strike out the word "other" from another sentence: "[T]hey are opposed to acquisition by any *other* government of any special right or privileges that would affect the independence or territorial integrity of China." Both Lansing and Ishii were aware that if "other" was eliminated, the declaration against acquisition of special rights and privileges applied to all governments, including the United States and Japan.[52] Finally, on November 2, 1917, Lansing and Ishii exchanged identical notes and signed the protocol. Having finished his duty, Ambassador Ishii departed for home on the following day.

The text of the notes exchanged between Lansing and Ishii was published simultaneously on November 6 in the United States and on the November 7 in Japan. The agreement consisted of two parts. One was a recognition by the United States that Japan possessed special interests in China. The agreement said, "The governments of the United States and Japan recognize that territorial propinquity creates special relations between countries, and, consequently, the government of the United States recognizes that Japan has special interests in China, particularly in the part to which her possessions are contiguous." The other consisted of mutual denials that either the United States or Japan had "any purpose to infringe in any way the independence or territorial integrity of China," adding a mutual pledge to support the principles of the Open Door and stating opposition to the granting of special rights or privileges to any government.[53]

When the agreement was published, Lansing's statement attached to the text gave the American people the impression that the latter part of the understanding was new and a triumph for American diplomacy. Lansing declared that the exchanged notes "not only contain a reaffirmation of the Open Door policy, but introduce a principle of non-interference with the sovereignty and territorial integrity of China." However, he made no comment on Japan's special interest clause. Instead, Lansing emphasized the importance of the agreement in its application to the Great War. "It not only swept away the mutual suspicion that had tended to produce ill feeling between the two governments," said Lansing, "but embraced an understanding that the Japanese government desired to do their part in the suppression of Prussian militarism and were eager to cooperate in every practical way to that end." To prove that U.S.-Japanese military cooperation against Germany was already a success, it was formally announced at the same time that "complete and satisfactory understanding upon the matter of naval cooperation in the Pacific for the purpose of attaining the common object against Germany and her Allies has been reached between the Representative of the Imperial Japanese navy who is attached to the Special Mission of Japan and the Representative of the United States navy."[54]

President Wilson did not make a public statement on the new agreement with Japan. Wilson's secretary, Joseph P. Tumulty, made the following statement after consultation with Wilson: "When the text of the pact is read, the President is confident that the country will be very much enlightened."[55]

The American press generally accepted the official explanation of Secretary Lansing at face value. The major newspapers in New York and Chicago and influential periodicals, such as *The Independent*, the *New Republic*, *The Outlook*, *Current History*, and *The Nation*, received the announcement of the agreement with approval. The *New Republic* defended the government's action strongly, regarding the American recognition of Japan's special interests as unavoidable. It said, "So long as Japan's special interests in China were unrecognized, it was inevitable that every move by Americans toward the commercial and industrial development of China should be viewed with suspicion in Japan." As for the assurance of the Open Door and the territorial integrity of China, the *New Republic* argued that "so long as there was likelihood that other Powers might violate the integrity of China, Japan had grounds in self-preservation for a policy of territorial encroachments, but that these grounds had been removed as far as the United States was concerned." The magazine concluded that with reaching cordial understanding, Japan and the United States would "be able to cooperate far more effectively than hitherto toward the winning of the war." The *New York Evening Post* went so far as to argue that the recognition of Japan's special interests was the recognition of a concrete fact that equality of opportunity "cannot be distorted to the disadvantage of the natural opportunities which Japan possesses by virtue of her proximity to the mainland of Asia and recent historic developments."[56]

Although welcoming the agreement, a few American newspapers expressed some concern about its implications for the future. The *New York Times* was prescient when it warned that "a misplacing of emphasis might make the agreement a cause for difference and discord." The *Times* argued that, between the two provisions, namely, the American recognition of Japan's special interests in China and noninterference with China's sovereignty and territorial integrity, "the one must not be put above the other." The *Times* concluded that "the agreement will be put to the test, not at once but when the commerce of the world resumes its flow in the usual volume and through natural channels after the war." Several newspapers in California, where people were generally more suspicious of the Japanese than were residents in other parts of the United States, had more critical views on the agreement. The *San Francisco Chronicle*, Republican in viewpoint, commented that no one questioned that the Japanese with their cheap labor and geographic position had any objection to the Open Door to China. "In return for something for which Japan cares nothing," said the *Chronicle*, "we have acknowledged that Japan has interests in China before which we must give way."[57]

On the other side of the Pacific, Japanese government officials and politicians declined to make public comments on the new agreement. Because there was no apparent reason to be dissatisfied with Ambassador Ishii's accomplishment, they preferred to let the text of the agreement speak for itself.

The Japanese press generally welcomed the agreement, calling it Viscount Ishii's great diplomatic victory, on the ground that it solved the cause of the friction between Japan and the United States. The *Japan Times*, a semiofficial paper, simply declared that the agreement was the most important document ever exchanged between the two countries and helped achieve "an incomparably vast improvement" in the East Asian situation. The *Tokyo Asahi* printed a more elaborate comment which seemed to reflect the mainstream beliefs of the Japanese leaders. It asserted that the most important feature of the agreement was America's formal recognition of Japan's special interests in China. The *Tokyo Asahi* argued that the fact that the United States publicly announced the recognition of Japan's special interests in China, but not those of other powers such as Russia and British India who were geographically contiguous to China, indicated that the United States had recognized that the entire relationship between China and Japan had recently changed, and that Japan's relationship with China had became "special and closer than any others" beyond the reason of territorial propinquity. As for the rest of the agreement, the *Asahi* said, "There is nothing of special consideration because they [the Americans] reaffirmed the principles of the Open Door and equal opportunity and territorial integrity of China which had been repeatedly declared by John Hay's notes of 1899 and by the Root-Takahira agreement of 1908. The only new addition is the pledge of respect for the independence of China."[58]

In China, Beijing government officials were embarrassed by the unexpected agreement by two powerful nations about Japan's special interests in their own country. Having received copies of the agreement from the Japanese minister on November 4, Premier Duan became concerned about the possible threat the precedent of this agreement had created for his country. He feared that Britain, France, and Russia might follow the Japanese example and insist on the recognition of their special interests in those parts of China where their possessions were contiguous to Chinese territory.[59]

The American legation was also dismayed and embarrassed by this new agreement. Minister Reinsch, who had been most active in trying to establish American leadership in China, had not been informed of the negotiations between Secretary Lansing and Ambassador Ishii. When the Japanese minister showed Reinsch the text of the agreement, the clause on the U.S. recognition of Japan's special interest in China at first sight struck Reinsch "in his face with stunning force." He felt that "it was inexcusable to fail to give the local representative the earliest possible information." Having learned that the Japanese minister had already handed to the Chinese government the copy of the agreement, Minister Reinsch telegraphed the State Department that his legation was in "a highly embarrassing position having received no information." When Lansing sent the copy of the agreement to Reinsch on November 5, he also directed the minister to deliver an explanatory note to the Chinese government. It read, "The statements in the notes require no explanation. They not only contain a reaffirmation of the open door policy but introduce a principle of noninterference with the sovereignty and territorial integrity of China." As to Japan's special interests, Lansing explained, "Japanese commercial and industrial enterprises in China manifestly have, on account of the geographical relation of the two countries, a certain advantage over similar enterprises on the part of the citizens or subjects of any other country."[60]

Contrary to Lansing's economic interpretation of Japan's "special interests" in China, the Japanese government offered broader interpretation in its explanation to the Chinese government. On November 8, Foreign Minister Motono directed Minister Hayashi to explain to the Chinese government the distinction between Japan whose home country was located in close proximity to China and other powers such as Russia, Britain, and France whose home countries were located far away from Chinese territory. The minister was instructed by Tokyo to tell the Chinese government that "this unique geographical position of Japan naturally creates special relations, *political*, economic, and social, with China. . . . The new agreement between Japan and the United States declared this fact, but there will be no change in Japan's policy toward China."[61] There is no doubt that the Terauchi cabinet felt some satisfaction at that moment, for, despite its ambiguity, the agreement could be construed as the first step toward the U.S. concession to Japan's superior position in China as the regional leader of East Asia.

Chinese high officials, who could not help feeling that "nothing very positive could be expected from the United States," decided to deliver a caveat against the new Japanese-American agreement. The Chinese note to Tokyo and Washington declared that "the Chinese government will not allow herself to be bound by any agreement entered into by other nations." When the Chinese minister in Washington, Wellington Koo, called on Lansing on November 12 to deliver the Chinese caveat, they engaged in a conversation that deserves attention. Lansing, who read the Chinese note, told Minister Koo that the memorandum was unnecessary because Viscount Ishii and he had no intention to bind China in any way. The Chinese minister said that his government was particularly disturbed by the American recognition of Japan's "special interests" in China and asked the meaning of those words. Lansing replied that "it was manifestly an axiom that geographical propinquity necessarily gave nations special interests in their neighbors." Koo then asked why this axiom had to be stated now. Lansing's answer was that "to concede a truth, which could not be successfully denied, in exchange for a declaration of a policy which restrained the other party was certainly a very desirable thing to do." The Chinese Minister thanked Lansing for his explanations and left without making further comment. The Chinese caveat was received by Japan and the United States not as a protest but as a declaration of the principle that China would not allow itself to be bound by any agreement entered into by other nations. Because China did not ask for an answer, its caveat was filed without being answered either by Japan or the United States.[62]

NOTES

1. Ian Nish, *Alliance in Decline: A Study in Anglo-Japanese Relations 1908–1923* (London: Athlone Press, 1972), 223; Burton F. Beers, *Vain Endeavor: Robert Lansing's Attempt to End the American-Japanese Rivalry* (Durham, N.C.: Duke University Press, 1962), 116–119.

2. Reinsch to Lansing, March 12, 1917, in Arthur S. Link, ed., *The Papers of Woodrow Wilson* (Princeton: Princeton University Press, 1966–1994), 41: 394. Hereafter cited as *PWW*; Reinsch to Lansing, March 18, 1917, in U.S. Department of State, *Papers Relating to the Foreign Relations of the United States*, 1917 Supplement (Washington, D.C., 1931), 1: 421. Hereafter cited as *FR*; Reinsch to Lansing, March 26, 1917, *FR*, 1917, 46.

3. *New York Times*, March 3, 1917.

4. Hayashi to Motono, May 11, 1917, in the Foreign Ministry of Japan, *Nihon gaiko bunsho* (Documents on Japanese foreign policy), 1917 (Tokyo, 1968), 3: 705–706. Hereafter cited as *NGB*.

5. Hayashi to Motono, May 16, 1917, *NGB*, 1917, 3: 710.

6. Motono to Hayashi, May 23, 1917, *NGB*, 1917, 3: 710–715.

7. Sato to Motono, May 15, 1917, *NGB*, 1917, 3: 708–709; Sato to Lansing, May 12, 1917, Lansing to Sato, May 15, 1917, *FR*, 1917, Supplement 2, 1: 63; Cabinet decision, May 22, 1917, *NGB* 1917, 3: 716–717.

8. Reinsch to Lansing, June 2, 1917, *FR*, 1917, 48; Robert Lansing, *War Memoirs of Robert Lansing* (Indianapolis, Ind.: Bobbs-Merrill Company, 1935), 287; Lansing to Reinsch, June 4, 1917, *FR*, 1917, 48–49.

9. Wheeler to Lansing, June 9, 1917, *FR*, 1917, 58; Motono to Sato, June 9, 1917, *NGB*, 1917, 3: 723; Robert Lansing, *War Memoirs*, 288.

10. *Tokyo Asahi*, June 19, 1917; *New York Times*, June 15, 1917; *Japan Times*, June 12, 1917.

11. Terauchi to Motono, June 12, 1917, *NGB*, 1917, 3: 729.

12. Sato to Lansing, June 15, 1917, *FR*, 1917, 72.

13. Bryan to Japanese Ambassador, March 13, 1915, *FR*, 1915, 111; Sato to Lansing, *FR*, 1917, 259.

14. Wheeler to Lansing, June 18, 1917, *FR*, 1917, 259; Sato to Motono, June 15, 1917, *NGB*, 1917, 3: 732; Motono to Sato, June 19, 1917, *NGB*, 1917, 3: 735; Lansing to Wheeler, June 29, 1917, *FR*, 1917, 78; Wheeler to Lansing, June 22, 1917, in U.S. Department of State, *Papers Relating to the Foreign Relations of*

the United States: The Lansing Papers 1914–1920 (Washington, D.C., 1940), 2: 430. Hereafter cited as *FRLP*.

15. Robert Lansing, *War Memoirs*, 289.

16. Wilson to Lansing, July 3, 1917, *FRLP*, 2: 431; *PWW*, 43: 80, emphasis in original.

17. Lansing to Sato, July 6, 1917, *FR*, 1917, 260–261.

18. Lansing to Wilson, July 5, 1917, *FRLP*, 2:339; *PWW*, 43: 106.

19. Kikujiro Ishii, *Gaiko yoroku (Diplomatic commentaries)*, trans. and ed. William R. Langdon (Baltimore: Johns Hopkins University Press, 1936), 112; Cabinet decision, July 24, 1917, *NGB*, 1917, 3: 743–744. English translation of the entire text of the instruction in Morinosuke Kajima, *The Diplomacy of Japan, 1894–1922*, 3 vols. (Tokyo: Kajima Institute of International Peace, 1980), 3: 302–306.

20. Cabinet decision, July 24, 1917, *NGB*, 1917, 3: 744–745; English translation in Morinosuke Kajima, *The Diplomacy of Japan*, 3: 304.

21. Motono to Sato, August 3, 1917, *NGB*, 1917, 3: 747.

22. Wheeler to Lansing, June 27, 1917, *FR*, 1917, Supplement 2, 1: 111.

23. Burton Beers, *Vain Endeavor*, 103.

24. *San Francisco Chronicle*, August 17, 1917.

25. "Welcoming Japan's Envoys," *Literary Digest*, September 1, 1917, 14; *San Francisco Chronicle*, August 17, 1917.

26. *New York Times*, August 23, 1917; "The Japanese Mission," *New Republic*, August 25, 1917, 94–95.

27. Kikujiro Ishii, *Diplomatic Commentaries*, 112–113.

28. Memorandum by Lansing, September 6, 1917, *FRLP*, 2: 433.

29. Sato to Motono, September 8, 1917, *NGB*, 1917, 3: 761; English translation in Morinosuke Kajima, *The Diplomacy of Japan*, 3: 309–310; Memorandum by Lansing, September 6, 1917, *FRLP*, 2: 434–435.

30. Sato to Motono, September 8, 1917, *NGB*, 1917, 3: 761–762.

31. See a detailed account on the establishment of the Advisory Council on Foreign Relations in Tatsuo Kobayashi, "Rinji gaiko chosa iinkai no secchi" (Establishment of the Advisory Council on Foreign Relations), *Kokusai seiji* 28 (1964): 53–71. The Advisory Council on Foreign Relations consisted of the premier; the ministers for foreign affairs, home affairs, the navy, and the army; the three privy councilors; the presidents of the Seiyukai and the Kokumin-to; the vice ministers for foreign affairs, the navy, and the army; and the secretary-general of the cabinet.

32. Lansing to Bryan, March 1, 1915, *FRLP*, 2: 408.

33. Arthur S. Link, *Woodrow Wilson: Revolution, War, and Peace* (Arlington Heights, Ill.: AHM Publishing Corporation, 1979), 16; Arthur S. Link, *Wilson: Campaigns for Progressivism and Peace, 1916–1917* (Princeton: Princeton University Press, 1965), 222; Edward M. House Papers, Diary entry, March 28, 1917; September 9, 1917.

34. Burton Beers, *Vain Endeavor*, 108; House Diary, April 29, 1917; Memorandum from Lansing to Wilson, April 30, 1917, cited in William R. Braisted, *The United States Navy in the Pacific, 1909–1922* (Austin: University of Texas Press, 1971), 327.

35. N. Gordon Levin Jr., *Woodrow Wilson and World Politics: America's Response to War and Revolution* (New York: Oxford University Press, 1968), 113; House Diary, January 9, 24; March 20, 23, 25; April 29; May 2, 10, 1917.

36. Child to House, June 7, 1917, Wilson Papers, Library of Congress, Microfilm, Series 2; House Diary, August 30, 1917.

37. House to Wilson, September 6, 1917, Wilson Papers, Library of Congress, Microfilm, Series 2.

38. House Diary, September 18, 1917; House to Wilson, September 18, 1917, *PWW*, 44: 213; Burton Beers, *Vain Endeavor*, 114.

39. Keiichiro Hara, ed., *Hara Kei nikki* (Diary of Takashi Hara) (Tokyo: Fukumura shuppan, 1965), 4: 316.

40. Motono to Sato, September 18, 1917, *NGB*, 1917, 3: 773–774.

41. Sato to Motono, September 23, 1917, *NGB*, 1917, 3: 775–776; *FRLP*, 2: 435–436.

42. *FRLP*, 2: 436; Robert Lansing, *War Memoirs*, 296.

43. Sato to Motono, September 23, 1917, *NGB*, 1917, 3: 776–777.

44. Kikujiro Ishii, *Diplomatic Commentaries*, 109–132.

45. Wilson to Lansing, undated, *FRLP*, 2: 438, emphasis in original; Sato to Motono, September 26, 1917, *NGB*, 1917, 3: 781.

46. Robert Lansing, *War Memoirs*, 297.

47. Memorandum by Lansing, September 26, 1917, *FRLP*, 2: 440; Sato to Motono, September 26, 1917, *NGB*, 1917, 3: 781.

48. *New York Times*, September 28, 1917; Kikujiro Ishii, *Diplomatic Commentaries*, 118; Carnegie Endowment for International Peace, *Imperial Japanese Mission 1917: A Record of the Reception Throughout the United States of the Special Mission Headed by Viscout Ishii* (Washington, D.C., 1918), 90–91.

49. Motono to Yada, September 30, 1917, *NGB*, 1917, 3:784; Motono to Sato, October 6, 1917, *NGB*, 1917, 3: 788–789.

50. Sato to Motono, October 9, Motono to Sato, October 10, 1917, *NGB*, 1917, 3: 791–792. Ronford S. Miller was the American consul general at Seoul in Korea and assigned as an aid to Ishii during the latter's trip to the United States.

51. Sato to Motono, October 13, 1917, *NGB*, 1917, 3: 799–800.

52. Sato to Motono, October 10, 12, 1917, *NGB*, 1917, 3: 792, 797; *FRLP*, 2: 442, emphasis by this writer; Robert Lansing, *War Memoirs*, 300.

53. Ishii to Lansing, November 2, 1917, *FR*, 1917, 265.

54. *New York Times*, November 7, 1917.

55. *San Francisco Chronicle*, November 7, 1917.

56. *New Republic*, November 10, 1917, 31; *Literary Digest*, November 17, 1917, 16.

57. *New York Times*, November 7, 1917; *San Francisco Chronicle*, November 7, 1917.

58. *Japan Times*, November 9, 1917; *Tokyo Asahi*, November 8, 1917.

59. Hayashi to Motono, November 5, 1917; *NGB*, 1917, 3: 826.

60. Reinsch, *An American Diplomat in China* (Garden City, NY.: Doubleday, Page & Company, 1922), 307–308; Reinsch to Lansing, November 5, 1917; Lansing to Reinsch, November 5, 1917, *FR*, 1917, 266, 268.

61. Motono to Hayashi, November 8, 1917, *NGB*, 1917, 3: 831–832, emphasis by this writer.

62. Reinsch, *An American Diplomat in China*, 313; *FR*, 1917, 270; *NGB*, 1917, 3: 833; Lansing's memorandum, November 12, 1917, *FRLP*, 2: 451–453; *New York Times*, November 14, 1917.

CHAPTER 5

Siberian Intervention

On November 7, 1917, the day the Lansing-Ishii agreement was made public, the Bolsheviks seized power in Petrograd. The revolution quickly spread eastward and not only threatened the Allied Eastern Front against the Central Powers but also the breakdown of the balance of power in East Asia. Rumors of a German-Bolshevik collaboration and Russia's subsequent separate peace treaty with Germany at Brest-Litovsk forced the desperate European Allies—Britain and France in particular—to urge Japan and the United States to reestablish an Eastern Front by sending troops through the Trans-Siberian Railway. As this chapter demonstrates, the irreconcilable views Japan and the United States held about the world and their roles in East Asia made it difficult for them to cooperate. President Wilson, who firmly believed the principles of self-determination, freedom, and democracy to be universal, tried to apply them to an unstable Russian Siberia. In his Fourteen Points Address on January 8, 1918, Wilson urged all belligerent powers to stay out of Russian territory in order to give the Russian people an opportunity to exercise self-determination.[1] The president refused to acknowledge Japan's responsibility as a dominant regional power in East Asia, and treated it as a potential threat to the Wilsonian liberal internationalism. The president and most of his advisers, except Secretary of State Robert Lansing, opposed any military operation independently or predominantly undertaken by the Japanese, not only because they suspected Japan's territorial ambitions in eastern Siberia and northern China,[2] but also because they were afraid that Japanese military intervention might force the Russians to side with the Germans for racial reasons. Yet, Wilson continued to use self-determination as an official explanation against any proposal for expedition.

Japanese leaders, on the other hand, felt that territorial propinquity gave their country as a great regional power the right to claim special interests and the obligation to maintain peace and stability in that region. Although the leaders were divided into interventionist and anti-interventionist factions, they had no interest in the reconstruction of the Eastern Front. If some sort of Allied military intervention was deemed necessary in Siberia, those who favored intervention wanted to receive an Allied mandate for Japan to act alone or to send an Allied joint expedition under Japanese command. Concerned about their own national and regional security, the interventionists were primarily interested in the creation of an anti-Bolshevik and pro-Japanese buffer state in Siberia and the expansion of Japan's influence into North Manchuria, which nominally belonged to China but was considered as Russia's sphere of influence at that time.

Diplomatic exchanges between Tokyo and Washington regarding the Siberian issue from December 1917 to the summer of 1918 also indicate that suspicion and rivalry prevailed in the thinking of the government officials on both sides. Because they paid more attention to critical reports on the opponent's activities, their suspicion kept growing; thus they miscalculated, and often exaggerated, the other's intentions and capabilities and imposed more strain on themselves than necessary. In the end, both sides increasingly felt pressed to take some sort of action.

On July 8, 1918, President Wilson reversed his policy and opted for a small-scale Japanese-American joint military expedition to Vladivostok. He proposed that the Japanese and American governments assemble "a military force at Vladivostok composed of approximately 7,000 Americans and 7,000 Japanese" for the limited purpose of guarding the Czechoslovak troops.[3] Instead of accepting the Allied proposal to create an Eastern Front, however, Wilson called for strictly limited military operations within the city of Vladivostok. Moreover, he proposed that the two governments make a public announcement that "the purpose of landing troops is to aid Czecho-Slovaks against German and Austrian prisoners, that there is no purpose to interfere with internal affairs of Russia, and that they guarantee not to impair the political or territorial sovereignty of Russia." The limited objective of Wilson's proposed expedition was further emphasized by his *aide-memoire* circulated among the Allied powers on July 17.[4] This document stated that the only admissible military action was "to help the Czecho-Slovaks consolidate their forces and get into successful cooperation with their Slavic kinsmen and to steady any efforts at self-government or self-defence in which the Russians themselves may be willing to accept assistance." The limited purpose of American troops should be to guard the Allied military stores in Vladivostok which might subsequently be needed by the people Wilson vaguely called "the Russians" to organize their own self-defense. Wilson warned that the United States would withdraw its forces should the proposed expedition later develop into something inconsistent with his policy. Thus, he attempted to prevent a large-scale Allied intervention in Siberia by altering its purpose.

The consequences of President Wilson's proposal for a joint venture turned out to be disastrous for Japanese-American relations. In Japan, the government of Premier Terauchi and the army, who had not been able to prevail over the anti-interventionists at home because of America's opposition to any military expedition, used Wilson's proposal as an excuse to carry out their larger version of a Siberian intervention to safeguard and expand Japan's interests in the region. The Terauchi government made a shrewd compromise with the anti-interventionists by ostensibly accepting the American proposal for the limited expedition on the surface but, at the same time, reserving its right to send reinforcements to areas beyond the city of Vladivostok. Under this ambiguous understanding with the United States, Japan systematically sent a far larger number of troops into eastern Siberia and northern Manchuria than the Americans had been led to believe would be sent. The Terauchi government eventually allowed the army to send 72,000 men (including 44,700 combatants) before Terauchi was replaced by the anti-interventionist Hara as premier in mid-September 1918. Although the Hara cabinet decided to reduce the number of Japanese troops in Siberia by over one half at the end of 1918,[5] the size of the Japanese force sent to Siberia during Terauchi's tenure in office had a chilling effect on the Wilson administration's relationship with Tokyo. After filing a series of complaints about the large number of Japanese troops in Siberia, the State Department warned Tokyo on November 16, 1918, that any monopoly of control in these areas "will arouse suspicion and prove open to the charges of exploitation."[6] Japan's breach of faith seriously offended Wilson who believed that nations had moralistic obligations. Later during the Paris Peace Conference, while the Council of Ten was deliberating whether Japan should receive the German Pacific islands as a mandate from the League of Nations, Wilson told David Hunter Miller that he did not trust the Japanese. Miller wrote in his diary that Wilson "had trusted them before,—in fact they had broken their agreement about Siberia. We had sent 7,000 troops to Siberia and they promised to send about the same number but had sent 70,000 and had occupied all the strategic points as far as Irkutsk, and that he would not trust them again."[7] In Wilson's eyes, Japan's image as an embodiment of an antithesis to Wilsonian liberal internationalism became complete.

Many historians have offered various reasons why President Wilson decided to propose a limited Japanese-American joint expedition to Vladivostok. Although most provide multi-causal explanations, the majority emphasize the urgent need to rescue and protect some fifty thousand Czechoslovak soldiers who had been trapped along the Trans-Siberian Railway by the Soviet forces since May 1918.[8] These historians also suggest other reasons for this action—such as continuing pressure upon Wilson from the British and French governments, and Wilson's serious concerns about the possibility of a Japanese-led expedition.[9] Still other historians argue that Wilson's decision to intervene was primarily motivated by his antagonism toward Bolshevism.[10]

Instead of reexamining this extensively scrutinized question regarding Wilson's motives behind his proposal for a limited Japanese-American military expedition, this chapter examines how and why Wilson's proposal set in motion unintended developments in the summer of 1918, and why his proposal should be considered misguided. If one reason for Wilson's decision to propose a limited joint expedition was to forestall a larger scale Japanese-led expedition, how did his proposal come to allow what he had been so eager to prevent? Knowing Japan's aspiration for hegemony in the Asian continent from America's unpleasant experiences with Japan in the crisis of the Twenty-one Demands and the negotiations for the controversial Lansing-Ishii agreement, why did Wilson take such a chance? How did he miscalculate? Was Wilson duped by the Japanese government? Did Wilson's proposal have inherent flaws? To pursue these questions, this chapter inquires into problems faced by the Wilson administration in its universalist and unilateralist approach to the crisis in Siberia—problems that suggest that the United States did not have adequate knowledge of internal affairs of the other participant. Certainly, both sides of the Pacific suffered from misperceptions and miscalculations, and perhaps both tended to assume unilateral attitudes. This chapter, however, mainly focuses on the problems of the Wilson administration, for President Wilson's decision to propose a limited Japanese-American joint expedition triggered the fiasco of the Siberian intervention in 1918. A close examination of Japan's internal conditions at that time will illuminate an obvious gap that existed between the Wilson administration's perception of the Japanese intentions and the reality in Tokyo.[11] President Wilson insisted on the rigid application of his ideas to the unfamiliar situation. This episode suggests that had President Wilson held an accurate understanding of Japan's decision-making process and its internal political conditions, he might not have offered the ill-advised joint expedition. There was a distinct possibility that Japan might not have sent any large-scale expeditionary forces against the wish of the United States if

Wilson had stayed firmly opposed to any idea of military intervention in Siberia until mid-September when the prointerventionist Terauchi cabinet was replaced by the anti-interventionist Hara cabinet. President Wilson's attempt to use a limited military action to achieve a political objective, on the surface, appeared to be clever, but, in reality, his failure to coordinate political ends effectively with military means[12] resulted in confusing and ineffective exercise of civilian control over the military operation in Siberia.

When the first serious discussion of the possibility of military intervention in Siberia took place at the inter-Allied conference in early December 1917, neither Japan nor the United States was ready to take any action. Both maintained an attitude of watchful waiting. Although the Bolsheviks' unilateral cancellation of the Russo-Japanese entente of 1916 upset Japanese leaders, they were deeply divided over the questions as to whether Japan should intervene, and if so, whether it should act alone, or jointly with the United States as the Allies requested. The Japanese army and a small group of civilians surrounding Premier Terauchi, including Foreign Minister Motono and Kamezo Nishihara, argued that Japan should send its troops to the Russian Maritime Territory, take over the Trans-Siberian Railways, and assist the anti-Bolshevik independence movement. When the Advisory Council on Foreign Relations, which held the key to Japan's foreign policy decisions, deliberated the Siberian issue, anti-interventionists barely managed to prevail over the foreign minister's proposal in favor of intervention. The leading advocates against intervention in the council were Takashi Hara, the head of the Seiyukai—the most powerful political party—and Nobuaki Makino, a privy counselor and former foreign minister. Behind them was the youngest genro, Kinmochi Saionji, who was generally considered a moderate liberal.[13]

The Wilson administration, although equally puzzled by the Bolshevik revolution, initially took a firm position of nonintervention. Colonel House, who attended the Supreme War Council in December 1917, believed that "so far as the United States was concerned, any effort at intervention, except at the request of the Russian Government, would be a mistake." Secretary of State Lansing, who is portrayed by historians as a hardheaded anti-Bolshevik, used the phrase "Do Nothing" to describe the American policy. He told the Japanese ambassador on December 27 that "it would be unwise for either the United States or Japan to send troops to Vladivostok as it would undoubtedly result in the unifying of the Russians under the Bolsheviks against foreign interference." President Wilson eloquently declared nonintervention in Russia and Russia's self-determination in his Fourteen Points Address to Congress on January 8, 1918. The main purpose of Wilson's speech was to make known to the world the high-minded universal war aims of the United States, but it was also designed as America's response to the Bolshevik invitation to a general peace conference with the Central Powers at Brest-Litovsk. Expressing sympathy for the Bolsheviks' sincerity in putting forward an open and liberal peace settlement, Wilson proposed in the sixth point of his fourteen-point peace program the "evacuation of all Russian territory," and "a sincere welcome into the society of free nations under institutions of her own choosing."[14]

However, instead of taking President Wilson's commitment to nonintervention seriously, Japanese leaders became increasingly suspicious of American intentions and jealously tried to protect Japan's leadership role in eastern Siberia. The Japanese government opposed any expedition led by the United States because of its concern about the spread of American influence in Siberia and insisted on Japan's taking charge of an expedition. As early as December 10, 1917, when British Foreign Secretary Arthur J. Balfour told Japanese Ambassador Chinda that an American expedition would be less objectionable to the Russians than a Japanese one, Chinda insisted that in case intervention was deemed necessary, Japan's geographic position naturally gave it the right and duty to undertake that task alone. Chinda warned that an American expedition would wound Japanese pride and arouse public opinion. In Tokyo, Foreign Minister Motono reiterated this position to the British ambassador, saying that should there be any need for some sort of measure to protect the Allied interests in East Asia, the duty should fall on the shoulders of Japan. Upon learning that the British government proposed to the American government to undertake a joint military action to protect the Allies' stores at Vladivostok, Motono reminded American ambassador Morris on January 16 that if "conditions should hereafter require occupation of Vladivostok and the lines of the Chinese Eastern and Amur Railways, Japan asks that this task be left to her alone."[15]

Foreign Minister Motono's statement to Ambassador Morris and the news that the total of four Japanese naval vessels were to be in the port of Vladivostok disturbed President Wilson and the State Department. Washington began to see in these Japanese moves "grave possibilities" of Japan's independent military action in Siberia. Wilson directed Lansing to "show very clearly" America's "distinct disapproval" of Japanese military action in Siberia. On January 20, Morris told Motono that "the presence of more than one Japanese war vessel at Vladivostok at present is likely to be misconstrued and create a feeling of mistrust as to the purposes of the Allied Government." Morris explained that America's objection to Japanese military action in Siberia was prompted by Washington's fear that Japan's intervention might force the Russians to throw in their lot with Germany.[16]

When the British government offered Washington a new proposal on January 28 that the Japanese troops occupy the Trans-Siberian Railway as the mandatory of the Allies, the Wilson administration flatly rejected the idea of any form of exclusive Japanese expedition either mandatory or independent. "Should such intervention unfortunately become necessary in the future," the United States insisted that any military expedition to Siberia "should be undertaken by international cooperation and not by any one power acting as the mandatory of the others." House wrote to Wilson that "it would be a great political mistake to send Japanese troops into Siberia," because House was seriously concerned about the racial problem between the Slavs and the Japanese. Wilson himself had no intention of giving any support to Japan's regionalist claim to justify its intervention. He wrote to Lansing, "[I]t seems to us unwise to make a request which would in itself give the Japanese a certain moral advantage with respect to any ultimate desires or purposes she may have with regard to the eastern Provinces of Siberia."[17]

Thus, the Wilson administration was against any Japanese military intervention in Siberia in the winter of 1918, but a series of misperceptions and miscalculations changed the direction of American policy during the next several months. The first grave miscalculation on the part of President Wilson and his advisers was their conviction that the United States held the key to Japan's decision to intervene and their overestimation of America's ability to control Japan's action. This American misperception came mainly from Washington's diplomatic exchanges with the Japanese and Allied governments between March and June in 1918, although nobody tried intentionally to mislead anyone.

In February 1918, reports coming from East Asia began to overwhelm the Wilson administration with the impression that Japan was about to undertake a military expedition to Siberia as a mandatory of the Allies. Japanese Foreign Minister Motono, who was frustrated by the Japanese senior statesmen's solid opposition to a Siberian intervention, personally tried to invite discussions among the Allies and the United States concerning a possible military expedition. When Motono suggested to American Ambassador Morris that "some plan of action ought to be agreed upon by the Allied powers to prevent the spread of German influence in Asia," despite his repeated emphasis on "the purely personal character of these tentative views," Motono failed to impress on Ambassador Morris that these views were literally "purely personal." Neither the Terauchi cabinet nor the Advisory Council on Foreign Relations had yet reached any consensus on the issue of Siberian intervention. However, assuming that Motono's suggestion was an unofficial proposal of his government, Morris reported to Washington that the Japanese government was "seriously discussing some plan of immediate action."[18] Morris's report prompted the Wilson administration to make an official objection to the Allied intervention in Siberia in unmistakable terms on February 13. The United States notes to the major Allied powers declared that the necessity for intervention did not exist and that should the Allies allow Japan a free hand in Siberia, it "might prove embarrassing to the cause of the powers at war with Germany."[19]

Toward the end of February, the Wilson administration was convinced that Japan's expedition to Siberia was imminent and that Japan was ready to act independently without America's consent. On February 23, Minister Reinsch in Beijing reported that Japan had proposed to the Chinese government "cooperation" between the two countries in restoring order in Siberia, and that the Chinese president had expressed "his approval of the principle." The next day, Morris reported from Tokyo that Foreign Minister Motono told the French ambassador that all preparations had been completed for immediate action and that Japan could act even without American consent if Britain and France agreed. Morris added that the "time would soon come when Japan would not be able to wait any longer." Morris again cabled Washington on February 27, "Japan is prepared to act at once, and may at any moment inquire of me the attitude of our Government."[20] On the same day, British Ambassador Rufus D. I. Reading met President Wilson and conveyed British Foreign Secretary Balfour's confidential telegram urging Wilson to join the Allies "in immediately inviting Japan to occupy the Siberian Railway" as far as Omsk.[21] Significantly, Balfour emphasized that "it is with the United States that the final decision appears now to rest," and that, if the United States failed to take common action, he feared that Japan would act alone without the "safeguards that would be provided by an Allied mandatory."

President Wilson, under the pressure from the British and the French governments, thought of raising "no objection" to Japan's being asked to undertake the expedition as a mandatory of the Allies; but he was later persuaded by William C. Bullitt and Colonel House to uphold America's moral position against the intervention. Bullitt, in particular, made a passionate moralistic appeal in his letter to the president, saying, "The President must oppose invasion of Siberia by Japan *in the name of democracy and liberalism*. He must act, or his position as moral leader of the liberals of the world will be lost." House also warned against Japanese intervention which might destroy "over night" the "fine moral position" that Wilson had built for the Allies.[22] Wilson, who was "much disturbed" over House's insistence on upholding the American moral position, decided to reverse his decision. On March 5, the American government notified the Japanese government that "the wisdom of intervention seems to it most questionable."[23] Should Japan undertake the intervention, the note said, Japan would have to give "the most explicit assurances," so that the Central Powers could not and would not "make it appear that Japan was doing in the East exactly what Germany is doing in the West."

The American objection to Japan's Siberian intervention produced a surprising response from Tokyo. In a confidential memorandum to Ambassador Morris on March 19, the Japanese government expressed its intention "to refrain from taking any action on which due understanding has not been reached between the United States and the other great powers of the Entente." Although, in the note, the Japanese government reserved its right to act independently in case hostile activities in Siberia endangered Japan's national security or vital interests, it assured Washington that its action in Siberia would be "wholly uninfluenced by any aggressive motives or tendencies."[24]

The Japanese note led Wilson and the State Department to believe that the information they had received earlier greatly exaggerated Japan's eagerness to intervene. Lansing apologetically explained to Tokyo that his government's attitude was "in no way based upon suspicion of the motives." Later, he also told Tokyo that the recent Japanese memorandum was "most gratifying and removes any possibility of misunderstanding which might otherwise arise."[25]

The optimistic view of President Wilson and the State Department of the Japanese willingness to comply with America's wish was further strengthened by another note from the Japanese government on June 26. The occasion that prompted Japan to deliver this note was the Allied Supreme War Council's decision on June 3 to propose a Japanese-American joint military intervention in Siberia on the condition that Japan accept the principles of territorial integrity of Russia and noninterference in Russia's internal politics.[26] The War Council's intent was to ensure that Japan agreed to the kind of expedition that the United States might be persuaded to accept. Incidentally, the War Council also made a decision to keep a portion of the Czech troops in Russia to make them cooperate with the Allied forces. British Under Secretary Robert Cecil had already told the Japanese ambassador on May 22 that the British government was discussing the possibility of using the 20,000 Czech soldiers in Vladivostok for the Allied expedition in Siberia and that they could be placed under Japanese command.[27]

In Tokyo, the Advisory Council on Foreign Relations deliberated the Supreme War Council's inquiry and decided to reemphasize the position Japan declared on March 19. Japan's formal reply stated that it attached "particular importance on the moral and material support of the United

States to any undertaking of military nature . . . in Siberia."[28] The Japanese government, therefore, declined to announce its decision concerning the proposed Allied intervention until "complete understanding is reached between the three Powers [Great Britain, France, and Italy] and the United States." Accordingly, on June 26, Japanese Ambassador Kikujiro Ishii explained to Secretary Lansing Tokyo's decision that Japan would not take action before "a complete and satisfactory understanding" on the Siberian question was reached between the Allies and the United States.[29]

Tokyo's message of June 26 no doubt strengthened Wilson's conviction that he held the key to the Allied intervention in Siberia. Even before receiving the Japanese note, Wilson had already believed that whether Japan would intervene depended on his decision. On May 29, Wilson told William Wiseman, the head of British intelligence operations in the United States, that he "realized that the U.S. Government held the key to the situation in that [the] Japanese Government would not intervene without their sanction."[30] Therefore, having read the reassuring note from Tokyo, Wilson wrote to Lansing, "I have read this communication with genuine pleasure."[31]

Wilson's perception of Japan's willingness to comply with America's wishes, however, was overly optimistic. Wilson assumed that the Japanese government's diplomatic notes represented the sound consensus among the Japanese leadership, both civilian and military. What Wilson did not know was that Japanese civilian and military leaders had been deeply divided into prointerventionist and anti-interventionist factions since the fall of 1917 and that the latter barely held the balance when Tokyo delivered the notes to Washington in both March and June. The anti-interventionists were able to prevail over their opponents because of America's constant and firm opposition to Japan's military intervention. Given their dependence on the U.S. opposition, the anti-interventionists would lose their ground when President Wilson himself proposed a joint expedition, even though it was for a limited purpose. Moreover, Wilson's proposal provided the Japanese interventionists with an opportunity to steal his thunder.

In Japan, the major driving force behind the movement for military intervention in Siberia was the army general staff. When the Bolsheviks did away with the Russo-Japanese Entente of 1916, Entente supporters on the general staff were stunned and quickly drew up a series of plans for military intervention. Starting with a November 1917 plan to send troops to the Russian Far East to protect Japanese nationals in northern Manchuria and the Maritime Territory, by the end of January 1918, the army general staff's plan had become conspicuously anti-Bolshevik and prointerventionist. The new January 1918 plan identified Japan's objective as "primarily to suppress the Bolshevik uprisings and hostile activity in the vicinity of the

Southern Ussuri and along the railroad in the Maritime Territory." The other equally important purpose was to protect Russian citizens in the Maritime Territory who held "moderate ideas" and "to assist their independence."[32] The army was clearly interested in the creation of a anti-Bolshevik buffer state in Siberia.

The ideas of an anti-Bolshevik military intervention in Siberia had a powerful civilian supporter in the foreign office—Foreign Minister Motono, who was eventually forced to resign in late April because of his stance on this issue. Undated policy drafts, believed to be written by the foreign minister and his secretaries sometime between November 1917 and March 1918, exist in the foreign ministry's archives. These documents recommend a Japanese expedition to eastern Siberia with or without the Allied participation in order to prevent Germany from penetrating into Russian Siberia and China. The documents also recommend that Japan support anti-German and antirevolutionary "moderate" elements in their efforts to gain autonomy.[33] As has been described earlier, a series of personal remarks and inquiries made by Motono in February 1918 to Ambassador Morris and the European Allied representatives misled them into believing that the Japanese government had already reached a decision to send troops to Siberia.

The first Japanese diplomatic note to the United States on March 19 was the outcome of the last minute political maneuvers by anti-interventionist leaders to silence the voices of their opponents. Among the members of the Advisory Council on Foreign Relations, the two most outspoken opponents of intervention were Hara and Makino. Surprised by Motono's unauthorized conversations with Ambassador Morris suggesting Japan's willingness to take action in Siberia, Hara and Makino confronted the foreign minister as well as the premier. To prevent interventionist officials in the foreign ministry from taking further unauthorized actions, Hara tried to use Japan's diplomatic reply to the United States as the council's formal resolution. He apparently persuaded the premier to have the pro-American faction in the foreign office draw a draft reply to the United States.[34] Hara's efforts were aided by a letter written two days before the council meeting by Aritomo Yamagata, then still the most influential genro, a senior statesman. In this letter Yamagata expressed his belief to Premier Terauchi that the spread of German influence in Russia was not enough reason to justify Japan's military intervention.[35] Yamagata warned that Japan's "interference" in Russian matters would lead to a major war not with the Germans but with the Russians. He added that Japan could not afford to wage such a war without material and financial support from the United States and Britain. Obviously, the American objection to Japanese intervention was a major concern of Yamagata.

Foreign Minister Motono resigned in frustration on April 22, but it was a defeat of an individual rather than a defeat of the interventionist policy. His successor, Shinpei Goto, was another strong advocate of Siberian expedition. His appointment reflected the contradictory policy of Premier Terauchi, who was personally sympathetic to the army's interventionist policy but was forced to take a more moderate approach for political reasons. The document that Goto wrote at the time of his appointment as foreign minister reveals that his East Asian policy objectives were not so different from those of the continental expansionists in the army general staff.[36] First, Goto supported Japanese intervention in Siberia for the purpose of stemming the tide of German forces in the Russian Far East and securing a firm foothold in the region before the Americans intervened. Second, he argued that Japan must conclude a Sino-Japanese defensive agreement and establish closer political, military, and economic relations with China to secure Japan's advantageous position over the Western powers in the postwar competition in China. The key to Japan's strategy, Goto believed, was to occupy the Chinese Eastern Railway and to seize control of North Manchuria—czarist Russia's virtual protectorate prior to the Bolshevik revolution, which not only would provide greater security against Bolshevism but also a base for the movement to create an anti-Bolshevik and pro-Japanese buffer state in Siberia. The Terauchi cabinet had another historical reason to seek control of the railway. In the summer of 1916, the czarist government agreed to sell to the Japanese government the branch line of the Chinese Eastern Railway between Zhangchun and the Sungari River (connected to the South Manchuria Railway) in exchange for Japanese military supplies. Japan provided weapons and munitions, but the deal for the transfer of the railroad was canceled when the Bolsheviks took over the government. Now that chaos was spreading in Siberia, the Terauchi government saw an opportunity to gain access to the railway. Goto's task as foreign minister was to pursue these goals without arousing the suspicion of the Western powers.

On June 3, the Allied Supreme War Council provided the new foreign minister with an opportunity to advance his cause. Contrary to the earlier decision of the Advisory Council on Foreign Relations, Goto now proposed that Japan should accept the Allied invitation for intervention regardless of American opposition. He recommended to the Advisory Council that Japan comply with the minimum conditions offered by the Allies and accept the principles of the territorial integrity of Russia and noninterference in Russia's internal politics. He considered Japan's holding of high command to be essential in case the Allies and the United States participated in the expedition, but rejected the idea of sending Japanese troops to western Siberia.[37]

Hara thought that it was a serious mistake to accept the Allied invitation without securing American consent. He rallied the support of Makino and some other members of the Advisory Council and persuaded the Terauchi government to reconsider Goto's proposal. When the Council reconvened on June 19, Hara was determined to block the government's attempt to declare its willingness to intervene. He firmly maintained that Japan should adhere to the position expressed in its note of March 19. He argued, "Whether Japan and the United States can establish friendly relations or not will almost determine our country's fate [and] . . . it is to Japan's interest to avoid any activity that might intensify America's suspicion about us."[38] The Advisory Council accepted Hara's motion and declined to make any commitment to the Allied proposal for intervention until the United States and the Allies reached a full understanding. Accordingly, the Japanese government notified the American government of its decision on June 26.

On the surface, the document Tokyo delivered to Washington signified the noninterventionists' victory over the army general staff and the Terauchi cabinet. What the document did not convey was the fact that Hara attained his victory by the narrowest margin. In his diary, Hara himself expressed his deep concern about the underlying desire of the army to find any pretext to send troops to Siberia.[39] He suspected that the army was constantly pressing Premier Terauchi to act and that most of the Terauchi cabinet members were sympathetic to the army's policy. Hara's fear was not unfounded. Sometime between the arrival of the Allied Supreme War Council's proposal and the Advisory Council's deliberation of the matter on June 17, the army general staff confidentially submitted to the Foreign Ministry "A Plan for a Siberian Expedition." The army proposed to occupy the territories east of Lake Baikal and key places along the Chinese Eastern Railway and assist the so-called "moderate elements" in Russia. According to the plan, first, one army division was to be sent to the Maritime Provinces, and three months later, to move to the province of Heilongjiang in Manchuria. Second, two and one-half divisions would advance to the Trans-Baikal Territory and reach Lake Baikal within six months. They were to lay the foundation of the westward advance of the Russian "moderate elements." In case of enemy reinforcements, the army estimated that an additional three and one-half divisions were to be sent to these areas.[40]

On July 3, the Political Bureau in the Foreign Ministry, too, produced the recommendation in favor of sending an independent Japanese expedition. The document, entitled "The Subject of the Empire's Russian Policy in Relation to the Issue of the Czechoslovaks," analyzed the American policy in

Russia and reached the conclusion that "there is no doubt that she [the United States] would sooner or later adopt some sort of forceful policy." If the United States sent a military expedition or economic commission without consulting with Japan, the document recommended, Japan should counter with the immediate execution of Japan's military intervention. Japan could not tolerate Siberia's becoming a field for competition between Germany and the United States. The document urged the government to use the recent Czech uprising as a pretext for the expedition and volunteered to assist the Czech forces in order to make them a shield against the German intrusion into East Asia, and at the same time to prevent the Czechs from becoming a tool of other countries who tried to extend their influence in Siberia.[41]

The second problem in President Wilson's perception of the Japanese government was his neglect of the shortcomings of the Japanese constitutional system, namely, the lack of civilian control over the military. Historian Frederick S. Calhoun's study demonstrates that Wilson's military interventions were limited operations specifically to pursue the objectives he defined. Calhoun argues that as commander-in-chief Wilson kept the armed forces "closely tied to his political goals" and "maintained an exceedingly tight control over the military, rejecting any attempt to broaden the role that he assigned."[42] Although his ability to coordinate effectively between his political goals and military means in Siberia was questionable, one can certainly consider Wilson's proposal to send a small-scale expedition to Vladivostok for a limited objective as an example of such an attempt by Wilson.

Regardless of the actual effectiveness of Wilson's use of the miliary to further his political objectives, he sincerely believed that he was carrying out policies which would ensure tight civilian control over the military as the U.S. constitutional system empowered the president to do so. He expected similar behavior from Japan and overestimated the Japanese civilian government's ability to dictate military operational matters. What Wilson did not know, or what the American embassy in Tokyo failed to communicate effectively, was the lack of civilian control over the military under the Meiji Constitution. The Japanese army and the navy, which were directly under the supreme command of the emperor, were not theoretically responsible to the civilian government which was also appointed by the emperor with recommendations from the genro. There was therefore a genuine possibility that the army and the navy might exercise their prerogative and act independently in case the civilian government and the military failed to reach an agreement over military decisions. The only force that could unify the two and dictate national policy had been the genro, but many of them had either passed away or retired from politics by World War I. To fill a power vacuum and maintain national unity in Japan's foreign policy during the war, the emperor's senior advisers established the Advisory Council on Foreign Relations under the direct control of the emperor. The Advisory Council's task was to put Japan's national interests and safety above all other political considerations; their decisions were supposed to be transcendental.[43]

The problem of the Advisory Council, however, was that it lacked a mechanism to enforce its decision upon the military. If the military acted in violation of the Advisory Council's decision, there was no legal or political means to stop them.

President Wilson's proposal for the limited joint expedition in July 1918 unwittingly touched the most vulnerable spot in Japan's ambiguous decision making process—the vaguely defined relationship between the supreme command of the military and the authority of the Advisory Council on Foreign Relations. Diplomatic negotiations with the United States undertaken by the Foreign Ministry were guided by the general decisions made by the Advisory Council. However, President Wilson's proposal required the Foreign Ministry to negotiate with the American government specific military strategic matters, such as the number of troops and the place of military operations. Therefore, the foreign office, and consequently the Advisory Council, had to deal with the issues that were considered as the prerogative of the supreme command.

Upon receiving America's proposal for the joint expedition on July 10, Foreign Minister Goto and Premier Terauchi decided to seize this opportunity to carry out a more vigorous policy in Siberia. The two men considered the limitations proposed by the Americans as unrealistic, and therefore, unacceptable. The Terauchi cabinet refused to limit the number of troops to be sent to Vladivostok, and wanted to reserve the right to send troops to other places on the grounds of self-defense. As a matter of fact, Terauchi had already come up with an approximate number of troops—one division (usually between 14,000 and 20,000 men) to Vladivostok and another division to eastern Siberia.[44]

When the Advisory Council met on July 16 to discuss the Terauchi cabinet's counterproposal to the United States, most of the members were supportive of the government position. However, Hara and Makino firmly opposed the government's idea of a large-scale intervention and insisted on the acceptance of America's proposal. Hara repeatedly emphasized his belief that cooperation with the United States was essential for Japan's future survival. He was even prepared to resign from the Council if it would not acquiesce to his position. Terauchi was equally adamant and insisted on the two-division idea. Their discussion was deadlocked.[45]

Why did Hara's opposition carry such great weight in the Advisory Council despite the fact that the majority of its members were in favor of the cabinet's proposal? As the leader of the powerful Seiyukai—the majority party in the Diet—Hara was capable of dissolving the Terauchi cabinet which was becoming increasingly unpopular because of its ineffective domestic economic policy. Moreover, the second largest political party, the Kenseikai, whose president, Takaaki Kato, refused to attend the Advisory Council for his own political reasons, supported Hara's position.[46]

With the discussion at a deadlock, Miyoji Ito, a member of the Advisory Council who was known as a shrewd tactician, struck a compromise between Hara and the Terauchi cabinet. He tried to obscure the differences between the American proposal and that of the Terauchi government, pointing out that everybody agreed to send an expedition to rescue the Czech troops. He argued that "the government is merely trying to incorporate part of the expedition plan for self-defense into the expedition proposed by the United States," and that "realistically speaking, it is also possible to regard the Siberian expedition as an inevitable consequence of the expedition to Vladivostok."[47] Therefore, he proposed that the Japanese government express its frank opinion to the United States and make an effort to negotiate more favorable conditions for Japan. The argument that nothing was wrong about exchanging opinions with the United States threw Hara and Makino off their guard.

The outcome was an ambiguous compromise between Hara's idea of cooperation with the United States and the Terauchi government's scheme to use the American proposal as an excuse to carry out a larger scale Japanese expedition to Siberia. The draft of Japan's declaration for the joint expedition approved by the Advisory Council best summarized this compromise. It said:

The Japanese Government, being anxious to fall in with the desires of the American Government, and also to act in harmony with their Allies, and having regard at the same time to the special position of Japan, have decided to proceed at once to the disposition of suitable forces for the proposed mission. A certain number of these troops will be sent forthwith to Vladivostok, and if called for by the further exigencies of the situation, another detachment will eventually be ordered to operate and to maintain order along the Siberian Railway.[48]

Whatever the wording of the document, the gist of the matter was that the Terauchi government refused to promise specifically how many troops it would send and where it would send them. In the end, Hara reluctantly consented to this, but it is important to note that he did so only after the premier gave assurances that the government would not send extra troops without conferring with the Advisory Council, and that the troops would be used only for protection of the railways. Hara and Ito wrote down a brief memorandum to keep the record straight. It stated that "the total of troops to be sent to Vladivostok and Siberia will not exceed two divisions."[49]

However, the army general staff had no intention of being bound by the Advisory Council's decision, and continued to pursue its own agenda. On July 16 and 17, for example, the very same time the Advisory Council discussed and reached the compromise resolution, the general staff decided to send at least one division to the Maritime Provinces and another division to the Trans-Baikal Territory. With the self-serving assumption that the United States would inevitably accept the need for reinforcements once the expedition began, the general staff made a conscious decision to "ignore" the American proposal. The instructions to the Twelfth Division, which was to be sent to Vladivostok, stated that the rescue operation of the Czechoslovaks was not the army's primary objective but would be used as an "excuse" because of the government's concerns about the relations with other powers.[50]

While the foreign office was anxiously waiting for the American response to its counterproposal, the army kept pressing the Terauchi government to make a final decision in favor of the army's plan. Terauchi had to assume the difficult task of persuading the army to meet him halfway. He met the vice chief of staff and the war minister on July 20, and somehow made them agree to send only one division to Vladivostok and its vicinity for the limited purpose of protecting the Czech troops for the moment, but he raised no objection to sending reinforcements to other areas later. Furthermore, the three men agreed that the time had come to invoke the provisions of the Sino-Japanese joint defensive agreement signed in May 1918, which meant the possibility of dispatching another division to northern Manchuria to guard the Chinese Eastern Railway.[51] Thus, Terauchi tacitly allowed the army to expand the scope of expedition in violation of the Advisory Council's resolution that the government must seek the Council's approval first in case it needed enforcement.

The negotiation between Tokyo and Washington was prolonged because of the latter's objection to Japan's attempt to expand the scale of expedition. According to Colonel House, President Wilson was "fretted with the Japanese attitude."[52] House thought that this was one of "all sorts of excuses" used by the Japanese who "have never wanted to intervene on an altruistic basis such as the President has insisted upon." Wilson directed Frank Polk, acting secretary of state, to give "a peremptory" reply to Tokyo. Polk told Japanese Ambassador Ishii on July 25 that Japan's reply was not an acceptance of the American proposal but "a new proposal" which was "indefinite as to numbers, not only now, but as to future reinforcement." Polk told Ishii that, although the American government had no objection to Japan's sending a division, a maximum of 10,000 to 12,000, or to Japan's having high command, it considered limitation on the number of troops as essential. He also made it clear that his government was firmly determined not to send troops beyond Vladivostok.[53]

Frustrated by America's objection to Japan's counterproposal, the army general staff began to consider the Advisory Council's seemingly pro-American decision as an obstacle to the army's efforts to carry out its mission. The staff complained about the government's attempts to meddle with the domain of the supreme command by restricting the strategic policies and plans that the general staff worked out. The officers expressed their "absolute" determination to prevent the occasion from becoming "a bad precedent of the government's encroachment on the supreme command."[54] Because the Terauchi government had been sympathetic to the army's interventionist position, the general staff's criticism was mainly directed at the Advisory Council. Kazushige Ugaki, one of the future architects of the Manchurian Incident of 1931, who participated in the preparation for the Siberian expedition, bitterly blamed the Advisory Council for letting the United States dictate Japan's military policy. He wrote in his diary that it was unconscionable for those who had no knowledge of military strategy to control when and where to send what size of forces.[55] Thus, the general staff was quite ready to dismiss the Advisory Council's decisions; and when it did, there was no mechanism for the Advisory Council to use to stop its actions.

Diplomatic correspondence between the American embassy in Tokyo and the State Department in Washington was silent on this matter. There is no indication from available sources that President Wilson was informed of the Japanese imperial army's authority to act independently from the civilian government with whom he was negotiating the size of the joint military expedition.

The third reason for the unintended outcome of Wilson's proposal for the limited expedition, which is closely related to the second reason, is a misunderstanding between Washington and Tokyo concerning the issue of military command of the proposed expeditionary force. Japan had repeatedly attempted to make the United States acknowledge Japan's special position in East Asia or the Asian Monroe Doctrine, as in the case of the Lansing-Ishii agreement of 1917, but President Wilson had been resisting Japan's efforts by revamping the Open Door policy with moralistic principles. He naively expected Japan to accept America's participation in the proposed *joint* expedition on an equal footing with Japan. Wilson did not anticipate how seriously the Japanese would consider the technical question as to who should have high command in the proposed joint expedition. There is no evidence that he paid any attention to the issue of high command until it was time to send troops. It is most likely that if Wilson had known that the Japanese army had the prerogative of making independent decisions without consulting the civilian government on matters related to actual military operations, he would not have consented to give Japan the high command.

On the other hand, ever conscious about their country's status as the regional great power in East Asia, Japanese leaders, both civilian and military, felt Japan was entitled to command a military expedition to the Asian continent on the ground of geographic propinquity. The Terauchi government and the military had been interested in securing the high command ever since the European Allies brought up the subject of an Allied joint intervention in Siberia. Although the army general staff and the ardent supporters of intervention in the Foreign Ministry initially preferred an independent expedition under the Japanese command, in the event that an Allied joint intervention became unavoidable, they considered Japan's acquisition of the high command vital to Japan's national defense and interests.

When the Japanese government realized that there was a possibility of a Japanese-American joint expedition in late April, Foreign Minister Goto began to make conscious efforts to secure America's consent to Japan's high command in such an eventuality. According to Japanese diplomatic records, at least three times between May and July the United States informally agreed to give the high command to Japan in the event that they agreed to undertake a joint expedition. The foreign ministry's summary of the U.S.-Japanese negotiations for the joint expedition, which was submitted to the Terauchi cabinet's key members on July 30, clearly shows the great importance the Japanese government attached to this matter. By the end of July, the Terauchi government and the army general staff apparently assumed that Japan was going to lead in the joint expedition, and this conviction further emboldened the army to make a self-serving decision to ignore the American proposal for the limitations on the expedition.

The first occasion that Japan obtained a positive response from the United States regarding the issue of military command was early May. In response to Secretary of State Lansing's inquiry on April 28, 1918, about "Japan's attitude" toward America's participation in the expedition,[56] Foreign Minister Goto conveyed Japan's willingness to consider the possibility of a joint expedition, but, significantly, he emphasized that Japan preferred to have the joint expeditionary force under the unified command of Japan.[57] When Ishii met Lansing on May 6, the secretary of state expressed his own personal opinion as follows: "The only reason for adding the Allied forces to Japanese troops is to alleviate the Russian people's suspicions about the expedition. In the event of a joint expedition, the high command should rightfully belong to Japan who would send the largest number of troops."[58] There is no indication that Lansing consulted with President Wilson concerning the issue of high command, but, undoubtedly, Lansing's opinion encouraged Tokyo to pursue this matter in the future.

The second occasion that Tokyo and Washington discussed the issue of military command was when Wilson proposed the limited joint expedition to Vladivostok on July 8. While the State Department was anxiously waiting for Japan's reply, Ambassador Ishii suggested to Lansing that "it might possibly expedite a decision" by his government "if some arrangement could be made as to the chief commander of the combined forces." Lansing, who had not yet discussed the subject with Wilson, later sought the president's advice, saying, "I am at loss what to say as I am sure the Japanese will expect to be in high command." After Lansing left on vacation, Ishii made the same suggestion to Acting Secretary of State Polk, who in turn advised Wilson: "I think if we were disposed to tell him that we had no objection to a Japanese officer being the senior military officer, and therefore in command of the troops, we would hear very shortly that the Japanese Government were willing to cooperate."[59]

On July 16, Wilson agree to let the Japanese have the supreme command when they landed in Vladivostok. On the same day, Polk met Ishii and explained that "no formal statement be given out" but that Japan should send "an officer of sufficient rank with their forces, and it would be understood that our forces would be under his command." Ishii reported the decision to Tokyo the next day, and Polk also cabled Ambassador Morris in Tokyo that "the Japanese will have the high command."[60]

Even after the Wilson administration discovered that Japan was trying to alter the purpose and the size of the joint expedition, it continued to confirm that Japan would have command of the expeditionary forces. When Polk met Ishii and expressed his objections to what his government considered Japan's "counterproposal" on July 25, the acting secretary still admitted that his government had recognized Japan's high command and agreed to allow Japan to double the number of troops to be sent.[61] Both the Foreign Ministry and the army general staff in Tokyo did not fail to miss this remark by Polk.

These two points that the Wilson administration conceded turned out to play a crucial role in the subsequent decisions made by Tokyo. The Terauchi cabinet members, bitterly disappointed by the American objection to Japan's counterproposal, were leaning toward a decision in favor of independent action in Siberia. Here again Miyoji Ito tried to smooth over the situation by creating an illusory understanding between the two governments. By pointing out to the foreign minister that the American government not only agreed to hand over to Japan the supreme command of the proposed expedition but also to allow Japan to double the number of troops, Ito argued that these concessions indicated that "although the Americans did not accept our proposal entirely on the surface, the implication of their words suggests their tacit acquiescence." However hollow and self-deceiving his argument was, Ito believed that an expedition in cooperation with the United States was better than an independent military action by Japan to which the Wilson administration would no doubt object openly.[62] With the same argument, Ito successfully persuaded the Advisory Council to accept the American proposal with an ambiguous qualification. Japan's final reply to the United States included the following passage: "in response to the American government's most recent reply, anticipating that in order to assist the Czech forces it will be necessary to dispatch troops beyond Vladivostok and send further reinforcements depending on developments in the situation, [the Japanese government] gladly accepts [the American proposal]."[63]

President Wilson and the State Department felt that Japan had taken advantage of them. According to Assistant Secretary of State William Phillips, Wilson was "indignant with the Japanese and thought that they had got the better of him," but Polk persuaded him to "let the matter stand as it is."[64] Interestingly, Wilson's announcement to the press on August 3 declared that "the Japanese Government has consented" to America's proposal that each send "a force of a few thousand men to Vladivostok, with the purpose of cooperating as a single force in the occupation of Vladivostok and in safeguarding . . . the rear of the westward-moving Czecho-Slovaks."[65]

However, in spite of high-sounding words from President Wilson, Japanese and American troops never acted as a single force. Major General William S. Graves, the commander of the American expedition to Vladivostok, was never told that the State Department had promised to give the Japanese the high command. According to Grave's recollection, a copy of President Wilson's *aide-memoire* of July 17, which Secretary of War Newton D. Baker handed to him, was virtually the only formal instruction he ever received at the commencement of his mission. During his first interview with the Japanese commander, General Kikuzo Otani, on September 2 at Vladivostok, Graves told Otani that he did not receive any instructions to the effect that Otani was to command American troops. Some ten years later, Graves still refused to accept the fact that the State Department had recognized Japan's high command. He wrote, "I feel that someone had led him [Otani] to believe that he was to be in command of all Allied troops."[66] The

Japanese and American forces in Vladivostok never cooperated "as a single force" as President Wilson declared.

It is not known exactly why General Graves did not receive instructions that the Japanese were to have high command. Secretary of War Newton D. Baker's statement in the *New York Times* on August 8, 1918, was evasive on this point. He said that Japan was going to send a higher ranking general but that he did not know whether "there will be any more definite Commander-in-chief."[67] According to Ambassador Ishii, however, Baker took part in making the decision to place American troops under a Japanese commander. Polk told Ishii on July 17 that "as a result of discussion among the three, namely, the president, the secretary of war, and himself, it was decided that should Japan send a senior officer to Vladivostok, they would have no objection to placing the American troops under his command."[68] It is conceivable that there were some sort of misunderstanding or miscommunication between the State and War Departments. In his foreword to General Graves's memoirs, Baker did not hesitate to admit it. He said, "Perhaps the State Department was more impressed than I was with some of the Allied views as to the desirability of cooperation beyond the scope of the *Aide Memoire*."[69]

In any case, this misunderstanding over the issue of high command further widened the differences between Tokyo and Washington concerning the proposed joint expedition. The Japanese and American forces never really cooperated in Siberia as President Wilson originally intended.

In conclusion, an examination of Japanese-American disagreements over the Siberian expedition confirms that the two countries' leaders held conflicting worldviews. The Terauchi government was determined to assert Japan's right to intervene as the leading regional power in East Asia, whereas President Wilson and his advisers refused to grant Japan such a status and held firmly on the issues of morality and principles. In response to the Czechoslovak troops' urgent circumstances that required some sort of action by the Allies in Siberia, President Wilson improvised an unrealistic halfway measure of a limited joint expedition. When the Japanese military took advantage of it and launched a large-scale expedition to pursue their own regional and national agenda, the president concluded that the Japanese government was acting in bad faith and therefore was untrustworthy. However, as this chapter has demonstrated, although the Terauchi government was opportunistic and self-deceiving, Wilson's proposal for the limited joint expedition, too, was an ill-advised policy based on the president's misperceptions, unilateral assumptions, and ignorance of his partner in East Asia. Wilson's miscalculations about Japan's intentions resulted from his lack of understanding of the internal politics and decision-making process of Japan. If he had been aware of the internal division in Tokyo and the lack of civilian control over military matters in Japan, he certainly would not have proposed the conditional joint expedition as he did. His unilateral attempt to dictate what he thought was right backfired in the end. Wilson's unpleasant experience in the Siberian expedition points to the dangers of proposing a joint action without fully understanding the motivation and constraints of the other party, especially Japan's unique conception of regional politics and strategies.

NOTES

1. Wilson's address to a joint session of Congress, January 8, 1918, in Arthur S. Link, ed., *The Papers of Woodrow Wilson* (Princeton: Princeton University Press, 1966–1994), 45: 537. Hereafter cited as *PWW*.

2. The best monographic study that illustrates this point is Betty Miller Unterberger, *America's Siberian Expedition, 1918–1920: A Study in National Policy* (Durham, N.C.: Duke University Press, 1956).

3. Memorandum by Lansing, July 6, 1918, in U.S Department of State, *Papers Relating to the Foreign Relaitons of the United States*, 1918, Russia (Washington, D.C., 1932), 2: 263. Hereafter cited as *FR*.

4. Lansing to the Allied Ambassadors, *FR*, 1918, Russia, 2: 287–290. Wilson's draft of the *aide-memoire* in *PWW*, 48: 624–627.

5. Uchida to Ishii, December 25, 1918, in the Foreign Ministry of Japan, *Nihon gaiko bunsho* (Documents on Japanese foreign policy), 1918 (Tokyo, 1968), 1: 1024–1025. Hereafter cited as *NGB*.

6. Lansing to Morris, November 16, 1918, *FR*, 1918, Russia, 2: 433–435.

7. Diary of David Hunter Miller, January 30, 1919, *PWW*, 54: 379.

8. The two best accounts on America's involvement in the Czech uprising in Siberia are Betty Miller Unterberger, *The United States, Revolutionary Russia, and the Rise of Czechoslovakia* (Chapel Hill: University of North Carolina Press, 1989); and George F. Kennan, *Soviet-American Relations, 1917–1920*, vol. 1, *Russia Leaves the War*, vol. 2, *The Decision to Intervene* (Princeton: Princeton University Press, 1956–1958). Unterberger offers a concise historiographical sketch of the works on the Siberian intervention in her review essay titled "Wilson vs. Bolsheviks" (*Diplomatic History* 21 [winter 1997]).

9. David F. Trask, *The United States in the Supreme War Council: American War Aims and Inter-Allied Strategy, 1917–1918* (Middletown: Wesleyan University Press, 1961); Wilton B. Fowler, *British-American Relations, 1917–1918: The Role of Sir William Wiseman* (Princeton: Princeton University Press, 1969); Unterberger, *America's Siberian Expedition*.

10. David S. Foglesong, *America's Secret War against Bolshevism: U.S. Intervention in the Russian Civil War, 1917–1920* (Chapel Hill: University of North Carolina Press, 1995); N. Gordon Levin Jr., *Woodrow Wilson and World Politics:*

America's *Response to War and Revolution* (New York: Oxford University Press, 1968).

11. James W. Morley, *The Japanese Thrust into Siberia, 1918* (New York: Columbia University Press, 1957), provides a detailed account of Japan's decision to intervene in Siberia.

12. The general concept of Wilson's poor coordination between political ends and military means is suggested by Lloyd E. Ambrosius in the context of Wilson's prosecution of World War I in Europe in *Wilsonian Statecraft: Theory and Practice of Liberal Internationalism during World War I* (Wilmington, Del.: Scholarly Resources, Inc., 1991), 135.

13. The positions of the army and Foreign Minister Motono are discussed later in this chapter. Nishihara's argument for intervention in Siberia is clearly outlined in his letters to Premier Terauchi. See Shiro Yamamoto, ed., *Terauchi Masatake naikaku kankei shiryo* (Documents relating to the cabinet of Masatake Terauchi) (Kyoto: Kyoto joshi daigaku, 1985), 2: 425–428; Hironao Kitamura, ed., *Yume no shichiju-yo-nen: Nishihara Kamezo jiden* (Seventy-some years in a dream: Autobiography of Kamezo Nishihara) (Tokyo: Heibonsha, 1965), 173–179. As for the deliberation by the Advisory Council on Foreign Relations, see Keiichiro Hara, ed., *Hara Kei nikki*, 4: 344–347, and *NGB*, 1917, 1: 661–664.

14. Charles Seymour, ed., *The Intimate Papers of Colonel House* (New York: Houghton Mifflin Company, 1926–1928), 3: 388; Wilton B. Fowler, *British-American Relations 1917–1918*, 165–166; *FR*, 1918, Russia, 2: 13; Wilson's Address to a Joint Session of Congress, January 8, 1918, *PWW*, 45: 534–537.

15. Chinda to Motono, December 12, 1917, Motono to Chinda, December 15, 1917, *NGB*, 1917, 1: 652, 660; Chinda to Motono, January 2, 1918, *NGB*, 1918, 1: 634–635; Morris to Lansing, January 17, 1918, *FR*, 1918, Russia, 2: 30.

16. Wilson to Lansing, January 20, 1918, *PWW*, 46: 46–47; U.S. Department of State, *Papers Relating to the Foreign Relations of the United States: The Lansing Papers 1914–1920* (Washington, D.C., 1940), 2: 351. Hereafter cited as *FRLP*; Polk to Morris, January 20, 1918, *FR*, 1918, Russia, 2:31.

17. The British Embassy to the Department of State, January 28, 1918, the Department of State to the British Embassy, February 2, 1918, *FR*, 1918, Russia, 2: 35–36, 41–42; House to Wilson, February 2, 1918, Wilson to Lansing, February 4, 1918, *PWW*, 46: 214–215, 236.

18. Morris to Lansing, February 18, 1918, *FR*, 1918, Russia, 2: 42–43.

19. Lansing to Page, February 13, 1918, *FR*, 1918, Russia, 2: 45–46.

20. Reinsch to Lansing, February 23, 1918; Morris to Lansing, February 24, 27, 1918, *FR*, 1918, Russia, 2: 55–57.

21. Reading to Wilson with enclosures, February 27, 1918, *PWW*, 46: 470–472.

22. A Draft of An Aide-Memoire, March 1, 1918, *PWW*, 46: 498–499; Bullitt to Polk, March 2; House to Wilson, March 3; House Diary March 3, 4, 5, 1918, *PWW*, 46: 510–513, 518–519, 532.

23. Polk to Morris, March 5, 1918, *FR*, 1918, Russia, 2: 67–68.

24. Morris to Lansing, March 19, 1918, *FR*, 1918, Russia, 2: 81–82.

25. Lansing to Morris, March 20, 22, 1918, *FR*, 1918, Russia, 2: 81–82.

26. Chinda to Goto, June 8, 1918, *NGB*, 1918, 1: 821–823.

27. Chinda to Goto, May 25, 1918, *NGB*, 1918, 1: 809–810.

28. Goto to Chinda, June 21, 1918, *NGB*, 1918, 1: 843–844.

29. Ishii to Lansing, June 25, 1918, *FRLP*, 2: 365.

30. Wiseman to Drummond, May 30, 1918, *PWW*, 48: 205.

31. Wilson to Lansing, June 28, 1918, *PWW*, 48: 457.

32. Sanbo honbu (Japanese Army General Staff), *Taisho 7–nen naishi 11–nen shiberia shuppei-shi* (History of the Siberian expedition, 1918–1922), (Tokyo: Sanbo honbu, 1924), 1: Appendixes 3 and 4, 29–36; English translation in Morley, *The Japanese Thrust into Siberia 1918,* Appendixes B and C, 329–333.

33. "Shiberia shuppei no kyumu" (Urgent need for a Siberian expedition); "Tobu shiberia suppei oyobi nisshi kyodo jiei jikko-an" (proposal for execution of an Eastern Siberian expedition and Sino-Japanese joint defense); "Teikoku gaiko no kiso kaihen no hitsuyo" (Need for a fundamental change in the empire's foreign policy); undated, *NGB*, 1918, 1: 744–756.

34. Keiichiro Hara, ed., *Hara Kei nikki* (Diary of Takashi Hara) (Tokyo: Fukumura shuppan, 1965), 4: 366–372; A Draft Recommendation, undated, *NGB*, 1918, 1: 702–704.

35. Iichiro Tokutomi, ed., *Koshaku Yamagata Aritomo den* (The biography of Prince Aritomo Yamagata) (Tokyo: Yamagata Aritomo ko kinen jigyokai, 1933), 3: 987–989.

36. Yusuke Tsurumi, ed., *Goto Shinpei* (Tokyo: Goto Shinpei haku denki hensankai, 1937), 3: 894–898.

37. Draft reply presented to the Advisory Council on Foreign Relations, June 17, 1918, *NGB*, 1918, 1: 845–847.

38. Keiichiro Hara, ed., *Hara Kei nikki*, 4: 404–407.

39. Ibid., 4: 404–408.

40. Confidential Plan for Siberian Expedition, *NGB*, 1918, 1: 859–860.

41. The Subject of the Empire's Russian Policy in Relation to the Issue of the Czechoslovaks, July 3, 1918, *NGB*, 1918, 1: 894–898.

42. Frederick S. Calhoun, *Power and Principle: Armed Intervention in Wilsonian Foreign Policy* (Kent, Ohio: Kent State University Press, 1986), 4.

43. Shoichi Amemiya, *Kindai nihon no senso shido* (Wartime leadership in modern Japan) (Tokyo: Yoshikawa kobunkan, 1997), 89–104.

44. Tatsuo Kobayashi, ed., *Suiuso nikki: Rinji gaiko chosa iinkai kaigi hikki to* (Diary of the green rain villa: Records of the Advisory Council on Foreign Relaitons, etc.) (Tokyo: Hara shobo, 1966), 126–128 (*Suiuso nikki* is a diary written by Miyoji Ito, a member of the Advisory Council on Foreign Relations); Chihiro Hosoya, *Shiberia shuppei no shiteki kenkyu* (A historical study of the Siberian expedition) (Tokyo: Yuhikaku, 1955; reprint, Tokyo: Shinsensha, 1976), 204–206; Hidenao Takahashi, "Hara naikaku no seiritsu to soryokusen seisaku" (The formation of the Hara cabinet and the total war policy), *Shirin* 68 (May 1985): 13.

45. Tatsuo Kobayashi, ed., *Suiuso nikki*, 138–149; Keiichiro Hara, ed., *Hara Kei nikki*, 4: 415–417.

46. Keiichiro Hara, ed., *Hara Kei nikki*, 4: 417.

47. Tatsuo Kobayashi, ed., *Suiuso nikki*, 152.

48. Goto to Ishii, July 19, 1918, *NGB*, 1918, 1: 924–925.

49. Tatsuo Kobayashi, *Suiuso nikki*, 153–155; Keiichiro Hara, *Hara Kei nikki*, 4: 418.

50. Sanbo honbu, *Taisho 7-nen naishi 11-nen shiberia shuppei-shi*, 1: 52–54.

51. Ibid., 1: 54–55.

52. Diary of House, July 25, 1918, *PWW*, 49: 96.

53. Polk to Wilson, July 26, 1918, *PWW*, 49: 107–109; Polk to Morris, July 27, 1918, *FR*, 1918, Russia, 2: 306–307; Ishii to Goto, July 26, 1918, *NGB*, 1918, 1: 933.

54. Sanbo honbu, *Taisho 7-nen naishi 11-nen shiberia shuppei-shi*, 1: 64.

55. Kazushige Ugaki, *Ugaki Kazushige nikki* (Diary of Kazushige Ugaki) (Tokyo: Misuzu shobo, 1968), 1: 173.

56. Lansing to Wilson, April 30, 1918, *FR*, 1918, Russia, 2: 144–145; *PWW*, 47: 459–461. Ishii to Goto, April 29, 30, 1918, *NGB*, 1918, 1: 792–794.

57. Goto to Ishii, May 1, 1918, *NGB*, 1918, 1: 795.

58. Ishii to Goto, May 7, 1918, *NGB*, 1918, 1: 800–801.

59. Lansing to Wilson, July 10, 1918, *FRLP*, 3: 373; *PWW*, 48: 579–580; Ishii to Goto, July 13, 1918, *NGB*, 1918, 1: 911; Polk to Wilson, July 15, 1918, *PWW*, 48: 621–622.

60. Ishii to Goto, July 17, 1918, *NGB*, 1918, 1: 921; Polk to Morris, July 17, 1918, *FR*, 1918, Russia, 2: 292.

61. Ishii to Goto, July 25, 1918, *NGB*, 1918, 1: 930–931.

62. Tatsuo Kobayashi, ed., *Suiuso nikki*, 167.

63. Ibid., 179–180; Goto to Ishii, August 1, 1918, *NGB*, 1918, 1: 935–936; James Morley, *The Japanese Thrust into Siberia*, 306.

64. Diary of William Phillips, August 3, 1918, *PWW*, 49: 178–179.

65. Press release, August 3, 1918, *PWW*, 49: 170–172.

66. William S. Graves, *America's Siberian Adventure 1918–1920* (New York: J. Cape & H. Smith, 1931), 4, 57–59.

67. *New York Times,* August 8, 1918, quoted in Unterberger, *America's Siberian Expedition*, 76.

68. Ishii to Goto, July 17, 1918, *NGB*, 1918, 1: 921.

69. William Graves, *America's Siberian Adventure*, foreword by Newton D. Baker, xiv.

CHAPTER 6

Wilsonian Idealism and Japanese Claims at the Paris Peace Conference

According to Ray Stannard Baker, head of the Press Bureau of the American Committee to Negotiate the Peace, the Paris Peace Conference in 1919 was a battlefield of two ideas: the "Old Diplomacy" practiced by the imperialists of the Old World and the "New Diplomacy" advocated by the idealistic internationalists under the leadership of President Woodrow Wilson.[1] As the previous chapters show, however, this dichotomy alone does not explain the reasons for the increasing tension and distrust between Japan and the United States at the end of World War I. To understand why President Wilson failed to fend off the Japanese challenge to the fundamental principles of Wilsonian internationalism envisaged in his Fourteen Points at the Paris Peace Conference, it is necessary to look beyond differences between Japanese imperialism in the tradition of the "Old Diplomacy" and the "New Diplomacy" based on Wilsonian liberal internationalism. This chapter argues that the ultimate reason for Japanese-American disagreements was the dichotomy between Wilsonian universalism and unilateralism and on the other hand an incipient particularistic regionalism and pluralism which arose from Japanese leaders' perception of the unique position of their own country in East Asia.

Wilson's frustration in his efforts to block Japanese claims at the peace conference was, in a sense, due to his own unshakable belief in the universality of his internationalist ideals. Once he assumed that his position was just, he considered the nations that failed to adhere to his ideals morally wrong. The moral indignation he felt against Japan because of his inability to control Japanese military action in the Siberian intervention demonstrated this point. It never occurred to him that the restricted joint expedition he had proposed in July 1918 was a misguided and impractical strategy in the eyes of the other party who had greater stakes in the venture because of its geographic proximity. He unilaterally applied his ideals to the East Asian situation without genuine comprehension of regional realities. At Paris, Wilson maintained the same attitude toward the issues that involved Japan. His knowledge of Japan and East Asia was limited and colored by reports from diplomats and "experts" who shared his universalist zeal for America's mission in East Asia. By treating Japan as a morally inferior state and turning America's rivalry with Japan in East Asia into a crusade against an uncivilized force, Wilson made it impossible to negotiate any workable compromise. Wilson's inflexible unilateralism was one of the limitations of his idealism.

Throughout the war, in search for a more independent and self-assertive policy toward the Asian continent, Japan's wartime leaders gradually developed a pluralistic and regionalist approach to justify Japan's hegemony in East Asia. They found in the rhetoric of an Asian Monroe Doctrine the ideological foundation for a Japanese version of imperialism that was regionalist and even anti-Western in motivation. By emphasizing the geopolitical separation of Asia from the West, they tried to argue that a nation's conduct could be based on principles other than those hitherto laid out by the Western great powers. Based on the idea that China and Japan had a "special relationship" because of geopolitical, economic, racial, and cultural commonalities, Japanese leaders defended their country's special position in China and the idea of Japanese "tutelage" over China.

The concept of an unequal partnership between China and Japan embraced by Genro Yamagata and other Japanese leaders, however, contained curiously ambivalent attitudes toward China. On the one hand, they believed that their country's national survival dictated that they must secure Japan's "lifeline" in the continent by any means possible, including exploitation of their weak neighbor through intimidation and coercion, so far as the great powers would permit. At the same time, as the only non-Western imperial power in East Asia, the Japanese also felt justified in claiming a special paternalistic position in the region on the grounds of geographic propinquity, as well as the common racial and cultural background. They arrogantly assumed that China would accept Japan's tutelage if they could make China understand Japan's true intentions. For example, when Yamagata proposed some sort of Sino-Japanese entente or agreement pledging "union and cooperation," his main goal was to encourage China's confidence in Japan through persistent persuasion and guidance. In doing so, he took it for granted that China would follow Japan's leadership and consult with Tokyo whenever China dealt with other foreign countries.

In these respects, the United States and Japan stood far apart in their views of the world when hostilities in Europe came to an end in November 1918. By the time President Wilson and the Japanese delegation assembled for the first meeting of the Supreme Council of the Peace Conference, both sides had diametrically opposite objectives based on incompatible visions of the postwar world.

The American delegation at the peace conference had as its objective a new world order as envisioned in President Wilson's Fourteen Points. As far as Wilson was concerned, the Fourteen Points were the only possible program for world peace. The realization of such principles as open diplomacy, freedom of the seas, free trade, and the self-determination of states, he declared to Congress in January 1918, hinged on the creation of a league of nations. He reiterated this position in his address on September 27, 1918, at the Metropolitan Opera House in New York, stating that "the constitution of that League of Nations and the clear definition of its objective must be . . . the most essential part of the peace settlement itself." Here and elsewhere, he insisted that "no special or separate interest of any single nation or any groups of nations can be made the basis of any part of the settlement which is not consistent with the common interest of all."[2] Having secured from both Germany and the European Allies a prearmistice agreement that they would, as a matter of principle, embrace the Fourteen Points as the basis of peace, Wilson presumed that the Fourteen Points would shape the peace conference, and, consequently, the postwar world.

Wilson gave the lowest priority to questions concerning the disposition of the German colonies. On the way to Paris, Wilson revealed to Colonel House and other chief members of the Inquiry his belief that the mandate system through the League of Nations would provide a satisfactory solution to the matter. (The Inquiry was a special commission directed by Colonel House to prepare the U.S. government's program for peace.) Wilson's plan was to make the German colonies "the common property of the League of Nations" to be "given to one of the smaller states to administer as the mandatory" of the League primarily in the interest of the natives. Wilson stressed that the peace conference would not tolerate "arrangements" made in "the old style," and that "only the adoption of a cleansing process would recreate or regenerate the world."[3] George L. Beer, an Inquiry member who was an expert on colonial questions, was disturbed by the president's suggestion, commenting in his diary that the president's mandatory idea was "a very dangerous and academic type of thinking."[4] Beer knew that colonial administration required skill and experience both in the governing state and the colony.

Prior to the peace conference, there is little evidence of Wilson's thinking about German rights and concessions in Shandong. This had been an extremely delicate subject between the Japanese and American governments since the crisis over the Twenty-one Demands in 1915. As chapter 2 has illustrated, the crisis aroused Wilson's suspicions concerning Japan's territorial ambition in China. The American government had refused to recognize the treaties signed between the Chinese and Japanese governments on May 25, 1915, in which the Chinese government promised to consent to any arrangement entered into between the Japanese and German governments at the end of the war concerning Germany's rights, interests, and concessions in the province of Shandong. In the summer of 1918, Wilson was again disturbed by the way Japan took advantage of his proposal for a joint military expedition to Vladivostok by dispatching a far larger number of troops than he had expected. Wilson therefore had no intention of accommodating Japanese interests at the expense of China. In November 1918, when Wilson had a brief interview with Chinese Minister Wellington Koo (one of the five Chinese plenipotentiaries at Paris), he expressed his willingness to support China's case at the coming peace conference.[5]

Prior to the Paris conference, the Inquiry offered little advice concerning the Shandong question because the organization lacked "qualified, trained scholars" capable of dealing with Asian problems. Lawrence E. Gelfand has suggested that the Inquiry's reports on East Asian issues, which were unsympathetic toward Japanese aspirations in Asia, were the products of nonexperts. Some thirty years after the conference, Charles Seymour recalled that even Stanley K. Hornbeck, chief of the Far Eastern Division of the Inquiry since September 1918, was inadequately prepared. Seymour commented, "Hornbeck knew something about the Far East but he learned most of it from 1919 on."[6]

Although the American embassy in Tokyo offered little insight into the thinking of the Japanese leadership to help formulate or modify American policy, alarming reports from Minister Reinsch in Beijing had a significant influence upon Hornbeck and other East Asian advisers at Paris just before the opening of the conference. Reinsch, who had been Hornbeck's mentor at the University of Wisconsin, was the embodiment of Wilsonian universal idealism and unilateralist internationalism. After alerting the State Department to Tokyo's alleged attempts to silence Chinese opposition to the Japanese claims at Paris, Reinsch made an unusual request to Washington on January 16, 1919, asking the State Department to transmit his telegram directly to President Wilson in Paris. In his message, Reinsch indicted Japan's wartime actions in China and appealed for Wilson's personal intervention, because the president had become "to the people of China the embodiment of their best hopes and aspirations." Reinsch said, "I have been forced through the experience of five years to the conclusion that the methods applied by the Japanese military masters can lead only to evil and destruction." He argued that "only the refusal to accept the result of Japanese secret manipulation in China during the last four years, particularly the establishment of Japanese political influence and privileged position in Shantung" could prevent China from becoming a dependent of Japan. He believed that German rights in Shandong "lapsed together with all Sino-German treaties upon the declaration of war," and that a succession of treaty rights from Germany to Japan was therefore impossible.[7]

Hornbeck gave unqualified support to Minister Reinsch's plea from Beijing. He believed that his mentor's observations on the East Asian situation were "uniformly and absolutely accurate," and that the solution suggested by Reinsch was that of a first-rate authority. Therefore, Hornbeck advised that Reinsch's opinion was "worthy of the most careful consideration of the Peace Commissioners." Edward T. Williams, the other Far Eastern technical expert of the American Mission, concurred. He commented that "the spirit of Japan is that of Prussia, whom Japanese leaders openly admire and whose government they deliberately chose for a model." Throughout its history, he continued, Japan's objective had been to dominate Asia, and the present cabinet of Takashi Hara was no exception. Employing Wilsonian rhetoric, Williams concluded that "Japan must be restrained if justice is to prevail or liberty survive in the Far East."[8]

The recommendations President Wilson received in the early stage of the peace conference in mid-February clearly reflected the anti-Japanese sentiments of the East Asian "experts" of the Inquiry and their unrealistic assessment of the situation. Their reports advised that Japan should be prohibited from control over the port of Qingdao, and that the entire German-leased territory in Jiaozhou and the Shandong Railway should be restored to China. With a view to freeing China from obligations under the Twenty-one Demands, the Inquiry recommended that all Sino-Japanese agreements concluded during the war involving the transfer or allocation of territory, special rights, or privileges should "be subject to screening for approval, revision, or rejection by the peace conference." The Inquiry went so far as to suggest that the peace conference review the Sino-Japanese treaties with regard to Japan's sphere of influence in South Manchuria and Eastern Inner Mongolia. The recommendation also included a rather unrealistic proposal to internationalize all railroads in Manchuria. To pacify Japanese expansionist zeal, but apparently without careful consideration, the Inquiry simply proposed that Japan be allowed to have the Russian maritime provinces in Siberia.[9]

There is no evidence to suggest that Wilson and his advisers, prior to their arrival in Europe, knew that Tokyo had secured secret agreements from the British and French governments to the effect that they would support Japan's claims both to the German rights in Shandong and the German islands in the Pacific north of the equator. In the spring of 1917, British Foreign Secretary Arthur J. Balfour had provided Colonel House with the text of various secret treaties which Great Britain had concluded with the Allies, but he had not enclosed the agreement with Japan over Shandong and the German islands in the Pacific. In the fall of 1917, Japan's special envoy, Kikujiro Ishii, had told Secretary of State Lansing that England had practically agreed that Japan would retain the German Pacific islands north of the equator and that England would keep those south of the equator.[10] When Wilson had met with British Prime Minister David Lloyd George on December 30, 1918, for "an informal interchange of views" on the issues to be discussed at the peace conference, the prime minister had revealed that his government "had definitely promised to Japan the Islands in the Northern Pacific." Wilson responded that "he was by no means prepared to accept the Japanese Treaty," and hinted that he meant to act "as a buffer to prevent" the Japanese from retaining those islands. Curiously, Lloyd George made no mention of his support for Japan's claims to the German concessions in Shandong. Several months earlier, in late October 1918, after the Japanese and Chinese governments had concluded an agreement regarding joint operation of the Shandong Railway, the Japanese embassy had informed the State Department of the substance of the agreement, but the question of the postwar disposition of Shandong was never discussed between Tokyo and Washington until the two countries' delegates met at Paris in 1919.[11]

In contrast to the Wilson administration's comprehensive peace program which dealt with problems at the global level, the Japanese government was concerned only with the issues that affected Japanese interests in East Asia and the Pacific. Tokyo's objectives at the peace conference narrowly concentrated on three areas: (1) succession to the German rights and concessions in Shandong; (2) acquisition of the German islands in the Pacific north of the equator (the Carolines, Marshalls, and Marianas); and (3) securing safeguards against racial discrimination in the event that the conference decided to establish the League of Nations.

As the previous chapters have demonstrated, the Japanese government painstakingly laid the groundwork for its territorial claims at the coming peace conference. The Sino-Japanese Treaty of May 25, 1915, gave Japan a free hand in the disposition of the German rights and concessions in Shandong. In the winter of 1917, Great Britain and France signed secret agreements to support Japan's claims both in Shandong and in the German Pacific islands north of the equator in exchange for Japanese naval assistance in the Mediterranean. In September 1918, a few days before his resignation, Premier Terauchi had further fortified Japan's claims to the Shandong Railway by concluding three new agreements with the Beijing government under Duan Qirui. Terauchi, who shared his mentor Genro Yamagata's vision of "the coexistence and co-prosperity of China and Japan," had worked during the war to instill in Chinese leaders a feeling of reliance on the Japanese Empire by providing wartime financial assistance known as the Nishihara Loans. Terauchi had used part of these loans to strike a deal with the Duan government on the Shandong Railway. In the Sino-Japanese agreement signed on September 24, 1918, the two countries agreed to place the Shandong Railway (between Jiaozhou and Jinan) under their joint management and to share police duty along the railway. One of the provisions, which later became controversial at the peace conference, stipulated that the Japanese were "to be employed at the headquarters of this police force, at the main stations, and at the police training school." In two other agreements signed on September 28, the Duan government accepted a loan of 40 million yen from the Japanese government: 20 million yen for military purposes and 20 million yen for the construction of four new railroads in Shandong, Manchuria, and Mongolia.[12]

On the following day, September 29, 1918, a moderate, Takashi Hara, became the first party politician to assume the premiership. Although Hara modified Japan's China policy somewhat, the new government did not alter Japan's fundamental objectives at the peace table. Hara opposed the aggressive military-oriented policy toward the Asian continent initiated by the Terauchi government in collaboration with the army, Japanese financiers, and the Duan government in Beijing. He also opposed the Siberian expedition and advocated cordial relations with the United States. However, as an astute political survivor, Premier Hara was fully aware that giving up Japan's foothold in Shandong would cost him his political career. Japan's policy throughout the war had focused on the acquisition of the German concessions in Shandong. For senior statesmen, the military, and the civilian bureaucracy, a reversal in that policy on the eve of the peace conference was unthinkable. Hara ultimately swam with the current, embracing the policy of the two preceding cabinets.

When the Japanese government learned that President Wilson's Fourteen Points were to become the basis of the peace settlement, the Advisory Council on Foreign Relations convened to discuss Japan's response. Members of the Advisory Council were concerned mainly with two issues. First,

Wilson's principle of self-determination seemed to pose a serious problem for the disposal of the German colonies. Although the council members had no idea of Wilson's specific views on Shandong and the Pacific islands, they were determined to press Japan's claim regardless of the American position.[13] By December 2, 1918, both the Advisory Council and the Hara cabinet formally decided that the Japanese government would return the territorial rights of Jiaozhou Bay to China only after Germany ceded the leased territory to Japan unconditionally. This would avoid the possibility of a direct restitution of the territory from Germany to China. The Advisory Council and Premier Hara also decided to insist on Japan's authority to settle the issue of retrocession directly with China without outside interference.[14]

What the Japanese really wanted to acquire, through the two-step procedure described above, were the railway and the mines in Shandong Province. War Minister Giichi Tanaka bluntly reminded the Advisory Council members that should Japan fail to obtain the Shandong Railway, it would lose control of Shandong Province as a whole, thereby losing "the artery that extends the power" of the Japanese Empire to the Asian continent. The Advisory Council overwhelmingly supported specific instructions to Japanese delegates at Paris, directing them to do their "very best" to secure the railway and the mines. In demanding the cession of these economic interests from Germany, the Japanese delegates were to set forth "a plain and straightforward political argument based on the rights of a victor."[15]

Senior Japanese statesmen shared a self-serving belief that China would accept Japan's tutelage if they could make China understand Japan's true intentions. When Japanese Foreign Minister Yasuya Uchida learned from Beijing that Chinese Foreign Minister Lu Zhengxiang intended to visit Tokyo on the way to Paris and make careful "preliminary arrangements" on the matter of Chinese peace terms with the Japanese authorities, he interpreted the report as the Chinese foreign minister's willingness to reach an understanding with Tokyo on the Shandong issue. Accordingly, the Advisory Council on Foreign Relations adopted a resolution to the effect that upon the Chinese foreign minister's arrival in Tokyo, "we will explain our decision [on the retrocession of Jiaozhou] and make him understand our just attitude and clear away misunderstandings; and we must take measures so that Japan and China can keep in step with each other in the coming peace conference."[16]

Leaders in Tokyo believed that Japan and China should take care of the issues between the two by themselves. The one thing the Japanese could not tolerate was Western intervention in Sino-Japanese affairs, especially if the interference might embarrass or hurt Japan's prestige in the eyes of the Chinese. The Shandong controversy at Paris turned out to be one of those occasions that the Japanese feared most. At the close of the Advisory Council's December 1918 meeting which forged Japan's official position on Shandong, Miyoji Ito expressed his concern: "Our national prestige will be impaired should we demand permanent retention of Qingdao and later be forced to withdraw that demand because of America's protest."[17]

The second and equally important question that the Advisory Council deliberated was President Wilson's proposal on the League of Nations. Documents from the Foreign Ministry and from the Advisory Council indicate that Japanese leaders were genuinely concerned about the possibility that the racial prejudice of Western powers might jeopardize Japan's position in the League of Nations and that they were resolved to prevent such a possibility. Draft guidelines prepared by the foreign office for the Japanese delegation at Paris urged indefinite postponement of plans to create a League of Nations on the grounds that "racial prejudice among nations" was widespread and that Western powers' control of the League threatened grave disadvantages to Japan. At the same time, the foreign office also concluded that "in case the League of Nations is to be established, the Empire cannot remain isolated outside the organization." Therefore, should the establishment of the League become unavoidable at the peace conference, the foreign office proposed "appropriate safeguards against disadvantages which the Empire may suffer because of the racial prejudice."[18]

The Advisory Council, too, expressed deep apprehension about the League of Nations. Council members were afraid that unless the principle of equality was absolutely guaranteed by the League, "the United States and the top-ranking nations in Europe" might use the League "to freeze the status quo and hold in check the development of second-rate and lower-ranked nations." Accordingly, the council unanimously supported a resolution to the effect that at the peace conference Japan would try to postpone the creation of the League of Nations because of its grave concern about racial prejudice among the Western nations; and in case the peace conference decided to organize the League, the Japanese delegation must seek safeguards against racial discrimination.[19]

In this way, Japanese objectives at the Paris Peace Conference challenged Wilsonian principles at two levels. Japan's territorial claims tested the Wilsonian ideal of self-determination and its unilateral application to the former German concession and colonies. Japan's efforts to secure safeguards against racial discrimination in the League of Nations raised questions about the effectiveness and the fairness of the fundamental principle of international federalism embodied in the League of Nations. Japanese regional and racial identities questioned the universality of the Western-oriented solution to international conflicts.

Once the peace conference began, the Japanese delegation discovered that the disposition of the German islands in the Pacific was the least divisive issue separating them from President Wilson. After Australia, New Zealand, and South Africa demanded annexation of the German colonies under their occupation, the Japanese simply asked for equal treatment in the Pacific north of the equator. While British and American negotiators tried to work out a compromise, Japan's delegates remained silent. President Wilson, who was determined to approve nothing less than a system of mandates under the supervision of the League of Nations, clashed with Prime Minister William Hughes of Australia. Eventually Wilson prevailed and Hughes agreed to accept the provisions of the "C-Mandate," which stipulated that the German islands were to be "administered under the laws of the mandatory states as integral portions [of the mandatory states] . . . in the interests of the indigenous population."[20]

The Hara government in Tokyo did not have much difficulty in accepting the provisions for mandatory status, including regulations for non-fortification and the open door in the islands. Nobuaki Makino, the leading member of the Japanese delegation at Paris, strongly urged his government to approve the mandatory proposal. After learning from Lloyd George that Australia and New Zealand were expected to accept the mandatory principle, Makino advised Tokyo that it would be unwise for Japan alone to oppose. He explained that the mandatory idea appeared to be intended as a face-saving gesture to Wilson by upholding the mandatory principle and at the same time securing the approval of the British Dominions through guaranteeing virtual annexation of these territories.[21] To Makino the deal was a realistic compromise.

Wilson expressed some uneasiness about granting the northern islands to Japan. On January 30, 1919, the day the decision was reached on the mandate system, he told David H. Miller that "these islands lie athwart the path from Hawaii to the Philippines and . . . that they could be fortified and made naval bases by Japan." Referring to the Japanese government's breach of faith with regard to the Siberian intervention, the president confided that he would not trust the Japanese again. He had also written to Colonel House earlier that "a line of islands in her [Japan's] possession would be very dangerous to the U.S." However, his concern was mitigated later when Tokyo accepted the provisions for a "C-Mandate" which prohibited construction of naval bases or fortifications on these islands.[22]

More problematic for Japan was the issue of race and the League of Nations, for Japan's attempt to include a racial equality clause in the League of Nations covenant was thwarted by unforeseen circumstances. Some contemporaries (and some later historians) have held that Japan used the racial equality proposal as a bargaining chip to obtain the German concessions in Shandong.[23] The Japanese concern about racial discrimination, however, was genuine; Tokyo's instructions on this issue were explicit from the very beginning. Certainly, Tokyo may have weighed the racial issue against Japanese interests in Shandong when both claims met with strong opposition at Paris. But Japan's decision to withdraw its proposal for racial equality was a result, primarily, of adamant objection from the British Dominions.

At the outset of the conference, the Japanese delegation worried that the United States might be the major obstacle to Japan's racial equality proposal. Makino knew how politically troublesome the racial issues could be for President Wilson on the West Coast of the United States. In 1913, Makino, as foreign minister, had negotiated in vain for the repeal of the alien land legislation in California, which banned Japanese immigrants from owning land in the state. However, when Makino and Sutemi Chinda opened informal negotiations with Colonel House, they found him surprisingly supportive of the Japanese proposal and learned from him that even President Wilson might approve a milder form of declaration on racial equality.[24]

The true stumbling block turned out to be staunch opposition from Australia's Prime Minister Hughes. By mid-February, Japanese delegates realized that the British would not agree to the proposal unless the Dominions changed their minds. In light of the British attitude, Tokyo was told, "evidently, it is going to be difficult to fulfill our wish." After negotiations with Colonel House and Lord Robert Cecil of Britain, Japanese delegates proposed a compromise to include in the preamble of the Covenant an endorsement of the principle of racial equality. When the prime ministers of the British Dominions deliberated on this proposal on March 25, all but Hughes agreed to accept it. Hughes rejected the repeated requests by the Japanese to discuss the proposal. Jan C. Smuts of South Africa, who tried to mediate between Hughes and the other Dominion representatives, told Makino that if Japan insisted on bringing up the race question at the plenary session and if Hughes opposed it, "I shall have to fall in line and vote with the Dominions, like a 'good Indian.' " Thus, by the end of March, Japan's efforts to negotiate with the British Dominions proved futile.[25]

In Tokyo, the Advisory Council on Foreign Relations met on March 30 to discuss how Japan could withdraw the racial equality proposal without losing its dignity. Foreign Minister Uchida insisted that the delegates must do their best to keep the record straight as to where Japan stood on the race issue at the peace conference. Premier Hara thought that some nominal manifestation of the principle would suffice as a face-saving gesture. He did not think the issue warranted Japan's withdrawal from the League of Nations.[26]

Following Tokyo's instructions, with a view to leaving Japan's position in a written record, Makino and Chinda asked the League of Nations Commission to vote on their amendment to the preamble. Eleven out of seventeen present voted in favor of the amendment. The United States abstained. President Wilson ruled that the amendment was not adopted because it had not received the unanimous approval of the Commission. Makino asked to record in the minutes the number of votes cast in favor of the Japanese amendment.[27]

Although the reasons why President Wilson abstained from voting on the racial question are not entirely clear, it is obvious that he did not fight for the principle of racial equality. At the meeting on April 11, he simply suggested that the wisest course for the United States would be not to press the matter. There are at least two possible explanations for Wilson's inaction and silence on this matter.

First, Wilson was well aware of strong opposition against the racial equality principle in his own country. He feared that its adoption by the League might provide Asians with grounds to demand the repeal of the laws banning or restricting Asian immigration. Wilson's opponents at home might claim that the League was interfering in America's domestic affairs.[28] The truth is that the American commissioners were reluctant to accept even the modified Japanese proposal for racial equality. As Dr. Cary T. Grayson put it, "[I]t was not necessary for the United States openly to oppose the suggested amendment because Australia and New Zealand through the British representatives had taken the position of positive opposition." Because of the outright objection of the British Dominions, the Japanese even felt grateful to Colonel House, on whom they called almost every day to work out a compromise. House wrote in his diary: "It has taken considerable finesse to lift the load from our shoulders and place it upon the British, but happily, it has been done."[29]

Second, caught in the cross fire between Japan's proposal and the opposition of the British Dominions, Wilson did not want a heated debate or publicity on this sensitive issue outside the conference room. He was so preoccupied with the establishment of the League of Nations that he did not want the question of race to become a divisive issue during the conference. "My own interest," Wilson said to the commission, "is to quiet discussion that raises national differences and racial prejudices. I would wish them, particularly at this juncture in the history of the relations with one another, to be forced as much as possible into the background." One of the limitations of Wilson's idealist approach to the League of Nations seems to have been his decision to let racial prejudices "play no part in the discussions connected with the establishment of this League."[30] To achieve his noble cause, he chose to close his eyes to one of the most serious factors contributing to political fragmentation in the world.

The settlement of the German rights and concessions in Shandong, Japan's primary objective at Paris, turned out to be one of the most controversial issues at the peace conference. It surprised and frustrated all the parties involved, especially the Japanese and Americans. As the conference unfolded, Japanese delegates who had not anticipated much difficulty in securing their claims to Shandong met with formidable opposition from both the Chinese and Americans. At the Council of Ten on January 27, Makino presented Japan's case for the unconditional cession to Japan of all German rights and concessions in Shandong, with the understanding that Japan would eventually return the territorial rights to China. Makino declared that Japan intended to keep Sino-Japanese negotiations strictly between the two countries and outside the peace conference. The Japanese were caught by surprise the following day when V. K. Wellington Koo demanded the direct restoration to China of the leased territory of Jiaozhou, the Shandong Railway, and all other rights Germany had possessed in Shandong Province prior to the war. Following Reinsch's earlier proposal to President Wilson, Koo argued that China considered all the agreements concluded during the war as provisional and subject to revision by the peace conference.[31] The Japanese felt betrayed by the Chinese, for they had relied on Chinese Foreign Minister Lu's promise that the Chinese delegation would act in concert with the Japanese.

The question of Shandong deeply troubled President Wilson. According to Ray S. Baker, "the Japanese crisis, while shorter and sharper, troubled the President more than any other—and the result of none, finally, satisfied him less." On one occasion Wilson told Baker that "he had been unable to sleep on the previous night for thinking of it."[32] He had great sympathy for China's plight and considered the Shandong question to be a prime case for self-determination. Moreover, Wilson's own experiences with the Japanese government during the war had convinced him not to trust it easily. His American advisers on East Asia, as well as Secretary of State Lansing, were united in opposition to the Japanese claims. The other American commissioners, except Colonel House whom the Japanese considered their "friend," also had little sympathy for Japan.

While the Council of Ten was making arrangements to deliberate the Sino-Japanese treaty and agreements of 1915 and 1918 concerning Shandong, China's anti-Japanese press campaign further aroused Wilson's suspicions of Japan and caused much bitter feelings on the part of the Japanese. When the Japanese foreign minister instructed his country's minister in Beijing to warn the Chinese government not to publish the secret agreements without consulting with Japan, the anti-Japanese faction within the Beijing government seized the opportunity to spread negative charges against Japan. On February 4, Wilson received a report that the Japanese intended to retain "the whole of Shang-Tung permanently," and were threatening "military intervention" and "the immediate withdrawal of all financial support" from China. He ordered Minister Reinsch to advise the Chinese government to stand firm; at the same time, he instructed the American ambassador in Tokyo to express "our distress that there should be these indications that the Japanese government is not willing to trust to the fairness and justness of the Peace Conference."[33]

Diplomatic exchanges between Tokyo and Beijing reveal the surprise and indignation felt by Japanese officials over the Chinese accusations. Although the acting Chinese foreign minister later corrected the erroneous press reports in Beijing, his action received little attention. In the end, China's anti-Japanese press campaign and its attempt to enlist the help of the United States in forcing Japan to abandon its claims served only to harden Japan's determination to carry out its objective at Paris. In Beijing, Japanese Minister Yukichi Obata told the Chinese foreign office that to succumb to the Chinese demands because of Western pressure would undermine Japan's international prestige and national self-respect, and that the Japanese people could not bear such a "humiliation."[34]

On this point, Edward T. Williams mistakenly commented that the publicity given to the activities of Minister Obata in Beijing "did lots of good" and that "there's nothing like public criticism to control the Japanese."[35] The American experts at Paris did not fully grasp the psychology of Japan's relations with China. Facing a hostile challenge from China and the United States, the Japanese no longer saw the Shandong settlement merely as a matter of expanding national interests; they regarded it as a matter of national prestige in the broader context of East Asian politics.

When the Council of Four began the final deliberation of the Shandong question in mid-April 1919, Japanese delegates realized that President Wilson's stance on this issue was the major obstacle to the fulfillment of their goal. Wilson clearly stated his position in the council: "My sympathies are on the side of China, and we must not forget that, in the future, the greatest dangers for the world can arise in the Pacific." Not knowing the specifics of the Sino-Japanese treaty and agreements, Wilson insisted that the council must first study them because, in his own words, "I know by experience that they [the Japanese] are very clever in the interpretation of treaties."[36] Makino and Chinda met privately with Wilson on April 21 and explained that some of the provisions of the treaty and the agreements in question were already in effect, and that the Shandong problem was only a matter of implementing them. The two Japanese told Wilson that "if the already existing and clearly stated treaty was disregarded and the problem was decided by a completely different mechanism for settlement, it was difficult to say whether in the end the plenipotentiaries would be able to sign the preliminary treaty or not." They also pointed out that, because of a breach of faith on the part of China and its hostile propaganda against Japan, the Shandong problem was no longer just a matter of leased territory but had become "a grave issue in the general political situation in the Far East."[37]

On the same day in Tokyo, the Advisory Council on Foreign Relations reached a crucial decision. Calling China's actions at Paris a "betrayal," Miyoji Ito argued that, should Japan's claim be defeated at the conference, "China would treat Japan with contempt" and that Japan would totally lose its prestige in the East. Ito, therefore, proposed that in the worst case the government should be prepared to withdraw from the League of Nations. The rest of the council members fell in line with his opinion, including Premier Hara, who stated that his government could put up with neither direct restitution to China nor trusteeship by the League of Nations.[38] That same day, Foreign Minister Uchida cabled to the Japanese delegation at Paris not to sign the Covenant of the League of Nations should Japan's Shandong claims be repudiated. He added, "[I]n order to maintain our government's dignity there shall be no room for conciliatory adjustment."[39] Tokyo's firm instruction gave the Japanese delegates no way out.

The following day, on April 22, after having heard the Japanese and Chinese cases separately, the Council of Four was leaning toward a decision in favor of Japan. First, both Lloyd George and Georges Clemenceau made it clear that they had definite wartime agreements with Japan. Second, Japanese delegates declared that they were under an explicit order from their government not to sign the treaty "unless they were placed in a position to carry out Japan's obligation to China." Although the Chinese delegation urged the council to undo the Sino-Japanese treaty of 1915 and the agreements signed in 1918, not only the British and French prime ministers but also President Wilson defended the "sacredness of treaties." Wilson had serious reservations about the Sino-Japanese treaty of 1915, but he could not question the validity of the British and French commitment to Japan's claim. Lloyd George stated that his country's engagement with Japan was "a solemn treaty" and that "Great Britain could not turn round to Japan now and say 'All right, thank you very much. We wanted your help, you gave it, but now we think that the treaty was a bad one and should not be carried out.'" Ironically, Wilson had to tell the Chinese delegation that "sacredness of treaties had been one of the motives of the war" and that "it had been necessary to show that treaties were not mere scraps of paper."[40]

Convinced that Japan's threat to withdraw from the peace conference was not a bluff, Wilson chose to compromise with the Japanese. This, he hoped, would provide an "outlet to permit the Japanese to save their face and let the League of Nations decide the matter later." As he put it to Lloyd George and Clemenceau, he believed "it is necessary to do everything to assure that she [Japan] joins the League of Nations." He was afraid that "if she stands aside, she would do all that she could want to do in the Far East."[41] He apparently believed that the League of Nations would police Japan's behavior in East Asia once it became a member, so that Japan would not violate China's territorial integrity and political independence.

The Shandong compromise, therefore, was a means to keep the influence of Wilsonian idealism alive in East Asia. It demonstrated Wilson's firm faith in the League of Nations and the universality of the international system and morality that his League represented. When the president said, "I am above all concerned not to create a chasm between the East and the West,"[42] he did not mean to create a federalism that would accommodate the hegemony of a regional power in the East. Wilson was thinking, instead, of an international mechanism that would unilaterally enforce his universal values as the League members saw fit. The problem was that Japan was apprehensive about, indeed repelled by, such an international body dominated by Western powers.

In the end, the Shandong compromise at Paris did not settle the differences between Wilson and the Japanese with regard to the details of the future disposition of Shandong. Both sides simply shelved the problem for the moment and signed the Treaty of Versailles on June 28, 1919. The gist of the compromise the Japanese and President Wilson agreed on was that, after the German rights had been ceded to Japan, Japan would return the Shandong Peninsula in full sovereignty to China, retaining only the economic privileges granted to Germany and the right to establish a settlement in Qingdao. Being jealous of protecting Japan's power and prestige in East Asia, the Japanese delegation asserted that this declaration must be "a voluntary expression of the Japanese delegates' interpretation" of the restitution of Shandong stipulated by the treaty of 1915 and that no impression should be given that this decision had been forced on Japan.

The picture that emerges from Wilson's encounter and dealings with Japanese claims at the Paris Peace Conference reveals the inadequacy of his idealistic policy toward East Asia. Wilson's absolute faith in the universality of his ideals, and his unyielding determination to turn his vision of a new world order into a reality, prevented him from understanding what was driving an emerging non-Western country like Japan to expand at the expense of weaker neighbors. Wilson's unilateral attempt to impose a new order, however righteous his intentions were, was doomed to a disappointing outcome.

Japanese leaders, who took advantage of the European war and tried to expand Japan's foothold in East Asia, considered Wilsonian opposition to Japanese claims at Paris as another attempt by Western powers to block the growth of an Asian regional power. Forgetting the blemishes in their conducts on the Asian continent, the Japanese felt that President Wilson's interference in Sino-Japanese negotiations over Shandong was humiliating and that his failure to support the principle of racial equality unjust. The Japanese viewed Wilsonian universal internationalism simply as hypocritical rhetoric that hindered the advancement of their country. Baron Makino, who later served Emperor Hirohito as lord keeper of the privy seal, commented in his memoirs about Wilson's unilateral approach at the peace conference. According to Makino, it was hard to associate Wilson's personality with democracy. The president seemed to him to be "a politician best suited to a dictatorship."[43]

NOTES

A substantial portion of this chapter was originally published as an article under the same title in the *Pacific Historical Review* 66 (November 1997): 503–526.

1. Ray Stannard Baker, *Woodrow Wilson and World Settlement*, 3 vols. (Garden City, N.Y.: Doubleday, Page & Company, Inc., 1923).

2. U.S. Department of State, *Papers Relating to the Foreign Relaitons of the United States*, 1918, Supplement (Washington, D.C., 1933), 1: 12–17. Hereafter cited as *FR*; Arthur S. Link, ed., *The Papers of Woodrow Wilson* (Princeton: Princeton University Press, 1966–1994), 45: 534–539, 51; 129–130. Hereafter cited as *PWW*.

3. Diary of William C. Bullitt, December 9[10], 1918, *PWW*, 53: 351; Memorandum by Isaiah Bowman, December 10, 1918, *PWW*, 53: 355.

4. Beer's Diary, December 10, 1918, quoted in James T. Shotwell, *At the Paris Peace Conference* (New York: Macmillan Company, 1937), 75.

5. Arthur Walworth, *Wilson and His Peacemakers: American Diplomacy at the Paris Peace Conference, 1919* (New York: W. W. Norton & Company, 1986), 360–361.

6. Lawrence E. Gelfand, *The Inquiry: American Preparation for Peace, 1917–1919* (New Haven: Yale University Press, 1963), 63–66, 227, 260–265, 315.

7. Polk to the Commission to Negotiate Peace, undated [received January 5, 1919]; Reinsch to Polk, January 6, 1919, the U.S. Department of State, *Papers Relating to the Foreign Relations of the United States 1919: The Paris Peace*

Conference (Washington, D.C.: U.S. Government Printing Office, 1942–1947), 1: 151–158. Hereafter cited as *FRPP*; *PWW*, 54: 77–82.

8. Hornbeck to the Commission to Negotiate Peace, undated, *FRPPC*, 2: 525–526; House papers cited in Roy W. Curry, *Woodrow Wilson and Far Eastern Policy, 1913–1921* (New York: Bookman Associates, 1957), 253; Burton F. Beers, *Vain Endeavor: Robert Lansing's Attempt to End the American-Japanese Rivalry* (Durham, N.C.: Duke University Press, 1962), 154.

9. "Black Book 2: Outline of Tentative Report and Recommendations Prepared by the Intelligence Section in accordance with Instructions, for the President and the Plenipotentiaries," February 13, 1919, Wilson Papers; Lawrence E. Gelfand, *The Inquiry*, 265–269, 322, 325.

10. *PWW*, 42: 156–157;U.S. Department of State, *Papers Relating to the Foreign Relations of the United States: The Lansing Papers 1914–1920* (Washington, D.C., 1940), 2: 433. Hereafter cited as *FRLP*.

11. Minutes of the British War Cabinet, December 30, 1918, *PWW*, 53: 562–563. Japanese Embassy to the Department of State, October 30, 1918, *FR*, 1918, 205.

12. Foreign Ministry of Japan, *Nihon gaiko nenpyo narabini shuyo bunsho* (A chronology and major documents of Japanese foreign policy) (Tokyo: Hara shobo, 1965), 1: 464–468; English translation in *FR*, 1919, 571–572.

13. Tatsuo Kobayashi, ed., *Suiuso nikki:Rinji gaiko chosa iinkai kaigi hikki to* (Diary of the green rain villa: Records of the Advisory Council on Foreign Relations, etc.) (Tokyo: Hara shobo, 1966), 284–293.

14. Cabinet decision, November 22, 1918, *NGB*, 1918, 3: 635. Tatsuo Kobayashi, ed., *Suiuso nikki*, 316–317.

15. Tatsuo Kobayashi, ed., *Suiuso nikki*, 318–324. Uchida to Chinda, December 26, 1918, NGB, 1918, in the Foreign Ministry of Japan, *Nihon gaiko bunsho* (Documents on Japanese foreign policy), 1918 (Tokyo, 1968). 3: 667–669. Hereafter cited as *NGB*.

16. Tatsuo Kobayashi, ed., *Suiuso nikki*, 316.

17. Ibid., 317.

18. Ibid., 286.

19. Ibid., 308–310.

20. Council of Ten, January 30, 1919, *FRPPC*, 3: 795–796, 799–800.

21. Tatsuo Kobayashi, ed., *Suiuso nikki*, 386–400; Uchida to Matsui, February 3, 1919, *NGB*, 1919, 3:382.

22. Diary of David Hunter Miller, January 30, 1919, *PWW*, 54: 379; *PWW*, 54: 347 n. 2.

23. Robert Lansing, *The Peace Negotiations: A Personal Narrative* (New York: Houghton Mifflin Company, 1921), 243; Ray S. Baker, *Woodrow Wilson and World Settlement*, 2: 239; Roy W. Curry, *Woodrow Wilson and Far Eastern Policy*, 257.

24. Matsui to Uchida, February 15, 1919, *NGB*, 1919, 3: 443–444; House Diary, February 4, 5, 1919, *PWW*, 54: 485, 500. President Wilson considered the

following compromise proposal to be acceptable: "The equality of nations being a basic principle of the League, the H.C.P. agree that concerning the aliens in their territories, they will accord them, so soon and so far as practicable, equal treatment and rights in law and in fact, without making any distinction on account of their race or nationality" (*PWW*, 54: 500).

25. House Diary, February 13, 1919, *PWW*, 55: 155; Matsui to Uchida, March 25, 30, 1919, *NGB*, 1919, 3: 483–485, 487–490; Stephen Bonsal, *Unfinished Business* (Garden City, N.Y.: Doubleday, Doran and Company, Inc., 1944), 169–170; Nobuaki Makino, *Kaikoroku* (Memoirs) (Tokyo: Chuokoronsha, 1978), 2: 205–206.

26. Keiichiro Hara, ed., *Hara Kei nikki* (Diary of Takashi Hara) (Tokyo: Fukumura shuppan, 1965), 5: 81.

27. Matsui to Uchida, April 13, 1919, *NGB*, 1919, 3: 496–497; Minutes of a meeting of the League of Nations Commission, April 11, 1919, *PWW*, 57: 259–265.

28. Diary of Cary T. Grayson, April 11, 1919, *PWW*, 57: 239–240.

29. Diary of Cary T. Grayson, April 11, 1919, *PWW*, 57: 240; House Diary, February 13, 1919, *PWW*, 55: 155.

30. Remarks upon the Clause for Racial Equality, April 11, 1919, *PWW*, 57: 268–269.

31. Council of Ten, January 27, 28, 1919, *FRPPC*, 3: 737–740, 749–757.

32. Ray S. Baker, *Woodrow Wilson and World Settlement*, 2: 223.

33. Uchida to Obata, January 31, 1919, *NGB*, 1919, 3: 119–121. Polk to Wilson and Lansing, February 4, 1919, *PWW*, 54: 474–476; Wilson to Lansing, February 7, 1919, *PWW*, 54: 548.

34. Obata to Uchida, February 3, 4, 13; Uchida to Obata, February 5, 1919, *NGB*, 1919, 3: 124–125, 127–130, 151–156.

35. Letter from Williams to Long, March 6, 1919, Long Papers, cited in Russell H. Fifield, *Woodrow Wilson and the Far East: The Diplomacy of the Shantung Question* (New York: Thomas Y. Crowell Company, 1952), 154.

36. Council of Four, April 15, 1919, *PWW*, 57: 358–359.

37. Matsui to Uchida, April 22, 1919, *NGB*, 1919, 3: 244–247; English translation in *PWW*, 57: 581–585.

38. Tatsuo Kobayashi, ed., *Suiuso nikki*, 464–467.

39. Uchida to Matsui, April 21, 1919, *NGB*, 1919, 3: 242.

40. Council of Four, April 22, 1919, *FRPPC*, 5: 139–148.

41. *PWW*, 58: 113; Council of Four, April 22, 1919, *PWW*, 57: 622–626; *FRPPC*, 5: 145.

42. Council of Four, April 22, 1919, *PWW*, 57: 626.

43. Nobuaki Makino, *Kaikoroku*, 2: 226.

Selected Bibliography

I. MANUSCRIPTS

A. The United States

Edward M. House Papers, Manuscripts, and Archives, Yale University Library.
The Papers of Woodrow Wilson, Library of Congress.
U.S. Department of State. *Confidential U.S. Diplomatic Post Records: Japan [1914–1941]*. University Publications of America. Microfilm.
U.S. Department of State. *Records of the Department of State Relating to the Internal Affairs of Japan, 1910–1929*. U.S. National Archives. Microfilm.

B. Japan

Japanese Foreign Ministry Archives, 1914–1919.
The Papers of Nobuaki Makino, National Diet Library

II. GOVERNMENT AND DOCUMENTARY PUBLICATIONS

A. The United States

Link, Arthur S., ed. *The Deliberations of the Council of Four (March 24–June 28, 1919): Notes of the Official Interpreter Paul Mantoux*. 2 vols. Princeton: Princeton University Press, 1992.
———, ed. *The Papers of Woodrow Wilson*. 69 vols. Princeton: Princeton University Press, 1966–1994.

MacMurray, John V., ed. *Treaties and Agareement with and Concerning China 1894–1919*. 2 vols. New York: Oxford University Press, 1921.

U.S. Department of State. *Papers Relating to the Foreign Relations of the United States*. 1914–1919 with supplements. Washington, D.C.: U.S. Government Printing Office, 1928–1934.

———. *Papers Relating to the Foreign Relations of the United States: Lansing Papers, 1914–1920*. 2 vols. Washington, D.C.: U.S. Government Printing Office, 1940.

———. *Papers Relating to the Foreign Relations of the United States 1919: The Paris Peace Conference*. 13 vols. Washington, D.C.: U.S. Government Printing Office, 1942–1947.

B. Japan

Gaimusho (Foreign Ministry of Japan). *Nihon gaiko bunsho* (Documents on Japanese foreign policy). 1914–1919 with supplements. Tokyo: Gaimusho, 1966–1971.

———. *Nihon gaiko nenpyo narabini shuyo bunsho* (A chronology and major documents of Japanese foreign policy). 2 vols. Tokyo: Hara shobo, 1965.

Sanbo honbu (Japanese Army General Staff). *Taisho 7–nen naishi 11–nen shiberia shuppei-shi* (History of the Siberian expedition, 1918–1922). 7 vols. Tokyo: Sanbo honbu, 1924.

III. PUBLISHED DIARIES, MEMOIRS, LETTERS, AND OTHER COLLECTED WORKS

A. The United States

Baker, Ray Stannard. *Woodrow Wilson: Life and Letters*. 8 vols. Garden City, N.Y.: Doubleday, Doran & Company, Inc., 1927–1939.

Bonsal, Stephen. *Suitors and Suppliants: The Little Nations at Versailles*. Introduction by Arthur Krock. New York: Prentice-Hall, Inc., 1946.

———. *Unfinished Business*. Introduction by Hugh Gibson. Garden City, N.Y.: Doubleday, Doran & Company, Inc., 1944.

Carnegie Endowment for International Peace. *Imperial Japanese Mission 1917: A Record of the Reception throughout the United States of the Special Mission Headed by Viscount Ishii*. Foreword by Elihu Root. Washington, D.C., 1918.

———. *Shantung: Treaties and Agreements*. Washington, D.C., 1921.

———. *The Sino-Japanese Negotiations of 1915*. Washington, D.C., 1921.

Cronon, E. David, ed. *The Cabinet Diaries of Josephus Daniels, 1913–1921*. Lincoln: University of Nebraska Press, 1963.

Graves, William S. *America*'s *Siberian Adventure, 1918–1920.* New York: J. Cape & H. Smith, 1931.

Houston, David E. *Eight Years with Wilson*'s *Cabinet 1913 to 1920.* 2 vols. Garden City, N.Y.: Doubleday, Page & Company, 1926.

Lansing, Robert. *The Peace Negotiations: A Personal Narrative.* Boston: Houghton Mifflin, 1921.

———. *War Memoirs of Robert Lansing.* Indianapolis, Ind.: The Bobbs-Merrill Company, 1935.

March, Peyton C. *The Nation at War.* Garden City, N.Y.: Doubleday, Doran & Company, 1932.

Reinsch, Paul S. An *American Diplomat in China.* Garden City, N.Y.: Doubleday, Page & Company, 1922.

Seymour, Charles, ed. *The Intimate Papers of Colonel House.* 4 vols. Boston: Houghton Mifflin, 1926–1928.

Shotwell, James T. *At the Paris Peace Conference.* New York: Macmillan Company, 1937.

Wilson, Edith Bolling. *My Memoir.* Indianapolis, Ind.: Bobbs-Merrill Company, 1938.

B. Japan

Hara, Keiichiro, ed. *Hara Kei nikki* (Diary of Takashi Hara). 5 vols. Tokyo: Fukumura shuppan, 1965.

Ishii, Kikujiro. *Gaiko Yoroku.* Tokyo: Iwanami shoten, 1930. English translation: *Diplomatic Commentaries.* Edited and translated by William R. Langdon. Baltimore: Johns Hopkins University Press, 1936.

Kajima, Morinosuke. *The Diplomacy of Japan 1894–1922.* 3 vols. Tokyo: Kajima Institute of International Peace, 1980. English translation of selected documents of the Japanese Foreign Ministry.

Kitamura, Hironao, ed. *Yume no shichiju-yo-nen: Nishihara Kamezo jiden* (Seventy-some years in a dream: Autobiography of Kamezo Nishihara). Tokyo: Heibonsha, 1965.

Kobayashi, Tatsuo, ed. *Suiuso nikki: Rinji gaiko chosa iinkai kaigi hikki to* (Diary of the green rain villa: Records of the Advisory Council on Foreign Relations, etc.). Tokyo: Hara shobo, 1966.

Makino, Nobuaki. *Kaikoroku* (Memoirs). 2 vols.Tokyo: Chuokoronsha, 1978.

Oyama, Azusa, ed. *Yamagata Aritomo ikensho* (Collection of memoranda of Aritomo Yamagata). Tokyo: Hara shobo, 1966.

Shigemitsu, Mamoru. *Sugamo nikki* (Sugamo diary). Tokyo: Bungeishunjushinsha, 1953.

Tanaka, Asakichi, ed. *Hara Kei zenshu* (Collected works of Takashi Hara). 2 vols. Tokyo: Hara shobo, 1969.

Ugaki, Kazushige. *Ugaki Kazushige nikki* (Diary of Kazushige Ugaki). 2 vols. Tokyo: Misuzu shobo, 1968.

Yamamoto, Shiro, ed. *Nishihara Kamezo nikki* (Diary of Kamezo Nishihara). Kyoto: Kyoto joshi daigaku, 1983.

————, ed. *Terauchi Masatake naikaku kankei shiryo* (Documents relating to the cabinet of Masatake Terauchi). Kyoto: Kyoto joshi daigaku, 1985.

C. Others

Grey, Edward. *Twenty-five Years, 1892–1916*. 2 vols. New York: Frederick A. Stokes Company, 1925.

Lensen, George Alexander, ed. *Revelations of a Russian Diplomat: The Memoirs of Dmitrii I. Abrikossow*. Seattle, University of Washington Press, 1964.

Lloyd George, David. *War Memoirs of David Lloyd George*. 6 vols. Boston: Little, Brown, and Company, 1935–1937.

Nicolson, Harold. *Peacemaking 1919: Being Reminiscences of the Paris Peace Conference*. Boston: Houghton Mifflin, 1933.

IV. NEWSPAPERS

A. The United States

New York Times.
San Francisco Chronicle.

B. Japan

Japan Times.
Kokumin shinbun.
Tokyo Asahi.

V. GENERAL WORKS AND SPECIAL STUDIES

A. The United States

Ambrosius, Lloyd E. *Wilsonian Statecraft: Theory and Practice of Liberal Internationalism during World War I*. Wilmington, Del.: Scholarly Resources Inc., 1991.

————. *Woodrow Wilson and American Diplomatic Tradition: The Treaty Fight in Perspective*. New York: Cambridge University Press, 1987.

Asada, Sadao. "Japan and the United States, 1915–1925" Ph.D. dissertation, Yale University, 1962.

————, ed. *Japan and the World, 1853–1952: A Bibliographic Guide to Japanese Scholarship in Foreign Relations*. New York: Columbia University Press, 1989.

Bailey, Thomas A. *Woodrow Wilson: The Lost Peace*. New York: Macmillan Company, 1944.

Baker, Ray Stannard. *Woodrow Wilson and World Settlement*. 3 vols. Garden City, N.Y.: Doubleday, Page & Company, Inc., 1923.

Barnhart, Michael A. *Japan and the World since 1868*. London: Edward Arnold, 1995.

Beers, Burton F. *Vain Endeavor: Robert Lansing's Attempt to End the American-Japanese Rivalry*. Durham, N.C.: Duke University Press, 1962.

Bemis, Samuel F. "The Yap Island Controversy." *Pacific Review* 2 (September 1921): 308–328.

Blaker, Michael. *Japanese International Negotiating Style*. New York: Columbia University Press, 1977.

Braisted, William R. *The United States Navy in the Pacific, 1909–1922*. Austin: University of Texas Press, 1971.

Buehrig, Edward H. *Woodrow Wilson and the Balance of Power*. Bloomington: Indiana University Press, 1955.

Calhoun, Frederick S. *Power and Principle: Armed Intervention in Wilsonian Foreign Policy*. Kent, Ohio:Kent State University Press, 1986.

Chi, Madeleine. *China Diplomacy, 1914–1918*. Cambridge: Harvard University Press, 1970.

Clements, Kendrick A. *Woodrow Wilson: World Statesman*. Boston: Twayne Publishers, 1987.

Cooper, John M. Jr. *The Warrior and the Priest: Woodrow Wilson and Theodore Roosevelt*. Cambridge: Harvard University Press, 1983.

Cooper, John M. Jr., and Charles E. Neu, eds. *The Wilson Era: Essays in Honor of Arthur S. Link*. Arlington Heights, Ill.: Harlan Davidson, Inc., 1991.

Coox, Alvin D., and Hilary Conroy, eds. *China and Japan: A Search for Balance since World War I*. Santa Barbara, Calif.: ABC-Clio, Inc., 1978.

Craft, Stephen G. "John Bassett Moore, Robert Lansing, and the Shandong Question." *Pacific Historical Review* 66 (May 1997): 231–249.

Crane, Daniel M., and Thomas A Breslin. *An Ordinary Relationship: American Opposition to Republican Revolution in China*. Miami: Florida International University Press, 1986.

Curry, George. "Woodrow Wilson, Jan Smuts, and the Versailles Settlement." *American Historical Review* 66 (1961): 968–986.

Curry, Roy W. *Woodrow Wilson and Far Eastern Policy, 1913–1921*. New York: Bookman Associates, 1957.

Duus, Peter, Ramon H. Myers, and Mark R. Peattie, eds. *The Japanese Informal Empire in China, 1895–1937*. Princeton: Princeton University Press, 1989.

Esthus, Raymond A. "The Changing Concept of the Open Door, 1899–1910." *Mississippi Valley Historical Review* 46 no. 3 (1959): 435–453.

Etzold, Thomas H., ed. *Aspects of Sino-American Relations since 1784*. New York: New Viewpoints, 1978.

Fifield, Russell H. "Disposal of the Carolines, Marshalls, and Marianas at the Paris Peace Conference." *American Historical Review* 51 (1946): 472–479.

———. "Documents: Japanese Policy toward the Shantung Question at the Paris Peace Conference." *Journal of Modern History* 23 (September 1951): 265–272.

———. "Secretary Hughes and the Shantung Question." *Pacific Historical Review* 23 no. 4 (1954): 373–385.

———. *Woodrow Wilson and the Far East: The Diplomacy of the Shantung Question*. New York: Thomas Y. Crowell Company, 1952; reprint, Hamden, Conn.: Archon Books, 1965.

Floto, Inga. *Colonel House in Paris: A Study of American Policy at the Paris Peace Conference 1919*. Princeton: Princeton University Press, 1980.

Foglesong, David S. *America's Secret War against Bolshevism: U.S. Intervention in the Russian Civil War, 1917–1920*. Chapel Hill: University of North Carolina Press, 1995.

Fowler, Wilton B. *British-American Relations 1917–1918: The Role of Sir William Wiseman*. Princeton: Princeton University Press, 1969.

Gardner, Lloyd. *Safe for Democracy: The Anglo-American Response to Revolution, 1913–1923*. New York: Oxford University Press, 1984.

Gelfand, Lawrence E. *The Inquiry: American Preparation for Peace, 1917–1919*. New Haven: Yale University Press, 1963.

Griswold, Whitney A. *The Far Eastern Policy of the United States*. New York: Harcourt, Brace and Company, 1938.

Heater, Derek. *National Self-Determination: Woodrow Wilson and His Legacy*. New York: St. Martin's Press, 1994.

Hogan, Michael J., and Thomas G. Paterson, eds. *Explaining the History of American Foreign Relations*. New York: Cambridge University Press, 1991.

Hunt, Michael H. *Ideology and U.S. Foreign Policy*. New Haven: Yale University Press, 1987.

———. *The Making of a Special Relationship: The United States and China to 1914*. New York: Columbia University Press, 1983.

Iriye, Akira. *Across the Pacific: An Inner History of American-East Asian Relations*. New York: Harcourt Brace Jovanovich, 1967.

———. *After Imperialism: The Search for a New Order in the Far East 1921–1931*. Cambridge: Harvard University Press, 1965.

———. *Cultural Internationalism and World Order*. Baltimore: Johns Hopkins University Press, 1997.

———. *Pacific Estrangement: Japan and American Expansion, 1897–1911*. Cambridge: Harvard University Press, 1972.

———, ed. *The Chinese and Japanese: Essays in Political and Cultural Interactions*. Princeton: Princeton University Press, 1980.

————, ed. *Mutual Images: Essays in American-Japanese Relations*. Cambridge: Harvard University Press, 1975.

Israel, Jerry. *Progressivism and the Open Door: America and China*. Pittsburgh: University of Pittsburgh Press, 1971.

Kawamura, Noriko. "Wilsonian Idealism and Japanese Claims at the Paris Peace Conference." *Pacific Historical Review* 66 (November 1997): 503–526.

Kennan, George F. *American Diplomacy*. Expanded edition. Chicago: Chicago University Press, 1984.

————. "The Sisson Documents." *Journal of Modern History* 28 (June 1956): 130–154.

————. *Soviet-American Relations, 1917–1920*. 2 vols. Princeton: Princeton University Press, 1956–1958.

King, Wunsz. *China at the Paris Peace Conference in 1919*. Jamaica, N.Y.: St. John's University Press, 1961.

Knock, Thomas J. *To End All Wars: Woodrow Wilson and the Quest for a New World Order*. New York: Oxford University Press, 1992.

LaFargue, Thomas E. *China and the World War*. Stanford: Stanford University Press, 1937.

LaFeber, Walter. *The Clash: A History of U.S.-Japan Relations*. New York: W. W. Norton & Company, 1997.

Langdon, Frank C. "Japan's Failure to Establish Friendly Relations with China in 1917–1918." Pacific Historical Review 26 (1957): 245–258.

Lasch, Christopher. "American Intervention in Siberia: Reinterpretation." *Political Science Quarterly* 77 no.2 (1962): 205–223.

Lauren, Paul G. "Human Rights in History: Diplomacy and Racial Equality at the Paris Peace Conference." *Diplomatic History* 2, no. 3 (1978): 257–278.

Levin, N. Gordon Jr. *Woodrow Wilson and World Politics: America's Response to War and Revolution*. New York: Oxford University Press, 1968.

Li, Tien-yi. *Woodrow Wilson's China Policy, 1913–1917*. Kansas City, Mo.: University of Kansas City Press, 1952.

Link, Arthur S. *The Higher Realism of Woodrow Wilson and Other Essays*. Nashville, Tenn.: Vanderbilt University Press, 1971.

————. *Wilson: Campaigns for Progressivism and Peace 1916–1917*. Princeton: Princeton University Press, 1965.

————. *Woodrow Wilson: Revolution, War, and Peace*. Arlington Heights, Ill.: AHM Publishing Corporation, 1979.

————. *Wilson: The Struggle for Neutrality 1914–1915*. Princeton: Princeton University Press, 1960.

Maddox, Robert J. *The Unknown War with Russia: Wilson's Siberian Intervention*. San Rafael, Calif.: Presidio Press, 1977.

May, Ernest R. "American Policy and Japan's Entrance into World War I." *Mississippi Valley Historical Review* 40, no. 2 (1953): 279–290.

————. *World War and American Isolation, 1914–1917*. Cambridge: Harvard University Press, 1959.

May, Ernest R., and Thomson, James C. Jr., eds. *American-East Asian Relations: A Survey*. Cambridge: Harvard University Press, 1972.

Mayer, Arno J. *Political Origins of the New Diplomacy 1917–1918*. New Haven: Yale University Press, 1959.

———. *Politics and Diplomacy of Peacemaking: Containment and Counterrevolution at Versailles, 1918–1919*. New York: Knopf, 1967.

McCormack, Gavan. *Chang Tso-Lin in Northeast China 1911–1918: China, Japan and the Manchurian Idea*. Stanford, Calif.: Stanford University Press, 1977.

Morley, James W. *The Japanese Thrust into Siberia, 1918*. New York: Columbia University Press, 1957.

———, ed. *Japan's Foreign Policy 1868–1941: A Research Guide*. New York: Columbia University Press, 1974.

Morton, William F. *Tanaka Giichi and Japan's China Policy*. New York: St. Martin's Press, 1980.

Nathan, Andrew J. *Peking Politics, 1918–1923: Factionalism and the Failure of Constitutionalism*. Berkeley: University of California Press, 1976.

Neu, Charles. *The Troubled Encounter: The United States and Japan*. New York: John Wiley & Sons, 1975.

Nevins, Allan. *Henry White: Thirty Years of American Diplomacy*. New York: Harper & Brothers Publishers, 1930.

Ninkovich, Frank. *Modernity and Power: A History of the Domino Theory in the Twentieth Century*. Chicago: University of chicago Press, 1994.

———. *The Wilsonian Century: U.S. Foreign Policy since 1900*. Chicago: University of Chicago Press, 1999.

Offner, Arnold A. *The Origins of the Second World War: American Foreign Policy and World Politics, 1917–1941*. New York: Praeger Publishers, 1975.

Palmer, Frederick. *Bliss, Peacemaker: The Life and Letters of General Tasker Howard Bliss*. New York: Dodd, Mead & Company, 1934.

Pugach, Noel H. *Paul S. Reinsch: Open Door Diplomat in Action*. Millwood, N.Y.: KTO Press, 1979.

Reed, James. *The Missionary Mind and American East Asia Policy, 1911–1915*. Cambridge: Harvard University Press, 1983.

Safford, Jeffrey J. "Experiment in Containment: The United States Steel Embargo and Japan, 1917–1918." *Pacific Historical Review* 39 (1970): 439–451.

———. *Wilsonian Maritime Diplomacy, 1913–1921*. New Brunswick, N.J.: Rutgers University Press, 1978.

Schild, Georg. *Between Ideology and Realpolitik: Woodrow Wilson and the Russian Revolution, 1917–1921*. Westport, Conn.: Greenwood Press, 1995.

Schmidt, Hans. "Democracy for China: American Propaganda and the May Fourth Movement." *Diplomatic History* 22 (winter 1998): 1–28.

Schmitt, Bernadotte E., and Harold C. Vedeler. *The World in the Crucible, 1914–1919*. New York: Harper & Row, Publishers, 1984.

Seymour, Charles. *American Diplomacy during the World War*. Baltimore: Johns Hopkins Press, 1934.

————. "The Paris Education of Woodrow Wilson." *Virginia Quarterly Review* 32 (1956): 578–593.

Silberman, Bernard S., and Harry D. Harootunian, eds. *Japan in Crirsis: Essays on Taisho Democracy*. Princeton: Princeton University Press, 1974.

Smith, Daniel M. *The Great Departure: The United States and World War I, 1914–1920*. New York: John Wiley and Sons, Inc., 1965.

Startt, James D. "Wilson's Mission to Paris: The Making of a Decision." *Historian* 30 (1968): 599–616.

Steigerwald, David. *Wilsonian Idealism in America*. Ithaca: Cornell University Press, 1994.

Tillman, Seth P. *Anglo-American Relations at the Paris Peace Conference of 1919*. Princeton: Princeton University Press, 1961.

Trani, Eugene P. "Woodrow Wilson and the Decision to Intervene in Russia: A Reconsideration." *Journal of Modern History* 48, no. 3 (1976): 440–461.

————. "Woodrow Wilson, China, and the Missionaries, 1913–1921." *Journal of Presbyterian History* 49 (winter 1971): 328–351.

Trask, David F. *The United States in the Supreme War Council: American War Aims and Inter-Allied Strategy, 1917–1918*. Middletown, Conn.: Wesleyan University Press, 1961.

Unterberger, Betty M. *America's Siberian Expedition, 1918–1920: A Study of National Policy*. Durham, N.C.: Duke University Press, 1956.

————. *The United States, Revolutionary Russia, and the Rise of Czechoslovakia*. Chapel Hill: University of North Carolina Press, 1989.

————, ed. *American Intervention in the Russian Civil War*. Lexington, Mass.: D. C. Heath and Company, 1969.

Vinson, John C. "The Annulment of the Lansing-Ishii Agreement." *Pacific Historical Review* 27 (1958): 57–69.

Walworth, Arthur. *America's Moment 1918: American Diplomacy at the End of World War I*. New York: W. W. Norton & Company, 1977.

————. *Wilson and His Peacemakers: American Diplomacy at the Paris Peace Conference, 1919*. New York: W. W. Norton & Company, 1986.

————. *Woodrow Wilson*. 2 vols. Third edition. New York: W. W. Norton & Company, 1978.

Widenor, William C. *Henry Cabot Lodge and the Search for an American Foreign Policy*. Berkeley: University of California Press, 1980.

Williams, William A. *The Tragedy of American Diplomacy*. Second revised and enlarged edition. New York: Dell Publishing Co., Inc., 1972.

Woodward, David R. "The British Government and Japanese Intervention in Russia during World War One." *Journal of Modern History* 46 no. 4 (1974): 663–685.

B. Japan

Amemiya, Shoichi. *Kindai nihon no senso shido* (Wartime leadership in modern Japan). Tokyo: Yoshikawa kobunkan, 1997.

Asada, Sadao. *Ryotaisen kan no nichibei kankei: Kaigun to seisaku kettei katei* (Japanese-American relations between the two world wars: The Navy and decision making process). Tokyo: Tokyo daigaku shuppankai, 1993.

Gaimusho Hyaku-nen-shi hensan iinkai, ed. *Gaimusho no hyaku-nen* (The foreign ministry centennial). 2 vols. Tokyo: Hara shobo, 1969.

Hara, Teruyuki. *Shiberia shuppei: Kakumei to kansho 1917–1922* (Siberian expedition: revolution and intervention 1917–1922). Tokyo: Chikuma shobo, 1989.

Hirama, Yoichi. *Daiichiji sekai taisen to nihon kaigun: Gaiko to junji tono rensetsu* (World War I and the Japanese Navy: Connection between diplomacy and military affairs). Tokyo: Keiogijuku daigaku shuppankai, 1998.

Horikawa, Takeo. *Kyokuto kokusai seiji-shi josetsu: 21 kajo yokyu no kenkyu* (An introduction to the history of Far Eastern international politics: A study of the Twenty-one Demands). Tokyo: Yuhikaku, 1958.

Hosoya, Chihiro. "Makino Nobuaki to berusaiyu kaigi" (Nobuaki Makino and the Versailles conference). *Chuo koron* (May 1965): 363–369.

———. *Roshia kakumei to nihon* (Russian revolution and Japan). Tokyo: Hara shobo, 1972.

———. *Ryotaisen kan no nihon gaiko* (Japanese diplomacy between the two world wars). Tokyo: Iwanami shoten, 1988.

———. *Shiberia shuppei no shiteki kenkyu* (A historical study of the Siberian expedition) (Tokyo: Yuhikaku, 1955; reprint ed., Tokyo: Shinsensha, 1976.

———. " '21-jo' yokyu to America no taio" (The Twenty-one Demands and America's response). *Hitotsubashi ronso* 43 (1960): 28–50.

Ikei, Masaru. *Nihon gaiko-shi gaisetsu* (A survey of Japanese diplomatic history). Tokyo: Keio tsushin, 1973.

———. "Pari heiwa kaigi to jinshu sabetsu teppai mondai" (The Paris Peace Conference and racial equality issue). *Kokusai seiji* 23 (1962): 44–58.

Iriye, Akira, and Tadashi Aruga, eds. *Senkanki no nihon gaiko* (Japanese diplomacy during the interwar period). Tokyo: Tokyo daigaku shuppankai, 1984.

Ito, Masanori, ed. *Kato Takaaki* (Biography of Takaaki Kato). 2 vols. Tokyo: Jitsubunkan, 1929.

Kitaoka, Shinichi. *Nihon rikugun to tairiku seisaku, 1906–1918 nen* (Japanese army and its continental policy, 1906–1918). Tokyo: Tokyo daigaku shuppankai, 1978.

———. "Nijuikkajo saiko" (The Twenty-one Demands reconsidered). *Kindai nihon kenkyu* 7 (1985): 119–150.

Kobayashi, Tatsuo. "Pari heiwa kaigi to nihon no gaiko" (The Paris Peace Conference and Japan's diplomacy). Edited by Toshio Ueda. *Kindai nihon gaiko-shi no kenkyu* (Studies of the diplomatic history of modern Japan). Tokyo: Yuhikaku, 1956.

————. "Rinji gaiko chosa iinkai no secchi" (Establishment of the advisory council on foreign relations). *Kokusai seiji* 28 (1964): 53–71.

Kobayashi, Yukio. "Oshu taisen to nihon no tairo seisaku" (The great war in Europe and Japanese policy toward Russia). *Kokusai seiji* 23 (1962): 28–43.

Masuda, Takeshi. "Hara Kei no chugoku kan" (Takashi Hara's view of China). *Kobe hogaku zasshi* 18 (March 1969): 413–460.

Mitani, Taichiro. *Kindai nihon no senso to seiji* (War and politics of modern Japan). Tokyo: Iwanami shoten, 1997.

————. "Tenkanki (1918–1921) no gaiko shido: Hara Kei oyobi Tanaka Giichi wo chushin to shite" (Foreign policy leadership at a turning point, 1918–1921: With particular reference to Takashi Hara and Giichi Tanaka). In Hajime, Shinohara, and Taichiro Mitani, eds. *Kindai nihon no seiji shido* (Political leadership in modern Japan). Tokyo: Tokyo daigaku shuppankai, 1965.

Miwa, Kimitada. "Japanese Opinion on Woodrow Wilson in War and Peace." *Monumenta Nipponica* 22 (1967): 368–389. In English.

Nagaoka, Shinjiro. "Daiichiji taisen niokeru santo hanto oyobi dokuryo minami taiheiyo shoto no senryo" (Occupation of Shandong Peninsula and the German Pacific Islands during World War I). *Gunji shigaku* 12 (December 1976): 24–33.

————. "Ishii-Ranshingu kyotei no seiritsu" (The making of the Lansing-Ishii agreement). *Kokusai seiji* 37 (1967): 54–71.

————. "Tai-ka nijuikkajo yokyu mondai no kettei to sono haikei" (The decision for the Twenty-one Demands and its background). *Nihon rekishi* no. 144 (June 1960): 66–80.

Obata Yukichi denki kanko kai, ed. *Obata Yukichi* (Biography of Yukichi Obata). Tokyo: Obata Yukichi denki kankokai, 1957.

Saito, Seiji. "Kaigun ni okeru daiichiji taisen kenkyu to sono hado" (A study of World War I by the Navy and its influence). *Rekishigaku kenkyu* (July 1984): 16–32.

————. "Nishihara Kamezo no tai chugoku koso" (Kamezo Nishihara's idea on China policy). *Kokusai seiji* 71 (August 1982): 54–51.

————. "Terauchi naikaku ni okeru endan seisaku kakuritsu no keii" (The circumstances under which the Terauchi cabinet adopted the policy to assist Duan). *Kokusai seiji* 83 (October 1986): 143–161.

————. "Terauchi naikaku to Nishihara Kamezo" (The Terauchi cabinet and Kamezo Nishihara). *Kokusai seiji* 75 (October 1983): 12–29.

Saito, Takashi. "Pari kowa kaigi to nihon" (The Paris Peace Conference and Japan). *Kokusai seiji* 6 (1958): 105–117.

Seki, Hiroharu. "1918–nen nicchu gunji kyotei seiritsu-shi joron" (An introduction to the history of the making of the Sino-Japanese military agreement of 1918). *Toyo bunka kenkyujo kiyo* 26 (February 1962): 111–312.

Seki, Shizuo. "Hara naikaku gaiko no kosoku yoin ni tsuite" (On binding factors of the Hara Cabinet's diplomacy). *Hogaku ronso* 101 (June 1977): 36–63; 103 (July 1978): 55–70.

Shidehara heiwa zaidan. *Shidehara Kijuro* (The biography of Kijuro Shidehara). Tokyo: Shidehara heiwa zaidan, 1955.

Shigemitsu, Osamu. "Ishii-Ranshingu kyotei" (The Lansing-Ishii agreement). *Kokusai seiji* 6 (1958): 66–78.

Shimizu, Hideko. "Santo mondai" (Shandong question). *Kokusai seiji* 56 (1976): 117–136.

Shinobu, Seizaburo. *Taisho seijishi* (The political history of the Taisho era). 4 vols. Tokyo: Kawaide shobo, 1951–1952.

Takahashi, Hidenao. "Hara naikaku no seiritsu to soryokusen seisaku" (The formation of the Hara cabinet and the total war policy). *Shirin* 68 (May 1985): 1–34.

Tanaka Giichi denki kankokai, ed. *Tanaka Giichi* (The biography of Giichi Tanaka). 2 vols. Tokyo: Tanaka Giichi denki kankokai, 1958–1960.

Tokutomi, Iichiro, ed. *Koshaku Yamagata Aritomo den* (The biography of Prince Aritomo Yamagata). 3 vols. Tokyo: Yamagata Aritomo kinen jigyokai, 1933.

Tsurumi, Yusuke, ed. *Goto Shinpei*. 4 vols. Tokyo: Goto Shinpei haku denki hensankai, 1937–1938.

Uchida Kosai denki hensan iinkai, ed. *Uchida Kosai*. Tokyo: Kajima shuppankai, 1969.

Uchiyama, Masakuma. "Nichidoku senso to santo mondai" (The Japanese-German war and the Shandong question). *Hogaku kenkyu* 33 (February 1960): 243–291.

Unno, Yoshiro. *Kokusai renmei to nihon* (The League of Nations and Japan). Tokyo: Hara shobo, 1972.

———. "Pari heiwa kaigi to gaimusho" (The Paris Peace Conference and the foreign ministry). *Rekishi kyoiku* 15 (January 1967): 46–53.

Usui, Katsumi. "Chugoku no taisen sanka to nihon no tachiba" (China's participation in the great war and Japan's position). *Rekishi kyoiku* 8 (1960): 22–34.

———. *Chugoku wo meguru kindai nihon no gaiko* (Diplomacy of modern Japan concerning China). Tokyo: chikuma shobo, 1983.

———. *Nihon to chugoku: Taisho jidai* (Japan and China: the Taisho era). Tokyo: Hara shobo, 1972.

Yamamoto, Shiro. "Sansen, Nijuikkajo yokyu to rikugun" (Japan's entry into the war, the Twenty-one Demands, and the Japanese army). *Shirin* 57 no. 3 (May 1974): 1–33.

C. Others

Beasley, William G. *Japanese Imperialism 1894–1945*. Oxford: Clarendon Press, 1987.

Dugdale, Blanche E. C. *Arthur James Balfour, First Earl of Balfour, G.G., O.M., F.R.S., Etc.* 2 vols. New York: G. P. Putnam's Sons, 1937.

Marston, Frank S. *The Peace Conference of 1919: Organization and Procedure.* London: Oxford University Press, 1940.

Nish, Ian. *Alliance in Decline: A Study in Anglo-Japanese Relations.* London: Athlone Press, 1972.

———. *Japanese Foreign Policy, 1869–1942: Kasumigaseki to Miyakezaka.* London: Routledge & Kegan Paul, 1977.

Yakhontoff, Victor A. *Russia and the Soviet Union in the Far East.* London: George Allen and Unwin Ltd., 1932.

Ye, Deng. "On China's Refusal to Sign the Treaty of Versailles at the Paris Peace Conference." *Social Science in China* 8 (1987): 125–148.

Index

About the Author

NORIKO KAWAMURA is Associate Professor of History at Washington State University. Educated in Japan and in the United States, her previous teaching assignments include the Virginia Military Institute. Her present research interests focus upon Emperor Hirohito and the Pacific War.